The Empire of
Civil Society

The Empire of Civil Society

A Critique of the Realist Theory of International Relations

JUSTIN ROSENBERG

VERSO

London • New York

This paperback edition published by Verso 2024
First published by Verso 1994
© Justin Rosenberg 1994
Afterword to the Second Edition © Justin Rosenberg 2024

13 5 7 9 10 8 6 4 2

Verso
UK: 6 Meard Street, London W1F 0EG
US: 388 Atlantic Avenue, Brooklyn, NY 11217
versobooks.com

Verso is the imprint of New Left Books

ISBN-13: 978-1-80429-597-7
ISBN-13: 978-1-80429-599-1 (US EBK)
ISBN-13: 978-1-80429-598-4 (UK EBK)

British Library Cataloguing in Publication Data
A catalogue record for this book is available from the British Library

Library of Congress Cataloging-in-Publication Data
A catalog record for this book is available from the Library of Congress

Printed and bound by CPI Group (UK) Ltd, Croydon CR0 4YY

Contents

To the memory of my mother,
Patricia Rosenberg (1925–1993),
who turned many an orthodoxy on its head
in her pursuit of human understanding

Acknowledgements

Such strengths as the argument which follows may possess owe a huge amount to the criticism, stimulation and advice of others. Ian Roxborough and Nicos Mouzelis were model PhD supervisors. Margot Light gave much helpful editorial assistance in the final stages of its preparation for submission as a thesis at the LSE. The argument benefited further from a generous yet searching doctoral examination by Ellen Wood, who identified several weak points which I was able to rectify – and several limitations that I could not. Finally, two individuals have been involved with this project from the outset, and deserve a special mention here. It was the example of Fred Halliday which first enticed me into the discipline of international relations. That example, and the warm encouragement given to this project, have been an inspiration ever since. Meanwhile, Simon Bromley has, at every stage, given unstintingly of his time, patience and formidable intellectual powers. I have drawn mightily on all of these, and happily acknowledge the debt. Had it not been for his support, the outcome would have been a very different, and a much poorer, work. Such weaknesses and omissions as remain are my own.

An earlier version of chapter 1 was published under the title 'What's the Matter with Realism?' in the *Review of International Studies*, 16 (4), 1990, pp. 285–303. Chapter 3 is a slightly revised version of 'Secret Origins of the State: The Structural Basis of *Raison d'Etat*', published in the *Review of International Studies*, 18 (2), 1992, pp. 131–59. Parts of chapter 5 were presented at the Political Studies Association conference at Queens University, Belfast, in the spring of 1992.

Introduction

The story is told of a Cambridge college, some years ago, which was presided over by a very conservative Master:

> It so happened that the College had just elected into a Fellowship a young man who ... had the temerity to propose, at the first Fellows' meeting in which he took part, a number of measures concerning College policy. The Master listened frowningly, and when the novice had finished, he said: 'Interesting ... but it would seem to me that your suggestions are a little contradictory to the tradition of the College.' 'Not at all, Master,' replied the aspiring reformer, 'I have studied the history of the College and I can assure you that my proposals are perfectly in keeping with the ways of the College over the last three hundred years.' 'This may well be,' said the Master, 'but wouldn't you agree that the last three hundred years have been, to say the least of them, rather exceptional?'[1]

And of course he was right. There is something about the last three hundred years which sets them apart from all other epochs in human history. In the field of international relations this is especially obvious since these centuries see for the first time the emergence of a states-system which covers the entire planet. But it is obvious everywhere else too. In fact, whenever we use the term 'modernity' we reiterate the claim that there is a huge gulf – a structural discontinuity – which separates the way the world used to be from the way it is now.

What is this discontinuity? This is arguably the first question of all social science – that is, of all attempts to develop a systematic understanding of the contemporary social world. And it preoccupied nearly all the major thinkers of the eighteenth and nineteenth centuries now regarded as the forerunners and founders of modern social thought – from the Scottish Enlightenment to Hegel, from English political economy to the post-revolutionary French sociologists. Whether they gave their answer in terms of the change from a society based on status to one based on contract, or one characterized by mechanical rather than organic relations, or the replacement of militant classes by industrial ones, or feudalism by capitalism – whatever the terms, nearly all these attempts to explore the character of the modern world begin by stressing how different it is from what went before.

Indeed, for many of them, it is this awareness of how great the change has been which makes social science, as distinct from political philosophy, possible at all. It does this by revealing how much of the world they had known was actually not part of a universal natural order of things, but was rather the daily outcome of historically specific social relations characterizing a particular kind of society. Augustine Thierry, writing in the aftermath of the French Revolution, is very eloquent on this point:

> There is not one amongst us children of the 19th century, who does not know more on the score of rebellion and conquests, of the dismemberment of empires, of the fall and restoration of monarchies, of popular revolution and the consequent reactions, than did Velly, Mably, or even Voltaire himself. ... [T]he events of the last fifty years, events hitherto unheard of, have taught us to understand the revolutions of the Middle Ages, to perceive the spirit beneath the letter of the chronicler, to draw from the writings of the Benedictines that which those learned men never saw, or saw only partially, without suspecting its significance. They lacked the comprehension and sentiment of great social transformations. They have studied with curiosity the laws, public acts, judicial formulae, private contracts, etc.; ... but the political sense, all that was living beneath the dead letter, the perception of society and its various elements ... escapes them. ... This perception, we have acquired through our experience; we owe it to the prodigious changes of power and society, which have taken place before us.[2]

And, of course, once this point is grasped with reference to the past, it cannot help but make one think about contemporary social forms which we take for granted – for example, the market, the state, and indeed the individual – in terms of historically specific social relations characteristic of a particular kind of society.

Depending perhaps on one's politics, that is either a very strong argument for bringing history and sociology together, or a very strong argument for keeping them apart. But either way, it is a striking feature of these early theorists of modernity that they did not think in terms of the partitioning of the social world between academic disciplines which we take for granted today. Smith can no more be squeezed into neoclassical economics with its relentless externalizing of all 'non-economic' factors than Marx can be accommodated within orthodox sociology. The reason for this is that the way the disciplines divide up social reality itself involves taking as natural (and therefore over-looking) certain basic things about the modern world which to both Smith and Marx seemed novel and needful of explanation. The clearest example of this is the disciplinary separation of politics and economics. This formal separation is now a century old, dating from the birth of pure economics in the aftermath of the so-called 'marginalist' revolution of the 1870s. Realist International Relations is one of several academic disciplines which are founded upon it, constituting itself as the study of political relations between states. (Hereafter, the *discipline* of international relations, as opposed to the *actual relations between states*, will be referred to as IR.) Over the years, many commentators (including, for example, E.H. Carr[3]) have pointed out that this division of labour can be unhelpful in trying to under-stand the real world. After all, states routinely intervene to regulate and constrain markets, and markets produce effects that influence the behaviour of states. More recently, this has led to the emergence of a new field of international political economy which focuses precisely on the causal interaction of international politics and international economics.[4] This is seen as an innovation which presses hard against the disciplinary boundaries of IR and economics.

Well, perhaps it does. And certainly the question 'What is the relationship between states and markets?' is an interesting and im-portant one. But it still takes *as its starting point* the observation that the international system comprises distinct institutional realms of politics and economics. Perhaps this starting point seems self-evident. In fact a historical review would show that it is more or less unique to the modern world.[5] And if these social forms really are new, then this points to a further question: exactly why does the modern inter-national system assume the distinctive form that it does – namely, states and markets? And since *this* question cannot be answered in terms of the irreducible properties of states and markets, we are led to ask what is surely a more fundamental question: in what kind of *society* do distinct institutional spheres of politics and economics open out in this way and why? What is really going on when this occurs? Answering these questions, as I hope to show later on, might tell us things about modern forms of social power which we could never see so long as we took states and economies to be the basic components of social reality.

For now, however, the point is simply that in order to pose this deeper question at all we need to step outside the existing disciplines and think as the earlier social theorists did in terms of the social world as a whole – as a social totality. We have to do this because it turns out that the disciplinary division of labour between the modern social sciences itself reflects uncritically and thereby naturalizes the distinctive social forms of modernity. States, markets, individuals – precisely the things we need to explain – are already assumed to be natural starting points. By conceptualizing particular structures of modern social relations in isolation from each other, this division of labour tends to reify them into self-sufficient actors with their own distinctive properties – hiding both the historical novelty of these forms and the specific social relations which constitute them. And it almost goes without saying that this also effects an ideological closure, a drawing in of the horizons of collective human possibility.

It is as if the modern social world arrived in Europe with a tremendous thundering and crashing which was unmistakable (even if not necessarily comprehensible) to those living there at the time – and then proceeded to cover up its tracks.

And, one could argue that the real task of social science is not to be complicit in this process, but rather the opposite: to *de*naturalize the world around us by showing how different it is from earlier societies; to dissolve the reified social forms of state and market back into the historically specific social relations between people which constitute them; and finally, to retrace our steps in order to rediscover the emergence and development of our modern social world as the history of these social relations between 'real, living individuals'.[6]

Now, if we define this as the labour of the social sciences as a whole, is there any reason why IR should be distinct methodologically in the exploration of its own subject matter? For many writers working in the still-dominant realist tradition, there most certainly is.

In their eyes, the discipline of IR is premised on the recognition of a fundamental *disjuncture* between internal political life, which is carried on under the co-ordinating and pacifying sovereignty of the state, and external politics, which is governed by the irresistible logic of anarchy. Exploring this logic of anarchy is held to be the distinctive task of IR theory – a task which must be kept more or less rigidly separate from the study of domestic politics which is governed by fundamentally different principles.[7] And attempts to explain international outcomes by reference to the internal character of the societies involved are (often rightly) seen as a crude reductionism which is blind to the operation of external factors. For these reasons, it has become almost axiomatic that whatever may be required in any empirical reconstruction, it is no part of IR *theory* to trace the connections between geopolitical systems and internal social structures. As Kenneth Waltz has put it:

> Students of international politics will do well to concentrate on separate theories of internal and external politics until someone figures out a way to unite them.[8]

The problem with this is that once the theory of external politics is cut adrift in this way, it becomes literally impossible to avoid the reification of social forms discussed above, because the social relations which compose them have been excluded from view under the heading of 'internal politics'. By definition, a separate theory of external politics must take states as its starting point.

The damage might be partially reversible if one were able to compare different geopolitical systems in history and see just how different they really were. For example, it is difficult to imagine how anyone would explain the role of dynastic diplomacy in feudal geopolitics – or its absence in the modern world – without reference to the internal character of the societies involved. But this review is blocked off by a remarkable neglect of historical contrast, which renders invisible the very modernity we ought to be trying to explain. Waltz is perhaps more extreme than most:

> The enduring character of international politics accounts for the striking sameness in the quality of international life through the millennia, a statement that will meet with wide assent.[9]

But he is far from being alone in this. Robert Gilpin asserted that 'the nature of international relations has not changed fundamentally over the millennia.'[10] And it is not unusual to see the Italian and Greek city-states-systems cited as examples of the timelessness of the balance of power.

As a result, critics often observe that realist IR ends up by reifying modern geopolitics, neglecting historical contrast, and producing a model of the states-system which is literally incapable of seeing historical change except as the rise and fall of great powers.

The aim of this book is to contribute to the reorientation of IR as a discipline in line with the common vocation of the social sciences as set out on page 4 above. That is, it seeks (a) to identify the ways in which the modern international system is different from all other geopolitical systems in history, (b) to integrate this contrast into a broader understanding of the dominant social structures of the modern world, and (c) to indicate how such a perspective might change the way we seek to recover the history of the international system, past and continuing. Each of these purposes requires a critical engagement with the realist orthodoxy at a slightly different point; but if there is a unifying theme to all three, it is the simple claim that geopolitical systems are not constituted independently of, and cannot be understood in isolation from, the wider structures of the production and reproduction of social life.

The argument of the book is divided into three principal parts, each comprising two chapters. The first part mounts a theoretical critique of the dominant theory in the academic study of international relations, namely realism. Chapter 1 uses three of the most influential texts of the school in order to focus successively on its descriptive, prescriptive and social theoretical articulations. Key weaknesses are identified in the unhistorical and presociological character of realist theory, and two categories in particular – sovereignty and anarchy – are marked out for future redefinition. Chapter 2 develops these points further: beginning with an example of how realist theory constricts any attempt to think historically about the international system, it argues that the unhistorical problematic of anarchy needs to be displaced by an alternative, sociological problematic of modernity. To this end, it reviews some key issues in contemporary social theory, outlines a broad historical materialist framework for analysis, and then challenges the realist axiom that the geopolitical core of the discipline's subject matter is ontologically distinct from the wider structures of social reproduction.

The second part of the argument comprises a series of historical explorations of the ways in which social structures have been implicated in geopolitical systems. Chapter 3 takes up the notion of the autonomy of the state, a notion central to the realist assertion of a separate geopolitical realm. By contrasting the modern capitalist states-system with those of Renaissance Italy and Classical Greece, it attempts to show that the surface similarities between them cannot be understood without seeing how in each case the form of the state is specific to a particular kind of society. This is an interrelation which also has important consequences for both the character of inter-state power and the developmental trajectory of the geopolitical system as a whole. The conventional use of these examples to argue for transhistorical continuities between states-systems *sui generis* is directly challenged. In chapter 4, the argument turns to some premodern equivalents of the contemporary world market – namely, the structures of exchange relations and forms of imperial expansion which characterized the Portuguese and Spanish empires of the absolutist period. Here it is demonstrated (in the Portuguese case) that the precapitalist character of the metropolitan society underpinned a set of exchange relations sharply contrasting with those of the modern world economy, while (in the Spanish case) both the dynamics of expansion and the forms of colonization bore the stamp of the originating social structures.

The third part of the argument returns finally to the contemporary epoch, and seeks to develop Marx's social theory of capitalist society into an alternative, non-realist framework for understanding the modern international system. In particular, the two core categories of the discipline earlier marked out for redefinition – sovereignty and anarchy – are now re-examined in the light of the foregoing historical and theoretical studies. In realist hands these categories had sealed the separation of the discipline from the broader social sciences; here they are reworked with the opposite intention – that is, to illuminate the ways in which the modern international system is unmistakably of a piece with the capitalist social structures which compose its leading constituent national societies. Chapter 5 redefines the concept of 'sovereignty' in the light of Marx's discussion of the abstraction of the state in capitalist society, and then goes on to suggest that Marx also provides an unremarked theory of 'anarchy' as the characteristic social form of capitalist modernity. Finally, chapter 6 develops Marx's discussion of 'the secret of primitive accumulation' to indicate an agenda of further historical research. This agenda points to a radically different historical narrative of the emergence and development of the international system to that assumed in the orthodox discipline.

One further observation may be in order at the outset. The chapters which follow have been left substantially unchanged, and in the order in which they were composed over four years of doctoral research. The disadvantage of this choice is clear enough: the argument developed over time, and the successive chapters reflect this. Indeed, were the book to be rewritten now from the vantage point of the concluding chapters, a different organization might suggest itself. Had the destination of the argument been known in advance, a more direct route could have been followed, from a more promising starting point than realist IR. On the other hand, the debate over the strengths and weaknesses of realism does remain the unavoidable starting point for students of IR. And for such readers, a work which begins ensnared in familiar debates and then struggles out onto a quite different intellectual terrain may actually be of more use than one which pitches its camp outside the recognized boundaries of the discipline. The argument which follows will therefore have served its purpose if, for all its unevenness and idiosyncratic turns, it traces one possible pathway out of realism.

1

The Trouble with Realism

The academic study of international relations is not known for its strength in the area of theory. It has no immediate equivalent to the rich contrasts of perspective generated in sociology by the legacy of Max Weber, Marx and Durkheim. So much so, that one of its most celebrated British exponents, Martin Wight, once wrote a paper called 'Why Is There No International Theory?'[1] His own answer was, in part, that there *is* nothing further to theorize after the discovery of the repetitive mechanisms of the balance of power. This was a sad conclusion for such an acute and creative mind to reach. But it does illustrate a central feature of this discipline. For a two-dimensional model of the balance of power, it can be argued, *is* the limit of any *realist* theory of international relations. And Wight's conclusion was perhaps more an index of the dominance of IR by a realist orthodoxy, than a reflection of the inherent properties of the international domain as an object of study.

What then does it mean to speak of a realist school of IR theory? In the postwar period the term realism has come to indicate a series of propositions underlying a distinctive approach to the study of international politics. These may be abbreviated as follows:

1. International politics is to be understood predominantly as the realm of interaction between sovereign authorities – a realm which is separate from that of domestic politics.
2. The distinctive character of this realm is given by the condition of 'anarchy' – meaning that the competitive pursuit of divergent 'national interests' takes place in the absence of regulation by a superordinate authority.
3. The result is a set of compulsions generic to relations between states which works, through the complex operation of the balance

9

of power, to determine how states behave internationally. To understand the balance of power is therefore also to explain international politics.

This chapter explores the adequacy of these premises as a starting point for understanding international relations. This exploration is divided into three sections, in which works by E.H. Carr, Hans Morgenthau and Kenneth Waltz are discussed as examples of (respectively) descriptive, axiomatic and theoretical articulations of realism.[2] It is argued that, as description, realism leaves too much out; as a set of prescriptive axioms, it lets too much in; and as social theory – well, that it is not a social theory at all: rather, it is an operator's manual posing as one. This technical assessment is followed by an ideological characterization of realism, and some preliminary suggestions as to how a redefinition of its core categories might alter the scope of IR theory.

Descriptive Realism: E.H. Carr and the State's-Eye View

The formulation of realism given above points immediately to a curious and suggestive paradox. Anyone seeking to reconstruct realism as a school might reasonably expect, on turning to its classic texts, to find these state-centric tenets argued for and grounded in a broader conception of political science – or at least stated in propositional form. Yet this is often not the case. Indeed, if we begin by turning to Carr, we discover not only an absence of any explicit defence of state-centricism, but also a discussion of 'realism' in which the latter is not even implicit.[3]

In the first half of *The Twenty Years' Crisis* Carr develops the idea of 'realism' as an intellectual tool especially suited to unmasking the ideological determination of political thought, a purpose to which he sets it in his impressive critique of the hopes for 'peace through law'. Time and again he demonstrates how liberal cosmopolitan values and the assertion of a fundamental harmony of interests between peoples have been successively the luxury, rationale and fatal delusion of materially and politically privileged groups. The utility of 'realism' for this critique is evidenced in its leading assumptions, as derived by Carr from Machiavelli (63–4). First, it conceives the historical process as a sequence of rationally discoverable causes and effects. Second, it holds that thought is not a faculty independent of the pragmatic needs of action; theory arises out of practice and can be analysed as a function of the latter. Third, inasmuch as ethical behaviour depends upon the expectation of reciprocity between actors, a reciprocity secured only by the presence of coercive authority, morality is a function of power and should be judged in that light. There is no visible commitment to a state-centric analysis here. Indeed, having added the later assertion of an immanent historical dynamic of progress as a fourth ingredient, Carr happily describes Marx – who would never have accepted the axiomatic separation of domestic and international politics – as a modern 'realist' (65). At this critical distance from the concerns of policy-making there is no overwhelming sense that, for example, power is constituted solely in the agency of the state.

How, then, is Carr a realist in our sense? Here the curiosity deepens; for of course by the time (in the second half of the book) he comes to construct his own understanding of international politics, the full panoply of realist assumptions has arrived unannounced.

In itself, there is nothing surprising in this. For Carr shared the urgent policy orientation of the 'idealists' he was criticizing: if their utopianism was an involuntary recoil from 1914, his own realist corrective was equally an injunction to learn the lessons of the 1930s. He was, after all, an ex-diplomat.[4] But as a result, Carr's is from the outset a discourse of *raison d'état*: as prescription, it is committed to a view of the state as subject; consequently, as explanation, its energies are directed to the illumination of international history as the half-mastered practice and partly staggered outcomes of state policy. Thus, theoretically, the agency of the state remains an irreducible category – not in the complexity of the challenges which it faces (Carr does not claim to offer easy policy answers), but very much with respect to the interweaving of international and transnational processes within which it is constituted. In short, Carr's 'science of international politics' poses questions not *of* the state but implicitly on its behalf. And this is, of course, a signature of realism. Its deepest assumptions are grounded in the ideological needs of the social practice – namely, diplomacy – whose norms it articulates.

Probably the first of these assumptions, then, is that political agency in the international system is concentrated almost exclusively in the state. (Historical *agency* is almost always reducible in realist writings to *policy*.) It therefore seems natural when he comes to define social power that Carr discusses it quite narrowly as the instrument or constraint of state policy. And although he allows that state power comprises diverse ideological, economic and military components, it is none the less measured and expressed in generic form as the nationally constituted capability of a state to influence international outcomes.[5]

We do not have to jump very far ahead to see the theoretical implication of this conception of power. If military, economic and ideological factors are seen as tributaries of a generic power (wielded by the state) which casts the pattern of international relations, if they attain significant international reach only through being mobilized as instruments of state policy, then the structure of relations between nation-states is not merely a specific moment of the international order: it actually defines the dynamics of that order. And the business of understanding world politics indeed resolves itself into the familiar realist task of describing the balance of power.

Now, we do need to understand economic, social, military and political power structures as parts of a global whole: arguably, that is the distinctive task of a theory of international relations. But can it really be done simply by collapsing them all into a model of politico-military competition between states? Can we give an adequate account of what international politics is about in these terms? This is what Carr attempts here, and we should look at some examples of why this is unsatisfactory.

For reasons which are evident (and which would have been especially pressing in 1939), 'the military instrument' appears to offer least resistance in this respect. If international politics is understood as the struggle for power between states and self-help is ultimately the only effective regulation of that struggle, then military power poses the quality of international competition most starkly, as it is directly controlled by states and most nearly conforms to the realist account of power. Thus it is here that Carr illustrates best the zero-sum mechanisms of international power politics: the prisoner's dilemma underlying 'the appetite for more power',[6] and the fragile complexity of the balance of power.[7]

However, the attempt to treat economic power along the same lines rapidly comes up against serious problems. Carr begins by observing that financial resources are a prerequisite of military power and that for this reason (among others) states conceive a strong interest in promoting economic growth. Building on this, and noting the historical expansion of government intervention in national economies, he proposes 'a general return to the term "political economy"' (116).

Now the utility of this phrase for thinking about international relations is that it suggests two vital perspectives simultaneously: an economics of political competition (exploring the role of the state in ordering, directing and taxing economic activity within its borders as a means of extending its power beyond) and a politics of the world economy (suggesting a set of shifting global economic relationships which traverse political boundaries and shape, via the transnational processes of uneven development, the forms and scope of political action). Evidently, we need to understand both of these. Similarly, when Carr adds that 'the science of economics presupposes a given political order' (117), this does not only signal the existence in every empirical instance of a ruling political elite which mobilizes economic resources; it also raises the theoretical question of the institutional relation of the state and state-system to the national and international economy.

Unfortunately, because he is considering 'economic weapons ... for use in the interests of national policy' (115), Carr's account is in both cases skewed heavily towards the former sense, with mercantilism presented as something like an ideal-type of economic policy. This is partly the result of his polemical focus, which identifies liberal theories of the market from Adam Smith onwards as the most persistent source of utopian thinking. But it also illustrates a more general weakness of the realist descriptive method, which *can* perceive that the modern state seeks to mobilize the economy, but not that the economy is also part of a transnational whole which produces important *political* effects independently of the agency of the state. Two examples may clarify this point.

Carr argues that the nineteenth-century doctrine of free trade posited a specious 'separation of economics from politics' which was not only belied by the reality of imperialism, but was later rudely shattered by unprecedented state control of the economy during the Great War: 'We have now returned therefore, after the important, but abnormal *laissez-faire* interlude of the nineteenth century, to the position where economics can be frankly recognized as a part of politics' (116). Within a pure realist perspective we do seem to have come full circle, nothing fundamental having altered since the closing years of European absolutism: states still compete for power in the international arena, mustering such economic and military resources as they can press into the service of policy (conceived generically as 'power maximizing'). In this, surely, Carr the ex-diplomat, who gauges the authenticity of political insight by its reconstruction of the dilemmas 'which are always present to the minds of those who have to solve problems of foreign policy in real life' (111), has got the better of Carr the historian. And we have a glimpse too of how realism, though heir to a huge fund of historical (or, more accurately, diplomatic) anecdote, is curiously insensitive to the processes of historical change.

For the implied image of the circle really does miss the wood for the trees. To picture the historical continuity of the nineteenth century we need at least to envision a spiral motion which incorporates the expansion of industrial capitalism as an international system as well as the related consolidation of the nation-state. If we ignore this transformation then 'the separation of economics from politics' will inevitably appear as simply the ideology of the status quo, and free trade as 'the mercantilism of the strongest'. Posed in a more familiar form, however, the separation of the political and the economic indicates precisely the central institutional linkage between the capitalist economy and the nation-state: that is, the legal structure of property rights which removes market relationships from direct political control or contestation and allows the flow of investment capital across national boundaries.[8] Carr is right to point to the state's use of economic resources for foreign policy purposes; but the economy is not, as military power is assumed to be, entirely a nationally constituted instrument ready at the disposal of the state.

The second example illustrates what is lost by regarding it in this way: Carr treats the export of capital solely as an instrument of state policy. No doubt there are many politicians on both sides of the Atlantic (and the Pacific) who wish that international capital flows could indeed be under the control of governments. However, private capital follows the highest returns; and when a currency appreciates because of the international competitiveness of the domestic economy, capital flows out in pursuit of the resultant cheap investment opportunities. Governments may seek to help or hinder this process, but the underlying mechanism is a fact about capitalism, not about states. And thus to construe the export of capital simply as an instrument of state policy is to place the international operation of the world economy and its complex interaction with the political order of nation-states outside the purview of his analysis.

A similar constriction arises from considering ideological aspects of international politics in terms of what Carr calls 'power over opinion'. Here the target of Carr's polemic is the liberal anticipation that international public opinion could become both judge and sanction in disputes between states. He is therefore concerned to show that universalist ideologies achieve effective power only when taken up by an interested national state, that public opinion is increasingly the *tool* of modern states, and that therefore 'international public opinion' may signal a temporary convergence of several national interests but cannot constitute itself as an autonomous agent in international affairs. All this is well argued and well taken. But this hardly closes the issue, for even the free trade credo which Carr dubs the ideology of the economically strong state hardly *emerged* as the contrived instrument of foreign policy. On the contrary, it evolved as the centrepiece of the domestic political and international economic aspirations of a self-conscious *class*[9] project. And its adoption by the state signalled both the victory of those interests and, yes, the ascendancy of British economic power: but where is the agency now?

This question has a much wider application. For if the course of international relations is grasped through the study of state policy, and public opinion is treated principally as the object of official manipulation, how are we to understand social revolutions and their prominence in international conflict? The point of this is not to construct an autonomy of 'public opinion' or deny the routine manipulation of nationalist currents by the state. It is simply to indicate how much remains unsaid about social ideology (even nationalism) as a dimension of international politics if it is conceived in purely instrumental terms.

So realism has serious defects when offered as an description of the dynamics of the international system. But its primary mode, as already suggested, is axiomatic: that is, it presents itself as a guide to policy-makers. How does it fare in this?

Axiomatic Realism: Morgenthau's Laws of Politics

It was suggested above that if we turn to *The Twenty Years' Crisis* for an exposition of the tenets of realism we find instead a 'realist' critique of utopianism followed by a proto-realist account of world politics. Our search for theoretical origins ends at the point where Carr (instinctively, it seems) collapses his discussion into the two-dimensional frame of the state's-eye view. And his guiding assumptions then become visible only in the light of subsequent criticism. This seems to illustrate a general feature of realism which becomes increasingly apparent as we review later attempts first to expound and then to theorize the precepts of *raison d'état*.

There is a well-known article by Stanley Hoffman which seeks to provide a sociological diagnosis of the intellectual symptoms of post-war US realist thought.[10] Hoffman considers (among other things) the sources of financial support for IR research, its close institutional connections with foreign policy-making during the global expansion of US power, and the prevailing positivist orthodoxy in the wider social sciences. And he argues that it was these factors which directed the American study of IR towards the search for general theories of world politics whose 'usefulness' would be measured by their ability to guide and predict policy. This perhaps explains why Hans Morgenthau's *Politics among Nations*, to a much greater extent than *The Twenty Years' Crisis*, is frankly a diplomats' manual of statecraft, which seeks in one extended argument to move from the assertion of laws of human nature to the elaboration of the Nine Rules of Diplomacy.

It is important to be clear how and why Morgenthau's attempt to derive axioms of political conduct from the premises of realism is ensnared from the start in circular arguments. For the truth is that realism can legitimate just about any course of action.

Morgenthau's repeated insistence on 'human nature as it actually is' forms more than a polemical allusion to the irresponsibility of idealist thought. For it is central to his account of the possibility of a 'science of international politics' that the empirically observable continuities of history point to objective causal laws of a universal and timeless kind. '[P]olitics ... is governed by objective laws that have their roots in human nature' (4).[11] Enquiry into this nature reveals 'those elemental bio-psychological drives by which in turn society is created. The drives to live, to propagate, and to dominate are common to all men' (39). And because the constitutive relation between human nature and the social world is one-way only ('social forces are the product of human nature in action' [20]), certain basic laws of political behaviour will persist throughout history.

It is on the existence of such laws that Morgenthau bases his claim for realist theory as scientific – and, relatedly, as both predictive and a sound guide to policy. What does he mean by a scientific theory? '[T]he natural aim of all scientific undertakings is to discover the forces underlying social phenomena and the mode of their operation' (18). In order to achieve this discovery, he advocates a broad positivist methodology: a rational hypothesis is constructed, positing a deter-minate causal relation between the social phenomena isolated; this is used to generate predictions which can then be tested against empirical evidence – and which, if successful, may be held to validate the original hypothesis. That is to say, the theory holds if it is 'consistent with the facts and within itself' (3). Morgenthau does not go as far explicitly as R.N. Rosecrance, for whom 'history is a laboratory in which our generalizations about international politics can be tested';[12] but the same assumptions are entailed.

The core of Morgenthau's theory is that states are by nature 'power maximizers'. They exist in a discrete world of 'the political', the latter being defined by its concern with power. In turn, power denotes 'anything that establishes and maintains the control of man over man' (11). Because each state conceives its interests in terms of the indefinite enhancement of this control, each is potentially predator or prey to any other. Moreover, the fact that, in the nature of this competition, states must ultimately look to self-help for their survival means that the contrivance of a favourable military position is the foremost concern of every state. Any group of states which endures as a plurality of sovereignties does so by virtue of what he calls 'a general social principle to which all societies composed of a number of autonomous units owe the autonomy of their component parts' (187) – namely, the balance of power. By this shifting equilibrium of multiple alliances, the independence of the units is preserved against the excessive accumulation of power at any one pole of the system.

Given this, sound policy can proceed only from a recognition of the power struggle at the heart of international life, and consists in using it to balance interests and alliances in the achievement of given ends. Too much power will call forth opponents in equal proportion; too little will make it impossible to uphold national interests – and may even invite aggression. Moral fastidiousness and moral fervour are equally inappropriate and dangerous to the rational calculation of interests and balances. Similarly, the study of politics must be grounded in the same recognition: its leading categories must enable the isolation and description of the dynamics of the power struggle. This is the claim made for the central assertion of *Politics among Nations*: 'We assume that statesmen think and act in terms of interest defined as power, and the evidence of history bears that assumption out' (5).

What does this tell us? We should turn again to the vexed issue of power. Viewed as a means, power takes myriad forms, depending on the type of political order, the nature of the ends to which it is directed and the particular social forces mobilized. Similarly, as a routinely exercised property of formalized relations of domination between individuals and collectivities, 'power' points our attention again to key social institutions specific to particular historical societies – obligations of fealty, the capitalist wage-labour contract, the sovereign authority of the state, and so on. In each case the meaning of the term power, beyond broad generalizations about control, is given by the context and the ends involved. But the offer of historical explanation based on power considered as an end in itself is altogether more difficult to make sense of. If, on a weak reading, it is taken to mean that all political agents must seek power (as a short-term end) in order to achieve their goals, then it is of little explanatory value for it must cover anything and everything. Morgenthau, however, also intends a stronger reading. For he argues (and this is of course necessary to the positivist goal of prediction) that the behaviour of states and the outcome of relations between them can be understood *sui generis* in terms of the fixed dynamics of power grouped around the compulsions originating in the balance.

Now, there *are* aspects of political and other forms of competition which are given by the number of competitors, the stakes, the means available and the degree of regulation involved. And states do perforce routinely pursue strategies in the international arena which must take into account the interests and behaviour of other states. It will therefore always be possible to point to interstate conflicts in history and describe this strategic dimension in terms of a 'balance of power'.

However, in order to pose the mechanism of the balance of power as the *explanation* of international politics, at least two further assumptions must be made. First, it must be assumed that the international scene is defined exclusively as a plurality of states conceived as unitary agents, each adjusting its power drive to the opportunities and dangers of the external environment. A consequence of this is that domestic political issues and the domestic configuration of power do not (or should not) shape foreign policy. If we seek to peer 'inside' the state we find not the complex of a society presided over by a political institution which faces both ways; instead we are returned to the image of the statesman, his gaze turned steadily outwards, calculating the external advantage of the ship of state, chafing at the querulous interference of 'public opinion' which threatens to distract from rational judgement. Only by sealing off the internal from the external in this way can the 'primacy of the international' (which simplifies the task of prediction by reducing the number of variables) be secured. Of course, most of the resources which the statesman brings to the negotiating table *derive* internally – but they are held to affect only the strength of his hand, not the rules of the game. Morgenthau does not offer to explain the processes by which powers attain and lose greatness, only how they will behave once they have arrived and (in the blunt imputation of a universal drive to dominate) what fuels the overall competition.

Second, the balance of power is of course a military balance. Its prominence is given by the self-help character of international anarchy. To define international politics in terms of the balance of power therefore involves posing a hierarchy of issues facing states internationally, of which only those connected or potentially connected with the use of force qualify as (power) political. Hence the statement: 'a nation is not normally engaged in international politics when it concludes an extradition treaty with another nation, when it exchanges goods and services with other nations' (32).

By this stage, however, the argument has become irretrievably circular: if power in a state system is ultimately military power, and the statesman is 'doing politics' only when attending to security-related issues, then the hypothesis that 'the statesman thinks and acts in terms of interest defined as power' becomes unfalsifiable.

Once the scope of political facts has been circumscribed in this way, the prediction that international politics is about 'interest defined as power' traces a great circle through history from Thucydides through Machiavelli to Kissinger and back again, skimming the tops of successive strategic climaxes and recovering the moral. For example, Charles V, Napoleon, Wilhelm II and Hitler all sought to dominate Europe and met the same fate. Moral: imperial ambitions in a state system generate overwhelming opposing coalitions. Another example: from the early sixteenth century to the mid twentieth century, Britain repeatedly changed sides in the Franco-German rivalry for control of the Continent. Moral: apparent fickleness in a nation's foreign policy may mask an underlying continuity given by its identity as 'holder of the balance'. Diplomatic relations in Europe after 1945 remained in a fixed pattern given by the overarching Soviet–American confrontation:[13] the conditions of a multipolar and a bipolar system differ in the scope of diplomatic mobility possible. Morgenthau gives a whole list of these examples; and they are held to illustrate the operation of the balance of power – but what has been explained about international politics?

The realist perspective highlights the similarities between Charles V, Napoleon, Wilhelm II and Hitler by superimposing on widely contrasting historical periods the logic of military competition in a state system. But in doing so it prejudges the form taken by political power, reducing it to its military climax, and thereby suppresses the differences. This is perfectly acceptable as a very general proposition about unregulated competition. But announcing it as a political explanation makes it reductionist. Further, because these events are explained by unchanging 'objective laws that have their roots in human nature'(4), the essence of international politics is unhistorical: there is only the unending accumulation of empirical instances reproducing the same range of scenarios with different participants. Yet while the realist is busy watching the statesmen playing the hands dealt them by the balance of power, those same international struggles are mediating a wholesale transformation of the form and conditions of social power in the world. One has only to consider the last hundred years and the relationship between imperial rivalries, the globalizing of a transnational capitalist economy and the emergence of a world nation-state system: it ought to be obvious that something more has been afoot internationally than can be captured in the maxims of Thucydides.

Thus what is perhaps the most widely debated and animating question in the broader social sciences, namely how we are to characterize the enormous and continuing historical transformations grouped, for want of any agreed explanation, under the heading of 'modernity', finds no echo at all in Morgenthau's realism. (A local and isolated exception to this is his recognition that the invention of nuclear weapons has complicated the use of force in the postwar world – but this remains an empirical observation.) As Kenneth Thompson puts it: 'The price one has to pay for identifying the "timeless features" of the political landscape is the sacrifice of understanding the processes of change in world affairs.'[14]

This is not just an unfortunate omission. It is a fundamental failure to grasp what an adequate social explanation would consist in. And the cause of this deficiency is traceable fairly directly to the doctrinal realist separation of domestic and international politics itself. For ignoring domestic non-state processes renders their actual transnational extension invisible. This in turn makes it impossible (or irrelevant) to conceive other global structures of power apart from the political – because the only visible agents are other states. And with so much of the substance of international politics cancelled at a stroke, it is little wonder that theories of indiscriminate power-maximizing and the endless security needs of anarchy step into the breach: what, otherwise, has all the fighting been about?

Returning to Morgenthau, the restrictive definition of the international is undertaken in an attempt to distil the purely political in order to make scientific statements. What then becomes of the goal of prescription? If the hypothesis about power is valid – and Morgenthau clearly believes that it is – then testing it against a wider and wider body of empirical data will progressively trace the outline of the laws of politics. Indeed, not only will it explain the past behaviour of the statesman: it may also provide 'the clue by which to predict his foreign policies' (6). As if this were not enough, realism is simultaneously a normative and a practical guide for the diplomat: since the responsibilities of government demand an ethic of prudence, and since only disaster awaits those who try to work against the forces determining political outcomes, the statesman is both morally and professionally obliged to pursue the national interest defined as power.

The problem, of course, is that a definition of power which produces an unfalsifiable hypothesis about the past is capable of legitimating an unlimited range of practical suggestions as to present policy. Morgenthau's later attempt to spell out the foreign policy implications of realism by distinguishing between 'the necessary and variable elements of the national interest'[15] leads no further than a rather unhelpful appeal for 'rational scrutiny' in order to identify and separate these. A similar attitude informs the gloss on the Fourth Fundamental Rule of Diplomacy: 'For minds not beclouded by the crusading zeal of a political religion and capable of viewing the national interests of both sides with objectivity, the delimitation of these vital interests should not prove too difficult' (588). Not only are the criteria for distinguishing these categories precisely what is contested – as his own later isolation on the issue of Vietnam was to indicate, even when it is commonly accepted that vital interests are at stake, the injunction to 'pursue the national interest' has no substantive content. Which statesperson, after all, ever thought he or she was doing anything *but* upholding the national interest? Certainly not the 'appeasers' of the 1930s, those whipping-boys of later realist writers. As Kennedy remarks of British foreign policy in the interwar years:

> these were the actions of a country with nothing to gain, and much to lose, by being involved in war. Peace, in such circumstances, was the greatest of national interests.[16]

And indeed the first edition of *The Twenty Years' Crisis* described Chamberlain's policy of appeasement as 'a reaction of realism against utopianism'.[17] This is an important point because it is part of the ideological self-definition of postwar realism to contrast itself with a supposed prewar idealist ascendancy in foreign policy-making which led inevitably to the shame of Munich and disaster beyond.[18] This is pure myth. Every realist consensus is, like the Roman Catholic distinction between the Church Spiritual and the Church Temporal, *post factum*. And while realism likes to think that it *guides* foreign policy, actually, it has often ended by simply legitimating it: its 'usefulness' has been of a rather different kind to what it had hoped.

This raises the interesting question: if idealism did not exist, would realism have to invent it? Any serious contention that a particular aspect of social life is (reductively) its 'dominant level' needs to be armed with some means of explaining behaviour and outcomes which do not conform to its expectations. And if international relations are patterned by the mechanical logic of the balance of power, if this shapes the thought and behaviour of the statesman, why does the latter need to be exhorted to hold fast to its lines? Morgenthau blithely resolves this difficulty by proposing 'a counter-theory of irrational politics' (7–9) of which the 'peace through law' school is one expression.[19] But the source of the difficulty remains all too apparent: realism inveterately confuses its own urgent desire for attention to the strategic aspects of interstate relations[20] with an explanation of international outcomes. And idealism then comes to represent anything which distracts from concentration on those pitfalls of the system which are deducible a priori, any concern with other issues which could lead to strategic errors. But of course it does not follow that those other factors are irrational; they may simply derive from other, connected realms of activity and determination in which the state is involved; they may involve, for example, domestic expenditures or foreign adventures conceived as necessary to the internal legitimacy of the state, or obligations which result from the regulative role played by the state in the international system, and so on.

For this reason there is, as has been widely remarked, considerable uncertainty attaching to the status of Morgenthau's 'interest defined as power': does it indicate an objective law of politics which determines political behaviour? This is certainly what he argues in describing it as a 'signpost' which 'reflects ... these objective laws' and enables prediction. Or is it rather an ideal-type concept which intuits (*verstehen*) the meaning to the agent of political action and registers its distortion by irrational or accidental factors? Again, this is how he defends against the charge that 'a perfect balance of power policy will scarcely be found in reality' (10). Or is it, finally, a normative precept whose achievement is quite contingent and for which statesmen are morally obliged to strive: 'foreign policy ought to be rational in view of its own moral and practical purposes'? Now it simply cannot be all three. The construction of ideal-types is part of an interpretive, not a predictive, methodology. Indeed, Weber premissed his use of them precisely on the denial of objective causal laws of human behaviour. Conversely, a deterministic account of human behaviour cannot be rescued from allegations of historical inaccuracy by 'a counter-theory of irrational politics' (7). And moral exhortation, a voluntarist intruder into the world of objective laws, is not accommodated easily within a concept which is claimed to show the world 'as it actually is'.[21]

These tensions break out into open contradiction in the first two chapters of the work. In chapter 1 Morgenthau stresses the importance to a theory of being 'consistent with the facts as they are' (3); such a theory 'allows us to retrace and anticipate, as it were, the steps a statesman – past, present or future – has taken or will take on the political scene' (5); it models itself on the achievements of the science of economics and seeks 'to contribute to a similar development in the field of politics' (16). By contrast, chapter 2 dwells on 'the ambiguity of the facts of international politics' (23); the 'first lesson' of international politics is that 'trustworthy prophecies (are) impossible'; and there is a general lament for the failure of the predictive power of economics. Not the least remarkable aspect of this confusion is the fact that chapter 1 was apparently written *after* chapter 2.

Waltz's Theoretical Realism:
Accidents Will Happen

Morgenthau's edifice of political realism was crumbling right from the start. Why *Politics among Nations* remained the leading textbook for so long is indeed a sociological rather than an intellectual question.[22] Yet the bulk of the criticism directed at Morgenthau was concerned not with attacking his realist premises, but rather with rescuing them from the idiosyncrasies of his *Weltanschauung*.[23] Morgenthau, it may be recalled, had some rather unflattering and unsophisticated views on human nature, and an embarrassing habit of parading them as the philosophical basis of realism. It must have been rather unsettling for diplomats to be told that the basis of postwar US foreign policy was not so much the defence of democracy as the pursuit of an 'elemental bio-psychological drive ... to dominate' (39), a drive which they might have in common with 'monkeys and chickens' (39n). And among the second generation of US realists, Kenneth Waltz, in his book *Man, the State and War*, undertook to secure the theoretical underpinnings of the concept of the balance of power by deriving it a priori in the more palatable form of a rational-choice model.[24] It should also be said that Waltz has an impressively clear grasp of what realism logically entails, and he therefore provides its most concise theoretical formulation.

Man, the State and War is not a general theory of international politics; it is an extended discussion of the 'level of analysis' problem which arises in attempting to explain the occurrence of war between states.[25] And Waltz's principal criticism of Morgenthau is a tactical one: by deriving the international power struggle from human nature, Morgenthau conflates the behaviour of agents who are driven by the distinctive pressures of unregulated competition with a supposed inherent will to power. This conflation opens liabilities on two fronts. First, it suffers the general flaw of arguments from human nature, namely that they cannot account for variation in the phenomena which they seek to explain – in this instance, why war is not a constant and pervasive feature of human life (29).[26] And second, it has difficulty confining its implications to the realm of explanation, and thus invites ethical challenges which distract it from its analytical purpose (37). By contrast, Waltz's alternative derivation of the balance of power from the anarchical properties of the international system enjoys the rigour and moral neutrality of a logical necessity grounded in mathematically given dilemmas of rational choice. This sanitizing of Morgenthau raises the inevitable question: in theorizing the precepts of realism does Waltz advance our understanding of international politics; or does he simply reproduce the assumptions of *raison d'état* at a higher level of abstraction?

Waltz's argument falls into three parts. First he derives the general principle that conflict is inscribed in any social system which lacks overarching authority. Next, he assesses how far states may be taken as discrete units involved in such a system. Finally, he establishes the connection between conflicts of interest and war, and reconstructs the balance of power as a function of an anarchical international social structure.

For the first part, Waltz uses a parable by Rousseau concerning five men in the presocial state of nature who are driven by hunger to co-operate in a stag-hunt. As they are on the point of trapping their quarry – which would be sufficient to feed all of them – a hare (which could feed only one) runs within their reach. One of the hunters lunges at the hare, a movement which puts the stag to flight.

The moral of this is taken by Waltz to be that in a condition of anarchy, co-operation between individuals each seeking his or her own interest is only *contingently* rational. Each must base his or her calculations on the possible actions of others, but without a common authority to guarantee agreements none can calculate with certainty what those actions will be. Therefore none can *afford* to be absolutely dependable. And the response of the hunter who disrupts the stag-hunt by seizing the hare cannot be called irrational since he had no means of knowing that he was not simply pre-empting his fellows. Rational self-interest would have dictated restraint only if the fidelity of his partners had been assured. And since it is precisely this which is ruled out by anarchy, the latter may be said to yield antinomies of political reason which establish the conflict between collective and individual interests as an inescapable feature of co-operation itself – so long as there is no authority to enforce contracts.

How far does the condition of states in the modern international system resemble the predicament of the hunters in Rousseau's parable? Clearly they interact without any common political authority. As to whether they constitute and behave as unitary agents, Waltz suggests that this condition is satisfied so long as *someone* is in charge. And since the state would not exist were this not the case, it necessarily holds for all states. It is irrelevant to this part of Waltz's argument that states are internally conflict-ridden, or that contingency and miscalculation are rife in politics. The question is simply whether those in power face conflicts of particular and general interest in their foreign policy-making which result from the effects of anarchy. To which the answer must of course be yes. Hence Rousseau's famous conclusion: 'it is not impossible that a Republic, though in itself well-governed, should enter upon an unjust war' (181–2). And this in turn underlies the logical core of Waltz's argument: 'That among particularities accidents will occur is not accidental but necessary. ... in anarchy there is no automatic harmony' (182). Moreover, since discord grows with interdependence, violence will be greatest in those situations where co-operation is necessary but supervening control and arbitration of the resultant conflicts is not available. This, says Rousseau (184) (and Waltz), corresponds to the political structure of the international system. To this extent, Waltz argues, the social structure itself plays a crucial causal role in producing collectively sub-optimal outcomes from an aggregate of individually rational choices.

The logic of the balance of power is then derived simply by interpolating into this anarchical structure an assumed desire by the state to maintain its own physical security. The means of achieving this goal are constrained by the condition of anarchy in that each state must provide for itself, and, as in a game of poker, 'Everybody's strategy depends on everybody else's' (201). Putting this maxim into practice necessarily involves at least a tacit reliance on a particular kind of behaviour from certain other agents – even if it does not issue formally in an alliance. Usually, however, where three or more units are involved, temporary coalitions result.

This much Waltz takes from the game theory of von Neumann and Morgenstern.[27] However, he is quite clear that in order for laws derived from such models to be applicable to states, they must be twice qualified. First, the game produced by the competitive pursuit of security is not necessarily defined in purely zero-sum terms. It may become a 'general' game in which one side's gain does not dictate the other's loss. There may even be times when the common goal becomes the maximization of collective security. (And the reasons why it may switch between these modes are not given within the rules of the game.) Second, states simultaneously play other games, both internally and externally, which compete for the political priority and the material resources accorded to the security game. This is an enormous caveat, for it concedes that within certain limits (which in practice turn out to be very wide indeed) the impact of anarchy on the behaviour of states varies according to determinations quite outside the purview of a realist theory. A state may choose or be forced to behave quite otherwise than predicted by the logic of the balance of power: it may be prepared to countenance large-scale retreat internationally in order to release resources for urgent domestic goals; it may undertake the military defence of a transnational socio-economic system which leads it routinely to exceed the requirements of the visible 'national interest'; in extreme cases, where it contends with serious internal challenges, it may even fail properly to resist an external aggressor. More routinely, certain security interests may simply be overridden because their pursuit is judged too costly in either domestic or international terms. But even if all the games which all the states play are governed by anarchical rules, we could still not predict the outcomes a priori, since the relative importance to each state of each game at any one time is contingent. And insofar as that is the case, both the predictive and the normative claims of realism virtually disappear; for realism does not pretend to possess the criteria for divining when pure balance of power considerations will be or should be overridden by other concerns: 'no set of rules can specify how important the (security) game should be considered!' (206). Waltz is quite explicit about the consequences of this:

> The reference to game theory does not imply that there is available a technique by which international politics can be approached mathematically. Balance-of-power politics, however, can profitably be described using the concepts of von Neumann and Morgenstern. (201n)

The implication is clearly that a theory of the balance of power is not a theory of international politics. And hence, no hard and fast rules may be drawn from it. In fact, we 'cannot say in the abstract that for peace a country must arm, or disarm, or compromise, or stand firm' (222).

What, then, is the explanatory scope of the theory? Paradoxically, Waltz's 'strong' realism is actually very weak in the scope of its claims. It purports to account for why war persists in the international system without any claim to explain why any particular war occurs. It isolates a permissive cause, as opposed to the efficient causes, of war. It is a contradiction of perpetual peace rather than a theory of international politics. And the purpose is simply to establish that there is a dimension of international politics, given by the absence of government, which conforms to Rousseau's parable: where knowledge of others' intentions is imperfect, and the use of force is not ruled out (these being the two immediate consequences of anarchy), rational calculation by any individual cannot afford to assume (and therefore cannot actualize) an assured harmony of interests. *Ergo*, the balance.

It is difficult not to feel that the mountain has laboured, and brought forth a molehill. Having rightly dispensed with the reductionism of Morgenthau, Waltz's theoretical realism is little more than a banality: *of course* states face recurrent prisoners' dilemmas in their attempts to manage their relations with other states – in all fields, particularly that of security. Truisms such as this, as the realists themselves like to point out, have been available to statesmen for millennia.

But there is perhaps a more significant question: is this as far as realism can go at the theoretical level – a barren choice between reductionism and banality? The question can be explored further by considering again what is involved in the realist assertion of the unitary agency of the state. For the latter is clearly connected with the belief that understanding the core of international politics is a matter of re-enacting the dilemmas faced by statesmen and tracing the recurrent techniques in the fitting of means to ends. This is especially clear in Waltz's use of the stag-hunter parable, where he allows the fiction of presocial individuals to persist even after he has supposedly debunked other fallacies of 'the state of nature'. Now, within such a perspective social structure is pictured as a set of external constraints which derive from the aggregate of individual, reciprocally calculated rational choices – that, after all, is supposedly how it is experienced by the politician. But such a model will take us no further than a charting of the mechanics of *realpolitik*. How calculations within the system are reckoned (ideally) by practitioners, and how determinations are set out in the model are identical: this is nothing more than a systematizing of *raison d'état*. (And, it might be added, a logical proof of the prisoner's dilemma is also a normative legitimation of *raison d'état*.)

It is precisely in this mechanical notion of structure that the inherent weaknesses of realism are most transparent. In particular, it is perhaps easier to see at this level how two key concepts, change and power, become deeply problematical. What is it then that accounts for realism's obliviousness to historical change?

The reason, it may be suggested, is that in order to conceive the state as a unit responding purely to the balance of power it must implicitly define it as ontologically anterior to the international system: and if the system is simply a set of external restraints given by the number and relative strength of the individual units comprising it, what could change *mean* beyond (reversible) variation in the numbers involved and the distribution of weight among them – where the mathematical possibilities are all given a priori?[28] But this of course is not what we mean by historical change. The shift from weak, territorially disaggregated fiefdoms in which the monarchical state shared authority and jurisdiction with Church and nobility to the modern, bordered, sovereign nation-state cannot be registered in these terms. Nor can the key role played in that shift by the convulsive interaction of domestic revolution and the international system. To conceive these it would be necessary to supply what cannot be derived from a rational-choice model: namely, an account of those conditions of social power within a system which result not from balancing the numbers involved but from the reproduction of the core institutions which reflect its historical character, which position the individuals in terms of access to resources and which define the terrain of interaction. And it involves the same 'state of nature' fallacy already referred to above to assume that there ever were social systems in which power could be understood without recognizing this dimension.

Waltz would presumably answer that the system of states is the one exception: such core institutions as property rights, the liberty of the person and the suppression of routine violence rely for their domestic reproduction on the availability of coercive authority in the hands of the civil state; but internationally, who will coerce the coercers? Short of world government, Waltz argues, no one. Since each state is therefore ultimately cast back solely on its own resources, a mechanical conception of structure is uniquely appropriate to the description of the society of states, however much it may need to be overlain by recognition of other, transnational processes in any historical study.

But this merely leads us back to the fallacy of collapsing our understanding of power into a military definition of international relations, since that is the only realm in which it is claimed that this mechanical structure applies. And once again, the argument has become circular.

Realism as Ideology

These recurrent circularities point to the need for an extra dimension, beyond a purely technical assessment, to any explanation of the part played by realism in IR. Something else, remarked near the start of this chapter, also points in the same direction: namely, the startling difference between the self-definition of realism and the properties which become visible only in the light of subsequent criticism. (As already suggested, the clarity of Waltz's exposition is exceptional.) And an intellectual position whose very propositional form is fiercely contested cannot help but invite consideration as an ideology.

To come to the point, there is something awry with the foundation myth of realism, the claim that the historical triumph over idealism involved something like an 'epistemological break' which marked the inauguration of the discipline of international relations. There is a sleight of hand being practised in the repetitive and apparently compulsive realist self-definition in contrast to idealism. Certainly, in rehearsing this 'Great Debate', opposing lists of assumptions are duly presented: there is the marshalling of *is* against *ought*, and *power* against *morality*; but what remain covert (because uncontested by either side) are those premises given by the fact that the 'Great Debate' has always been fundamentally a policy debate. And as such it tacitly reproduces the premises of the unitary agency of the state, the international 'state of nature' and the insulated autonomy of the political sphere taken over from the tradition of normative political theory. In important ways, realism never did break with idealism, which partly explains why its central premisses remain unannounced. For this reason the question of how to theorize the state within a broader understanding of world politics, surely a central question facing IR theory, simply does not arise as an issue for realism because it stands squarely in the common ground it shares with idealism.

Realism, then, is not simply a focusing of attention on the state-political aspect of international relations. It is a determinate construction of political reality which entails a series of hidden propositions and symptomatic silences.

Realism is the conservative ideology of the exercise of modern state power: it provides a terminology of international relations which dramatizes the dilemmas, legitimizes the priorities and rehearses the means of *realpolitik*. (Liberal, socialist and revolutionary governments also use realist arguments to justify unpopular state policies; but they do not, if they can help it, embrace realism as overall explanation. For it clashes with their alternative ideology, the 'society-centred', instrumentalist conception of the state.)

Fundamental to this role is the positing of a discrete environment of 'the international' in which the behaviour of states can be explained *sui generis* – requiring the insulation of the international from the domestic. This is what enables 'the autonomy of the political' – whether the latter is conceived as a self-sufficient explanation of outcomes (as in Morgenthau) or alternatively as the bare framework (and sole possible theory) of world politics (as in Waltz). The borders and landscape of this environment are set and policed by the twin concepts of sovereignty and anarchy. Quite restrictive definitions of these are needed to keep the environment sealed. The realist concept of sovereignty wavers between a military fact, a legal claim and a theoretical category; but in each case its 'indivisibility' defines societies as bounded entities whose interaction is channelled through the agency of the state. It does not, however, thereby become a window on to the society over which the state presides: on the contrary, by assuming the state to be co-extensive with the society for the purposes of foreign policy, this conception of sovereignty must factor out the operation of socio-economic forces which are not convertible into state power.[29]

The fact that in the logic of realism this sovereignty of the state precedes the theoretical formulation of its interaction with other states is of considerable importance. Under the plausible cover of conforming to the experience of the statesman, it achieves two things. It poses the state as a completed social order such that its foreign interests are

THE TROUBLE WITH REALISM

constituted entirely internationally – thereby removing interpretation of the 'national interest' from domestic political contestation. And it clears the field for a purely interstate theory – since any other global structures or international agents which might complicate the picture could only be the result of the transnational extension of (domestic) sub-state socio-economic relations, which are not recognized. If sovereignty were not anterior in this way, and in addition were seen as a form of rule particular to the societies whose governments dominate the states-system, then the role of that system in upholding domestic social orders would come into view and the use of the term 'anarchy' to denote its overriding 'structural principle' would have to be re-worked. As it is, for the purposes of international politics, states are seen to have only each other to deal with; and the theoretical atomism entailed by their analytical priority as completed orders dictates a mechanical conception of structure. And so on.

For these reasons, we shall make the explicit redefinition of these categories of sovereignty and anarchy central to our construction of a non-realist perspective in the last third of this book.

Why then does realism have such 'staying power' as an ideology? Four major reasons may be suggested. First, although the discrete realm of 'the international' is a fiction, the distinctive social form of the modern state – expressed in its sovereign legal, territorial and violent aspects – does indeed have to be addressed theoretically. The historical fact of the differentiation of the state from civil society, and the specificity of the sovereign state-form which resulted from this, cannot be understood by 'reducing' it to economic factors, any more than it can be understood by conceiving it in isolation from the rest of society. Realism may end by misconstruing the specificity of the state; but it does at least gesture at something of considerable importance.

Second, realism *sounds plausible* because it articulates commonly held common-sense assumptions about world politics. This is not surprising since it mimics the vocabulary of the state's rationalization of its own behaviour, and forms in that sense a ruling ideology *par excellence*. Its conception of the unitary, sovereign agency of the state sits easily with the popular nationalist identification with the home state which comprises most individuals' participation in the international system. This is a notion which is reinforced from all sides in public discussion of the international scene, through the media presentation of 'news' and the regular commentary of diplomats and politicians. And realism's celebration of the professionalism of diplomacy chimes with the nationalist premiss that there exists a permanent 'national interest', and that the conduct of international relations is therefore predominantly about the techniques and the means (not the political ends) of the operator:

> although I appreciated the idealism of those who march and demonstrate for 'peace', my admiration is reserved for that community of grey, inconspicuous, overworked men and women of all nations – bureaucrats, diplomats, lawyers, businessmen and political leaders, sitting behind desks overflowing with paper – whose boring work, prudent foresight and hardwon mutual understanding across cultural barriers actually preserves it.[30]

Third, to the extent that IR remains, in terms of the sheer weight of numbers, resources and publications 'an American social science', the persistence of realism seems assured. This is so mainly as a result of the interaction and mutual reinforcement of three factors which distinguish the American discipline: the demand for policy-relevant studies which provides the financial supports of the discipline and thereby installs the state's-eye view as the natural perspective; the unique role played by the American state which requires special justification in the light of its extensive global interventions at all levels of the system; and the positivist methodologies, adopted in the effort to emulate the 'usefulness' of other sciences, which tend to accept uncritically the received categories of realist common sense – provided by the state.

The fourth major strength of realism is what Waltz might term a 'permissive cause': it consists in the absence of any recognized alternative conceptualization of the political structure of the global system to the one extrapolated from normative political theory, and the (related) behaviour of the critics of realism. It has become a commonplace in recent years to remark the 'absence in liberal sociology and in Marx's writings … of a systematic interpretation of the rise of the territorially bounded nation-state and its association with military power'.[31] Whatever the reasons for this, the contrast with the plethora of theories of the domestic activity of the state is striking: there appears to be no parallel as yet within IR to the way in which the tradition of normative political theory was overtaken by political sociology.[32] On the day that mainstream IR theory too breaks with the classical problematic of 'why must we support the coercive activities of the state?', and asks instead 'how are we to understand the distinctive social form of the modern state?' – on that day the stranglehold of realism on IR as a social science will begin to loosen.

For the moment, however, the commanding position of realism – reproduced also through the broader ideology of nationalism, the language of the media and the testimony of practitioners – continues to have a disorganizing effect on its critics. Indeed, one could almost say that realism has been able to organize them into certain familiar areas of contestation which reinforce its own dominance. At any rate the persistence of forms of anti-realist argument which are clearly self-defeating is an index of how far realism is still able to set the terms of debate within the discipline. Among these forms, two stand out in particular. First, there is the outright denial of any specificity to either the political behaviour or the institutional form of the state. In the case of political behaviour, a clear instance is the ringing pronouncement of Jenkins and Minnerup:

> Conflicts between states are in reality not conflicts between states at all, but conflicts between specific social and class interests using those states for their purposes. ... Stripped of its class content as defined by its ruling class, the nation-state is no more than a shell, a form, an organizing principle of political sovereignty: a unit in the vertical division of humankind, devoid of any inherent dynamic which would set one against the other, and as compatible with federal association 'above' as with decentralizing devolution 'below' it.[33]

Plenty of similar examples could be drawn from the longer history of liberal internationalism. As for the state's institutional form, calls for the democratization and even dissolution of centralized controls of the means of violence and the distinct foreign policy-making arm of government have an equally long history; they range across a broad political spectrum, from Cobden's slogan of 'No Foreign Policies!', through Lenin's (and Engels's) anticipation of 'a self-acting armed organization of the population', to the advocacy in parts of the 1980s peace movement of 'détente from below' as a means of reducing international tensions. In each case the outright denial of the autonomy of the political points to the need for an alternative theorizing of the state which, however, the critique does not supply. The net effect is therefore to perpetuate the realist claim to sole occupancy.

A second form of polemical suicide in the face of realist orthodoxy involves endorsing the notion of a discrete political realm but challenging realist prescriptions on ethical grounds. Moral attacks on the untroubled acceptance of power politics, on the rationale of arms racing, on the use of military force and war – all these, when unsupported by analytical criticisms, are so much bread and butter to realism: for they legitimate the contrast of 'is' and 'ought' which is so central to its ideological self-definition. And the louder the moral protest, the more attention is diverted from the two most dubious claims of realism: that its conception of power has any significant explanatory (as opposed to rhetorical) force; and that it rests on a value-free empiricism. Both this and the previous type of criticism unwittingly rehearse the 'Great Debate', and thereby automatically reproduce the terms of the realist ascendancy.

Conclusions: What's Missing?

It was suggested above that the interlocking of the emphasis on anarchy with the restrictive definition of sovereignty forms a kind of stranglehold on the development of IR theory. It remains therefore to give some preliminary indication of what new perspectives come into view when this grip is prised open.

Let us take the question of anarchy first. In chapter 5 we shall mount a systematic redefinition of anarchy, one which allows us to pose its centrality to the modern states-system in non-realist terms. In the meantime, however, we may begin by displacing the existing realist category. As we have seen, a rigorously interstate theory of international politics pushes this conception of anarchy to the fore, and blocks consideration of how much interstate behaviour is determined by – and is concerned with managing – other, domestic political processes. It is not just that the international offers an arena for exploits to bolster domestic legitimacy. Rather, the description of the state, of its position within the global political order – and hence the overall character of that order too – is simply distorted without the recognition that the same agent is simultaneously central to the constitution and management of international and domestic politics.

One of the clearest and most important illustrations of this claim concerns the phenomenon of revolution.[34] On a strict realist view there is no necessary reason why domestic revolution should impact significantly on the international system. If any instability is introduced into the balance of power it must be associated with the weakening of the state concerned; hence revolutionary states should calculate a strong interest in peace with their neighbours. However, this is not the case. The foreign policies of revolutionary states are generally hostile to foreign ruling establishments, which are perceived as representing the same oppressive social forces as have been overthrown domestically; they are unwilling (for the same reason) to recognize the legitimacy of conventional diplomatic channels; and they frequently seek to export the revolution via transnational links and assistance to insurgents in other countries. Generally too, the social conflict which they seek to export is taken up at the interstate level by counterrevolutionary alliances of other states, often prepared to intervene directly or indirectly to restore 'order'. But a counter-revolutionary foreign policy is rarely just a foreign policy. To a degree which varies with individual cases it is also directed inwards, a nationalist identification of certain programmes of domestic political change with a foreign threat. The Cold War, for example, always partook of this three-dimensionality.

All this might seem innocuous enough to the realist until it is recalled just how much of the history of the states-system has been distracted by such internationalization of social conflict – that is, through how much of the history of 'international' conflict it is necessary to speak of the states involved as mediating the agency of social forces. Martin Wight found '256 years of international revolution to 212 unrevolutionary' since 1492 – and that calculation was made in 1960. So, however much states are compelled to prepare against the possible behaviour of other states, 'the international' has also been very much about the management of change in domestic political orders. In the aftermath of great wars this aspect generally needs to be reasserted: Wight noted that '[s]ince Bismarck's time, every war between great powers has ended with a revolution on the losing side'.[35] And both world wars were followed by a period of sustained, internationally concerted counterrevolution. (Nor has the states-system acted uniformly as a brake on social change; in many instances the opposite applies: witness the drastic impact of European imperialism, or the imposition from outside of liberal democracy in Germany and Japan.)

This does not mean that the state is 'no more than a shell'. For when we approach it from the perspective of transnational political (and other) movements and forces, the materiality of its power is indeed of enormous significance. Revolutionaries in power moderate their support for comrades abroad in accordance with *raison d'état*. When they do attempt to carry the revolution beyond their borders by force of arms, they stir up currents of nationalist resistance which contradict their solidarist doctrine. And indeed the very process of 'liberation' is an extension of the power of the revolutionary state, which is generally appropriated in nationalist terms. The attempt to use the agency of the state in the promotion of the transnational spread of revolution has proved endlessly problematic.

However, the important point here is that in both cases what is specific to the political realm, the manner in which the role of the state overdetermines other political projects and conflicts, is not visible if the state is conceived as a 'national-territorial totality'[36] responding purely to external determinations in the shape of other states. The plurality of sovereignties is indeed a fundamental aspect of the modern world system. But it does not follow that anarchy – conceived in realist terms – forms its core identity. On the contrary, as we have seen, such a claim cannot be consistently maintained without emptying the history of the states-system of its actual political content. Perhaps this is the price that must be paid in order to construct a general theory of the states-system. If so, it is not a price worth paying.

Turning to the issue of sovereignty, Morgenthau explains that

> sovereignty points to a political fact. That fact is the existence of a person or a group of persons who, within the limits of a given territory, are more powerful than any competing person or group of persons and whose power, institutionalized as it must be in order to last, manifests itself as the supreme authority to enact and enforce legal rules within that territory.[37]

There have been states which were not sovereign – medieval monarchs had to share jurisdiction with Church and nobility. (In Waltz's atomistic version of realism, however, even this does not mar the conception of the international.) To this extent, sovereignty is recognized as a historically contingent fact which in turn enables us to date the modern states-system. But it remains a quantitative measure of authority, rather than a qualitative characterization of a specific form of rule. Moreover, it is an all-or-nothing fact: either it obtains or it does not; and if it does, the realist conception of the international is held to be relevant. Hence the ease of recourse to Thucydides.

Again, what is missing is any sense that the history of the states-system is more than the accumulation of successive power-struggles, any awareness that those competitions between great powers have mediated the continuing evolution, geographical expansion and global consolidation of a world political structure which in many ways is continuous with the changing *domestic* form, legitimacy and powers of the state: that the meaning of sovereignty itself is historically specific.

The long decline of British (and European) ascendancy was associated with the military occupation of almost every stretch of territory not already claimed by one of the European states or settler-colonies. The subsequent rise of American world power coincided in turn with the creation of a hundred-odd new states. Now evidently, the Europeans did not carve up the planet in order to extend the states-system. But they did install the colonial state apparatuses for their own purposes of exploitation and control; these did shape and become the focus of nationalist resistance; and the mobilization for independence was supplemented from the outside by American pressure for unrestricted economic access, clothed in a rhetoric of freedom and self-determination. For their part, US planners recognized by May 1942 that 'the British Empire ... will never reappear and that the United States may have to take its place'; that in the light of growing nationalism there was a need to 'avoid conventional forms of imperialism' and that new institutions of international management, such as a United Nations organization, should be developed to meet this need.[38] What we see here is not just a change in the identity of the hegemonic power in the system, but also a transformation in the historical character of the system itself. Playing the directive role in a global nation-state system is already hugely removed from policing a colonial periphery – and what either of them has in common with Thucydides' Athens is something of a distraction.

In short, if we displace for the moment the realist concern with anarchy, we see that the history of the states-system has a live political content; a moment's glance at this content, and it is apparent that to understand the realm of the political we need a conception of historical agency as a dispersed property of human societies which state organizations will always attempt to mobilize, but which is never reducible to state policy. If, secondly, we redefine sovereignty in the manner suggested, we start to make sense of power as a category because we specify it as a determinate historical configuration of social relations. This in turn throws into relief the changing institutional form of the state, and with it the essential novelty of 'international' power. And at a certain point in this overall process of reformulation, something else comes into view which realism is incapable of showing us: the emergence and historical formation of a global nation-state system. What has realism to tell us about the *differentia specifica* of this unprecedented development? And yet where else is its significance to be registered if not in IR theory?

2

Social Structures and Geopolitical Systems

Since we are proposing to develop an alternative theoretical perspective for thinking about international relations, it might help to reflect a little upon both the nature of our subject matter and the tools available to us for constructing social theories. The considerations which follow are guided by two related assumptions. On the one hand, if we are to avoid the shortcomings of general theories of the states-system, with their blindness to the great social transformations of modern world history, then the theoretical categories which we develop in order to understand geopolitical systems must be historical categories.[1] That is, they must enable us to distinguish and explain particular historical forms – particular forms of state, for example – rather than pointing to generalizations wide enough to cover all cases. On the other hand, it rapidly becomes clear that such categories cannot be formulated without addressing the wider structures of society whose development over time underlies (and explains) the changing historical form of the geopolitical system. Thus any historical investigation needs in turn to be informed by a theoretical understanding of social structures in general, coupled with some conception of how they might be implicated in the reproduction of geopolitical systems in particular. The recurrent inability of realism to provide such a social theory (in either the abstract or the substantive modes just distinguished) has been perhaps the single greatest technical obstacle to the development of IR as a non-positivist social science.

The argument of this chapter is set out in four parts. The first part illustrates the pitfalls of anachronism and the need for historical categories by challenging the conventional reading of a celebrated event in IR: the Treaty of Utrecht of 1713. This is followed by a brief interrogation of one attempt to think historically about the emergence of the modern international system – the failure of which is traced to the realist theoretical assumptions covertly informing it. This failure prompts, in the third part, a general theoretical discussion of social structure, followed by a brief discussion of the character of historical materialism as a substantive social theory. Finally, and on the basis of this, the axiomatic realist separation of geopolitical system from social structure (and hence of external from internal) is questioned theoretically, as a prelude to the substantive historical challenges developed in chapters 3 and 4 below.

Utrecht, 1713

Let us begin, then, with our first point: if geopolitical systems change over time, then our theoretical categories must also be historical categories. In order to illustrate this point, we shall take a famous historical example: the Treaty of Utrecht of 1713. Utrecht is generally remembered in IR as the first occasion on which the establishment of a balance of power in Europe appears as an explicit aim of a peace settlement. As the preamble to the Treaty has it, the aim was

> to establish an equilibrium between the powers of such a kind as to prevent the union of many in a single one, so that the balance of equality, which it is desired to assure, could not incline to the advantage of one of these powers to the risk and injury of the others.[2]

Utrecht falls therefore at the tail-end of that venerable procession of treaties which is generally held to mediate the historical emergence of the states-system. Thus, the Peace of Lodi (1454) 'founded the Italian Concert and the first system of collective security';[3] the treaty of Augsburg (1555) established the principle of *cujus regio, ejus religio* – a partial secularizing of the states-system, later completed at Westphalia (1648), which asserted the sovereign rights of the German princes against Pope and Emperor alike.[4] 'By the time of the Congress of Utrecht', says Wight, 'the states-system is there.'[5] That is to say, the replacement of Church and Empire by the secular sovereign state as the foundation of diplomatic organization is well established; and the diplomatic machinery for the collective self-organization of a plurality of state apparatuses stretching across the European continent is available and in periodic use. We are in home waters; the modern identity of the system is complete in its essentials. But is it? What was Utrecht actually about? How material was the prescription of the balance of power to the content of the settlement? A closer look at the terms seems to warrant a degree of scepticism.

The first three items on the list are as follows.[6] France agrees to recognize the Protestant Succession in England. We shall return to this. Next, Spain cedes to Britain 'the exclusive monopoly of the slave trade, or rights of the *Asiento*'. Third, France yields up 'contested possessions in America – Hudson's Bay, Newfoundland with Nova Scotia, & St Christopher'. Some way further down the list comes the most frequently cited 'balance of power' provision: the ban on French fortifications at Dunkirk. What is interesting about this is not simply the unearthing of seedy provisions in the small print of a venerable treaty: a realist might well contend that the pursuit of vile lucre is a fairly universal activity, and that territorial expansionism as an aspect of strategic competition between states needs no special explanation. But monopoly rights to the *Asiento* were not simply an additional source of revenue in the manner of an extra territory added to a feudal royal estate.[7] They brought Britain closer to the levers of a process which had a very specific – and inevitably to modern eyes exaggerated – role in the intercontinental system of absolutist Europe: the production and control of bullion. In turn this intercontinental system, this patterning of state and mercantile institutions and practices, cannot be understood without reference to the constraints on trade imposed by the dominant structural features of European societies.

Failure to recognize the importance of this proviso has sometimes led modern writers to dismiss mercantilist doctrine as an intellectual error. Even some of the more historically minded commentators have argued that it 'grossly misunderstood the true means to and the nature of plenty'.[8] The zero-sum model of international trade, the obsession with specie and the extensive use of military means to create and bolster commercial monopolies – these have been seen as indicative of the rude prehistory of the modern science of wealth creation. It might be more illuminating, however, to say that they reflect characteristics recognizable in all precapitalist trade, and that in premodern social orders 'the true means to plenty' necessarily entailed strategies very different from free trade, price competition and waged labour. In short, whereas much modern capitalist trade connects centres of production competitively, increasing the pressure for surplus extraction in the labour process, precapitalist trade connects a centre of production with a distant market and reaps windfall profits by setting prices monopolistically.[9] And because the profits are gleaned in the realm of exchange, physical control over the circulation of commodities becomes a precondition of profit – and one which, for obvious reasons, tends to necessitate more or less elaborate territorial strategies of segregation backed up by direct military force. In practice, these ranged from the straightforward English Navigation Acts confining all English and colonial trade to English ships and ports,[10] to the sixteenth-century Spanish practice of assembling all licit contact with the American empire in two annual massed fleets under the supervision of the *Casa de Contratacion*,[11] to the extraordinary measures taken by the Dutch East India Company to segregate and regulate the production of spices in the Moluccas.[12]

This being the nature of long-distance trade, it made little difference where the 'carrying' was conducted; indeed, Braudel tells us[13] that '[t]he greatest source of wealth in the East' was not the carriage of luxury goods to Europe, but rather the cornering of 'trade between regions of Asia that were economically different from each other and very far apart' – the so-called 'country trade'. India's consumption of fine spices was double that of the whole of Europe. There was, however, one important difference: moving into this trade proved difficult for the Europeans because of the age-old deficit of East–West trade: 'In the end, the Europeans had to have recourse to precious metals, particularly American silver, which was the "open sesame" of these trades.' This partly explains why, in the Caribbean, the Dutch and the English were so eager to expand their contraband trade with Spanish settlers on the mainland:

> The Dutch and the English were thus able to tap the flow of Spanish silver through the open veins of the Caribbean. At the end of the seventeenth century, the amount of Spanish silver drawn off through the Jamaican trade alone is estimated at ... about half the amount of bullion exported annually to the Far East by the British East India Company.[14]

Given that the total volume of world trade was increasing only slowly,[15] and that the scale of production and markets was constrained directly by 'the great frozen ice-cap of the world's traditional agrarian systems and rural social relations',[16] the equations describing the means of expanding surpluses indeed begin to look close to zero-sum. Thus the strategic importance of silver in facilitating the expansion of East–West trade, and the particular mechanisms for increasing access to that resource (of which the gaining of the *Asiento* was one), cannot be understood on the assumption of the contemporary capitalist world market, which does not experience the same blockages.

Similar qualifications must be entered with respect to the other terms of Utrecht mentioned above. For example, the Anglo-French disputes over North American territories emphatically were not instances of a military competition which spilled over into territorial expansionism in the periphery, in the spirit of George Canning's later boast.[17] Quite the reverse: they resulted from a commercial competition for control of the fur trade which assumed a strategic dimension because of the territorial preconditions of an effective monopoly.[18] It was a distinctive feature of the fur trade that as the East Coast beaver populations became depleted, its quadrangular complex of social and ecological relations (comprising Anglo-French rivalry for commercial relations with those native tribes currently in control of beaver hunting territories) moved steadily westward, leapfrogging successive local political fixes and throwing up new tribal intermediaries and possibilities for strategic manoeuvre. The activity of the English Hudson Bay Company which benefited directly from Utrecht formed part of just such a manoeuvre. Its purpose was not primarily to accumulate territories; rather, the mobility of the extractive social relations it sought to monopolize dictated that strategy.

Finally, the first of the terms mentioned above (French recognition of the Protestant Succession) calls to mind the fact that the conflict resolved at Utrecht was the War of Spanish *Succession*. To be sure, one would not argue that the states involved were therefore simply feudal organizations in the medieval sense. But the very fact that this principle of political legitimacy was still strong enough to determine the moments of danger in the continuity of state organizations suggests that it would be premature to speak of sovereignty in any completed sense. A full eighty years later, Immanuel Kant still felt impelled to stipulate in the Preliminary Articles of *Perpetual Peace*: 'No independent nation, be it large or small, may be acquired by another nation by inheritance.'[19]

Thus, on reflection, neither the political agencies nor the social processes arbitrated in the settlement at Utrecht can be understood in terms of their modern equivalents. We see here neither nation-states nor capitalism: we see dynastic and oligarchic state-organizations, in collaboration with mercantile groups, deploying territorial strategies to secure monopoly control over resources (mostly the trade in luxury goods) to supplement the income from their agricultural estates. We see joint-stock companies (in India and the Far East) exercising the prerogatives of states, and an extra-European environment in which no separate sovereignty was recognized.[20] What does it actually tell us to say that 'the states-system is here'? Do such features really characterize our states-system? If not, which states-system is this? IR as a discipline *begins*, it may be suggested, when we move beyond the ahistorical generalizations of realism, and start to map out something like a periodization of the successive institutional forms, agents and scope of 'international power' which have accompanied the precursors of today's global nation-state system.[21] Were we to do this, we might stand a better chance of seeing what it is that is so different about modern geopolitics. And this in turn would redefine what it is that we need to explain.

Historical periodization is a notoriously fraught enterprise which cannot help but cast some events and processes into shadow even as it illuminates others. Nevertheless it remains an indispensable tool for defining and testing our understanding of both the historical specificity and the key structural mechanisms of the modern social world. What tools are available within realism for the construction of such a periodization?

Wight and the Limits of Realist History

In the low-key style which marked many of his sharpest insights, Martin Wight once observed how closely interdependent were the two tasks of dating the origins of the states-system and defining its overall historical identity:

> If [the states-system] is seen as beginning after 1648 rather than after 1494 ... [s]ecularized politics, *raison d'état* or national interest, and a multiple balance of power become the norm, and the ideological strife of the French Revolutionary period and the twentieth century an aberration. If we go back to 1494 ... we watch the states-system being shaped by the strains of four generations of doctrinal conflict, and of a bipolar balance of power.[22]

It is therefore of some interest to ask why, when he came in a separate essay to offer his own preferred choice, he should have fixed not on the 1730s, nor 1713, nor 1648, 1494 – nor even 1454, but rather on 1414.[23] The argument developed to support this choice has three parts. Wight first defines a states-system in terms of six 'internal marks ...: sovereign states ... their mutual recognition ... their accepted hierarchy ... their means of regular communication ... their framework of law and their means of defending their common interests'.[24] He next observes that these conditions are wholly absent before the fifteenth century and fully visible by 1713. The intervening three centuries therefore bear the transition from the (mythical?) lost union of Christendom to the systematized anarchy of high absolutist Europe. Wight has too much a historian's instincts to insist that this transition moves along a single axis in causal terms or is accomplished simultaneously in its different aspects. None the less, he accepts the challenge of locating a precise turning point; and because the plurality of 'national' actors is the key indicator in his definition, he is led finally to identify 1414 as 'the real break'.[25] For this year witnessed the first Church Council to be organized along 'national' lines (which was also the last to be presided over by an emperor):

> The modern secular sovereign states-system arose from the ruins of the medieval international papal monarchy. The dividing line between the two is clearly marked by the Council of Constance.[26]

The peculiarity of this position may be seen if we turn Wight's implicit question, cited above, on to his own dating: what historical character of the states-system is emphasized by this periodization? The short answer, explicit already in his six-point definition, is: none – unless it be the simple fact of multiple political actors and the progressive legal recognition of their separateness. The system exists 'in itself' from the moment that Christendom is sundered ('The first lamentations about international anarchy are heard' in the first half of the fifteenth century), though it takes some two centuries for the diplomatic accoutrements of a states-system 'for itself' to accumulate ('At Westphalia, the states-system does not come into existence: it comes of age.'[27]) The historical manner in which these conditions were contingently realized in Europe at this time, their production of and by wider social transformations, is immaterial: for the period-ization is constructed not as a historical explanation of how the modern system arose but as a bare dating of when one of its descriptive attributes appears. It might equally have appeared in ancient Greece, China in the period of the Warring States or India before the Moghul conquests. In fact, according to Wight, it did.[28] When a putatively historical definition pans out so readily across the centuries, one must perforce reconsider what is being defined, and what relation it bears to the attempt to understand the history of the international system.

For the 'internal marks' listed by Wight are in fact external: they indicate merely mutual interaction between and regulation of discrete political entities. On this definition (in contrast to his speculation cited at the start of this section above), it is impossible to see where 'doc-trinal conflict', the French Revolution or anything like the global struggles of the twentieth century could come from. But there is no mystery here: we are firmly locked inside the familiar realist strait-jacket. When it contemplates the modern world, realist theory sees only what appears to be the timeless mechanics of an anarchical states-system. Consequently (since this is what it takes as the explanandum), when it turns its gaze on the past, it finds at most the constitutional history of that system's emergence, a blindness which restricts it to 'a juristic survey, innocent of any sociological enquiry'.[29] And of course it is as much a fallacy to suggest that the historical rise of the modern international system can be captured in the formal shift from Christendom to anarchy (purely by external indicators) as it is to assume that the identity of the contemporary international system is given solely by anarchy. Thus Wight's essay opens up the prospect of a historical characterization of the international, only to close it down again by posing the issue in realist terms.

The question then arises: in what alternative terms should the issue be posed? For once the orthodox definition of the international as a separate realm governed by the timeless dynamics of a states-system is given up, the mere addition of the domestic political scene as an extra source of pressures determining the behaviour of states will not suffice.[30] If the international system is not a separate realm moving according to its own autonomous determinations, then it needs to be understood – and theorized – as a level, or dimension, of a broader, more inclusive social order. And if this is so, then the characterization of a states-system itself cannot be contained at the level of the international, because its institutions and practices will inevitably reflect the forms of social power given by a historically specific social structure. This is a strong claim – though not, perhaps, one that would raise many eyebrows outside IR. Giddens is surely not alone in his scepticism:

> the very notion of a distinctive field of international relations, separated somehow from what goes on inside nations or 'societies', is in some part symptomatic of the limitations in social thought I have described ... . Although there must be divisions of labour and specialism within the social sciences, there can be no justification for the theoretical aberrations which this particular disciplinary partitioning tends to perpetuate.[31]

We find, then, that if we dispense with realism, we have suddenly to address that series of questions which animates the social sciences as a whole. We cannot avoid asking of our states-system: what kind of societies are involved? What are the core institutions and practices comprised in their material and political reproduction? How specific are the forms of their interrelation to this historical identity? And can we therefore distinguish the broad structural mechanisms of the modern international system? What is it that makes it different from previous geopolitical systems?

In short, the break with realism necessitates not just a different set of answers to the questions which have defined the discipline: what are the causes (and justifications) of war? how far do (and should) considerations of power govern the behaviour of states? what are the systemic properties and institutional needs of an unregulated, multi-actor system? and so on.[32] It necessitates something more fundamental: the wholesale transposition of IR theory out of this formal/legal problematic which takes the condition of anarchy as its starting point, and into a historical problematic whose starting point is the identification of what is distinctive in the social forms of modernity. In implying a problematic of 'modernity', reference is not intended to either the schema of liberal modernization theory or the contemporary debates on modernism/postmodernism. Rather it is suggested that what we need to recover is that profound awareness of structural transformation and of a radical break with the past which stimulated the historical cast of the early social sciences.[33]

Effecting this transposition would have two major benefits. First, as already indicated, it would redefine the historical objects of IR theory and at last render visible that which needs to be explained: Wight's conviction that there is no international theory because there is nothing to theorize is meaningless outside the realist problematic. Conversely, addressing the questions which compose our alternative problematic may reveal that there is a great deal more to our states-system than realism can ever tell us. Second, the assimilation of IR to the other social sciences promises to be very fruitful in a more general sense: not only will it make available to us the rich theoretical traditions of political economy and sociology; it also challenges us to develop them in new directions, to draw out their implications for thinking about international politics. It would probably be an exaggeration to say that the addition of an international perspective raises as many questions for political sociology as the recognition of sociology does for IR; but a review of some recent historical sociological work on the state suggests, at any rate, that we need not fear that we will replicate the work of other disciplines.[34] To say that IR should be reconstituted as a social science does not entail that it either should or would disappear into sociology.

Social Theory and Social Structure

How do we go about understanding historical societies? Giving some answer, however preliminary, to this question seems to become unavoidable at this point – if only for methodological reasons. We need to formulate some general perception of the relationship between social structure and geopolitical systems, a perception which will guide the historical work in the chapters to follow. In order to do this, however, we must first say what we mean by social structure.

The problems involved in defining social structure in relation to human activity underlie one of the key fissures in the literature of social theory.[35] However, it is not a debate that seems capable of resolution at that level of abstraction where it is formulated *sui generis*. Thus, for example, Giddens's structuration theory – explicitly presented as an attempt to replace the dualism of agency and structure with 'the duality of structure' – often amounts to little more than a series of (important but not unfamiliar) methodological injunctions about how the conduct of knowledgeable human agents may be theorized, woven into a descriptive and critical survey of the sociological perspectives in which they apply.[36] Since these perspectives range from the primal constitution of consciousness right through to the articulation of the global political system, the effect is undeniably impressive. But it cannot actually achieve what it prescribes because it is not itself a substantive social theory offering to explain determinate historical phenomena: rather, as already suggested, it is a tour of the modalities of human agency and social reproduction. In a sense, therefore, the task of defining what we mean by social structure is better undertaken at the next level 'down', where the varied *use* of structural explanations entails definite ontological and epistemological premises which can be assessed in terms of both rational and evidential criteria.

At this level the definition of structure moves beyond the observation that many features of social reality both pre-exist and outlive the agency of the individuals through which they are reproduced. And its concern is no longer to provide a theoretical resolution of the tension between the concepts of agency and structure. It concentrates instead on specifying the actual social relationships themselves which comprise the fabric of any society – and on tracing the particular institutional forms and distribution of resources which are reproduced by those relationships.

Let us take as an example the relation between feudal lord and serf which obtained as a structural principle of rule and material appropriation across some areas of medieval Europe. This relation institutionalized a set of rights, obligations and resources governing the interaction of rulers and ruled – allocated differentially according to social position. In its simplest sense, this is what 'structure' denotes:

a regularized relation between social positions which places individuals with respect to determinate resources (of various kinds). It is an abstraction posed in order to illuminate the form and properties of a definite set of relationships – rather than a law which operates from without to manipulate the individuals concerned. This in turn makes it possible to define the historical character of a social order. This is done by examining the structures of relations involved in its reproduction, by specifying the mechanisms of social power, the sites of routine political contestation to which they give rise, the kinds of social development within reach and those ruled out by the existing structuring of material interests, and so on. For example, it makes little sense to expect medieval mercantile groups to have invested their profits in expanding the production of commodities. Not only were they not free to buy labour at will, since labour was tied to agrarian property relations; but also their interests were in regulating production to maximize profits in a limited market:

> The experience of centuries had shown that the highest profits were not to be got in technical progress or even in production. They had adapted themselves to business activities in the comparatively narrow field which remained for them once one left aside the majority of the population of Europe as 'economically neutral'.[37]

If anything, given that they traded agrarian surpluses and luxury goods, they were parasitic on the existing aristocratic ascendancy and social structures.

This kind of analysis, then, points up how the reproduction of social structures shapes the horizons and behaviour of the individuals concerned. But it does not entail that there is anything automatic or self-explanatory about that reproduction: on the contrary, the struggle against seigneurial encroachments on common rights was routine – not to mention the 'peasant uprisings which reached a crescendo with the intensification of labour services in the context of labour shortage in the 14th century'.[38] Thus, while all societies promote an ideological naturalization of existing social structures, few social theorists would pretend that social order lives on normative consensus alone. It also involves the enforcement of compliance through routine deployment of a range of sanctions by concretely located actors. How these sanctions are mobilized, the form they take, the purchase they have on the capacities of those they seek to constrain – all these are specific to the structure of relationships involved. The forms of legitimate sanction available to a feudal lord differ enormously from those exercised by a capitalist employer — which differ fundamentally again from the disciplinary sanctions used by works managers in state socialist societies. The difference is not just that between physical coercion, redundancy and compulsory relocation. It concerns rather the structured distribution of resources between different social groups which gives the sanctions their leverage: unemployment held no terrors for the peasantry of medieval Europe, for they were in possession of the means of subsistence; 'free' labour is dependent in ways that tied labour never was.

But this is to make the obvious point that these sanctions do not activate themselves. Indeed, sometimes they fail to work because structured relations of power have shifted, yielding a new impunity to dominated groups. Sometimes it proves impossible to mobilize them at all – as when an embattled state organization is faced with a complete evaporation of its repressive apparatus. (The Shah's Iran springs to mind.) There is a more general point here. One of the explanatory axioms of Giddens's structuration theory is the notion of the 'dialectic of control'. Briefly stated, this refers to a nearly universal feature of power relations given by the character of human agency:[39] short of conditions of mass murder, the need of those in power to secure the *active* compliance of the dominated always gives the latter a leverage which can be developed into a counter-sanction. Strikes in the capital–labour relation provide the clearest example of this, but it has a much wider scope. As a result, strategies of rule are subject to continuous modification in order to maintain their effectiveness in the face of struggle, innovation and manoeuvre. The implication of this emphasis on human agency is that the reproduction of social structures can never be assumed. It always needs to be explained as a contingent outcome of the practices involved – and of their wider context.[40] Perhaps above all, then, functionalist forms of explanation are ruled out. Apart from the purely theoretical objections to this type of explanation,[41] the historical record is full of instances of functional requirements which were not met – prompting the need for an alternative form of explanation. If ever there was a dire functional requirement confronting a social system, it was epitomized in the urgent need of the eighteenth-century Polish nobility to generate an absolutist state organization in the face of the military threat posed by its neighbours. Instead,

> jealously preserving the individual rights of every squireen against every other, and all against any dynasty, the Polish gentry committed suicide. Their pathological fear of a central state power institutionalized a nobiliary

anarchy. The result was predictable: Poland was wiped off the map by its neighbours.[42]

More generally, the vast majority of states in history have been destroyed[43] – and our own age has witnessed the widespread collapse and transformation of social structures. Yet survival, just as much as dissolution, needs to be explained. History, as Giddens notes,[44] is not to be confused with change.

We have slipped, without explicitly registering the shift, from discussing a single set of relationships – a structure – to discussing social orders in the fuller sense – societies. Is this legitimate? That is to say, can it be argued that some structures of relationships are more deeply 'ontologically embedded' than others – meaning that their reproduction is not only more fundamental to the stable reproduction of the social formation as a whole, but also that it is consequential for the ordering and form of other social structures, and hence legitimately assumes a key role in the explanation of wider social development?[45] And if societies *are* of this nature – complex but recognizable totalities – how do we distinguish the 'strategic relationships'[46] which define their historical identity?

The answer given by Giddens is, it must be said, too general. It tells us what to look for without telling us how to identify it:

> 'Societies' then, in sum, are social systems which 'stand out' in bas-relief from a background of a range of other systemic relationships in which they are embedded. They stand out because definite structural principles serve to produce a specifiable overall 'clustering of institutions' across time and space.[47]

Once again, we need to descend to the level of substantive social theory in order to see how particular explanatory strategies are assembled, elaborated and applied. An especially clear example of this is provided by Eric Wolf's elegant presentation – all the more interesting for the anthropological ambiance of his statement of premises – of the *modus operandi* of historical materialism.[48]

Wolf begins with the linked observations that '[t]he human species is an outgrowth of natural processes; at the same time, the species is naturally social.' That is to say, however much humans may be defined (on account of their consciousness) over against the natural world, they nevertheless subsist materially in and through their interaction with nature; further, this interaction is carried on characteristically in groups made up of individuals connected to each other. These two facts are linked insofar as the interaction with nature is *organized* – that is, it comprises also a regularized social interaction (or relation) between individuals. There is both an analytic and an empirical simultaneity to the processes linked here – one which demands a single dynamic category for its expression. This, says Wolf, is the purpose of the Marxian category of 'labour'. Where labour is involved – as distinct from the solitary activity of 'work' – the physical act of production by individuals is always at the same time the social act of *re*production of the historically specific set of social relations organizing production. Labour, and the division of labour, entails co-ordinated social roles, regularized relations of authority and subordination, shared cognitive schemata and so on.

These observations are, we may say, just that: observations listing the multiple aspects (cognitive, organizational and physical) of the (social) labour process. The overall point is profound, but not controversial: it is a generic point about human agency and its relation to social structure which could equally be made about any organized human activity.[49] The fact that *this* activity (labour) comprises 'the universal condition for the metabolic interaction between man and nature, the everlasting nature-imposed condition of human existence',[50] does not at this stage of the argument set it apart from any others. And yet in Marx's hands this descriptive observation is transformed into a full-blown substantive claim about how to understand and explain historical societies:

> The specific economic form in which unpaid surplus labour is pumped out of direct producers, determines the relationship of rulers to ruled. ... *It is always the direct relationship of the owners of the conditions of production to the direct producers ... which reveals the innermost secret, the hidden basis of the entire social structure,* and with it the political form of the relation of sovereignty and dependence, in short the corresponding specific form of the state.[51]

Wolf calls this the strategic relationship – partly because the lines connecting the interaction of the society with the material world, on the one hand, and the structured interaction of individuals which comprises the society, on the other, all cross here. As a result, it is claimed that this relation composes a kind of fault-line running though any historical society – because it is the place where conflict over the appropriation of surplus labour is routine: destabilize this relation, and the result – slave rebellion, peasant revolt, general strike – threatens the whole social order. A political crisis of the mode of surplus extraction is a crisis of the material reproduction of the society as a whole because the two are accomplished in the same relation. At the same time, this relation also assumes a strategic significance in explanation. Here, for example, Marx explicitly claims to be able to illuminate the character of the state by tracing the connections between its varying social form in different societies and the corresponding variation in the relations of production. (This, incidentally, is a startling claim, for the state is conventionally assumed to be a blind spot of historical materialism, and Marxist theories of international relations are generally associated not with the reinterpretation of the state, but rather with its displacement in favour of 'class relations'.)

But how did we get from the incontrovertible fact that labour involves social organization to the claim that the way to explain a social order is by studying it as a mode of surplus extraction? The second does not follow with logical necessity from the first.[52] It is consistent with it, but so are many alternative starting points for a substantive social theory. One might, for example, begin instead with the authoritative dimension involved in all forms of human social organization and contrast collectivities in terms of different principles of legitimation and domination. It would not be implausible to discuss the work of Max Weber in such terms.[53] Language and the communication of meanings have on occasion provided yet another starting point. In the terminology of the foregoing discussion, these positions could almost be understood as contradictory assertions about the 'ontological embeddedness' of the particular structure of social relations which each prioritizes.

So how do we choose between these premises and the explanatory frameworks they imply? How, in other words, do we assess the relative merits of two or more substantive social theories making competing claims about social reality? Craib cites three criteria. First, the propositions comprising a theory should be mutually consistent. Second, the theory 'must in some way be measured against evidence'. And finally, '[t]he better theory will be able to specify in more detail the causal processes at work and the situations in which causal mechanisms come into operation.'[54]

It cannot be said that any one of these criteria – rational, evidential, explanatory – is less crucial than the others. For a substantive theoretical argument must remain permanently open to the threat of empirical refutation – otherwise it must give up its claim to be engaging with historical realities. Similarly, we cannot relax the ban on internal contradiction without giving up the fundamental goal of any social theory: *systematic* knowledge of the social world. None the less, it is sometimes striking how little the ability to satisfy these two criteria tells us about the adequacy of a social theory. The logical rigour of

Waltz's work, for example, is the despair of his critics; and his central propositions about the behaviour of modern states have not suffered systematic empirical refutation. The problem, as discussed in the previous chapter, is how little he actually explains. For this reason, much of the argument against realism which follows concentrates on Craib's third criterion: that is, it tries to elaborate an alternative theoretical approach which is demonstrably superior in explanatory power. These observations also entail that, in the long run, the adoption of a broad historical materialist framework is not axiomatic. It is contingent upon the claim – which remains to be validated – that this framework allows us to explain in greater detail and more consistently the historical objects and processes, causes and outcomes which constitute our field of study. As this formulation suggests, such a validation can only be retrospective. In the end, the ultimate judgement we can make of a substantive social theory is whether it enables us to write better history.

One further proviso may be worth making at this stage. On the understanding of it used in these pages, the central claim of historical materialism is emphatically not what it is often taken to be, even by many Marxists, namely that economic relations determine political relations.[35] It is important to clarify this point at the start. If this were the core premiss, we could make a nonsense out of it immediately. All we would need to do is step outside of the modern West into virtually any other historical society, European feudalism for example, and ask: 'Where is the economy?' We would have only to look at the institution of serfdom and ask 'Is that an economic relation or a political relation?', or dynastic diplomacy and ask: 'Is that politics or economics?'

These questions are of course meaningless, because they involve imposing distinctively modern categories on a completely different kind of social world. And we do not find Marx wasting his time trying to answer them. This is because the central thesis of historical materialism is not economic determinism; it is the centrality of those relations which organize material production to the wider institutional *re*production of social orders. And exactly what those relations are in any given society is always an empirical question. We have to look and see. In the *Grundrisse* it turns out that they can include kinship relations, 'communality of blood, language, customs'.[36] In fact, it is uniquely in the modern Western world that they appear to constitute a distinct institutional sphere of 'purely economic' relations, separated off from the state. We cannot therefore assume the distinctness of 'economic' relations and categories in the way that 'base–superstructure' models of historical materialism seem to require: on the contrary, as we shall see later, their apparent distinctness in modern Western society is part of what we have to explain.[57]

Social Structures and Geopolitical Systems

> Do international relations precede or follow (logically) fundamental social relations? There can be no doubt that they follow.
>
> GRAMSCI[58]

It has been argued above that we understand societies by conceiving the set of historically specific structures of social relationships involved in their stable reproduction over time. These structured social relations do not sustain themselves; they are contingently reproduced by concretely located, knowledgeable human agents. However, they do have determinate properties, preconditions and consequences which define the mechanisms and forms of social power, the distribution of resources and the institutional sites of routine social conflict. By specifying these for any particular society, we begin to elaborate its historical identity.

In the case of IR as a discipline, however, there remains one more theoretical question which must be addressed before we can begin our historical explorations, namely: what does all this have to do with IR? The question arises because the foregoing discussion of social theory has been concentrated almost entirely at the level of social relations *internal* to particular societies, rather than addressing the issue of relations *between* societies. As we saw in chapter 1, this distinction has been central to the orthodox definition of IR as a discipline. And it persists as a justification for holding that IR theory is distinct from social theory more generally. It may be, however, that the question is most appropriately dealt with by turning it around. For the burden of proof here lies surely with the other party: is there any reason why we should *revise* our broad methodology when we turn to the subject matter of IR? To put the matter more directly: if societies are to be analysed in terms of determinate structures of social relationships, does it make any sense to say that a whole dimension of these societies' reproduction – one indeed by virtue of which they comprise part of a wider *society* – will not submit to such an analysis? Why not? Is there an ontological difference between 'societies' and 'the international system' (even supposing they could be conceived independently of each other) in the way that there indubitably *is* between societies and individual humans, on the one hand, and humans and inanimate objects, on the other? As Craib, among many others, points out, the fact that a society is neither a conscious individual nor an inanimate object but rather a set of social relationships does entail that the kind of theory we use to explain social phenomena is different from that which would be appropriate in either psychology or physics.

Now, what would have to hold in order to justify an equivalent autonomy of IR theory from social theory, of the kind implied by the realist separation of domestic and international? The realist claim is that multiple sovereign rights of violence without superordinate regulation distinguish fundamentally the character of 'the international' from that of 'the domestic'. Yet it should hardly need to be spelled out that this is not an ontological difference, but merely a different form of structured social relationship. What after all *is* the international system but a society – meaning not (necessarily) that its formal institutions uphold a normatively appropriated community of interest among its members,[39] but rather that it is actively reproduced as (and is therefore to be analysed as) a set of social relationships?

If this is so, then we are now in a position to ask the underlying question of this chapter directly: how do we formulate the connection between social structure and the implied 'structure' of the international system? As already noted above, if we reject the realist separation of domestic and international into two separate spheres, we do not resolve our difficulty by substituting a model (however flexible) of a causal relationship between the two sectors and postulating ways in which 'the domestic' impacts on 'the international' and vice versa to the *n*th degree of complexity. The search for causal explanation in this form prejudges the issue by allowing that the two can be spoken of as if they were constituted separately. Now there are plenty of occasions in political and short-run historical analysis where this assumption is not at all disabling. For example, we might wish to focus on how separate internal and external causes interacted in the build-up to a political crisis. However, given our purpose here – which is to rehistoricize the study of international relations by identifying the *continuities* between domestic social structures and geopolitical systems – this assumption of separateness is precisely what we have to get beyond. We have instead to find ways of seeing the form of our states-system as the geopolitical expression of a wider social totality.

The quotation from Marx above points to one way of doing this. For if the character of political relations and the form of the state vary from one kind of society to another in ways that correspond to the changing form of the relations of production, then might not something similar apply to the character of *geo*political relations and the form of the states-*system*? If so, then the significance of the abstraction Marx calls 'the innermost secret' should be visible, and should have powerful explanatory potential at the geopolitical level – or else, alternatively, it will be shown to be a far less powerful abstraction than is claimed for it. In other words, rather than producing yet another general theory of states-systems, it should enable us to show how the character and dynamics of our international system reflect at the level of geopolitics the particular social structures distinctive of modern societies. To do this would be to address the third criterion suggested by Craib above for evaluating a social theory. For we would be using it successfully 'to specify in more detail the causal processes at work and the situations in which causal mechanisms come into operation'. By definition, a theory of states-systems *sui generis*, which seeks to encompass a range of disparate historical examples, is prevented from generating this kind of understanding. But how are we to operationalize Marx's social theory in so as to address the subject matter of IR?

Giddens writes the existence of a nation-state system into his definition of the nation-state.[60] This seems a very wise procedure. In attempting to elaborate a historical materialist understanding of the international, let us adopt the same approach. The difference it makes is simply this. We do not pose the issue in the form: 'If a particular state is a capitalist (or feudal, or state-socialist) state, how will this affect the way it behaves in its relations with other states?' That is to presuppose the states-system as anterior to social structure: that way realism lies. Rather we ask: 'If the dominant social structures of a particular geopolitical system are capitalist etc., what consequences does this have for the form that its political institutions will assume, and what kinds of geopolitical power will result?' For – to repeat our earlier criticism of both Waltz and Wight – the character of a geopolitical system is no more to be understood as given simply by the plurality of competing units (however sophisticated our account of the mix of the internal and external goals and determinations of behaviour) than the character of a society in the conventional sense is understood as the outcome of a plurality of pre-constituted individuals.[61] In both cases, the social system shows structural properties not deducible from the logic of rational choice – properties which comprise its historical identity, and whose delineation is an essential precondition of explanation. And Marx's claim, a strong one indeed, is that it is these properties which are to be understood by observing the dominant form of productive relations. If he is right, then when we conceive the modern international system, just as much as when we conceive any social formation, we need to understand how its political dimension – in this case, the sovereign states-system itself – is of a piece with the basic social structures which distinguish modern societies.

In fact, Marx would be far from alone in making such a stipulation. From the eighteenth century onwards, social thinkers posited a constitutive relation between the new social structures distinguishing modern societies and the parallel transformation of the character and dynamics of the international system. But this fact has been somewhat obscured by the way in which these themes are remembered today. For within sociology the writings of Comte and St Simon among others, associating predatory warfare with a now passing feudal social order, have been recalled above all in the debates on militarism.[62] There they are frequently used as cautionary examples to decorate the argument that internal social change does not resolve the problem of war in an anarchical states-system. Yet the primary purpose of these writers was much broader than speculation on the causes of war. It was to identify the structural specificity of the societies that were emerging around them and to understand the difference this would make to the character of the geopolitical system.[63] And while it may be true that the consolidation of classical sociology during the Hundred Years' Peace of nineteenth-century Europe caused it to underestimate the importance of war in social development, this argument too can be turned around. For when all is said and done, the Hundred Years' Peace itself needs explaining – rather than simply being invoked as a contingent and aberrant historical circumstance which led the early sociologists into irenic delusions. For it was, as Polanyi noted, 'a phenomenon unheard of in the annals of Western Civilization' and 'certainly not the result of an absence of grave causes for conflict'.[64]

The theoretical conclusions reached in this chapter are of a very general kind. We have discussed the conceptualizing of social structure and have drawn out a historical materialist guideline for research; we have reviewed briefly the criteria for assessing the adequacy of a substantive social theory, and we have asserted the ontological status of our material. We have not, however, sought to give a falsifiable answer to the question of exactly what the relation between social structure and geopolitical system comprises. The reason is that ultimately this is not a theoretical question. It is an empirical, historical question. To seek to resolve it at this level would be to dehistoricize it. This by no means entails that the question cannot be answered. But abstract social theory of this kind can only take us so far on its own. Pressed too far, it passes all too easily into theoreticism. Lest we fall into this trap, the rest must be history.

3

Secret Origins of
the State

The Historical Legitimation of Realism

The Italian Renaissance city-state system occupies a special place in the canon of orthodox IR. For, as Martin Wight says,

> it was among the Italian powers that feudal relationships first disappeared and the efficient, self-sufficient secular state was evolved, and the Italian powers invented the diplomatic system.[1]

And of course this was not all they invented. In addition to the earliest modern discourse of *realpolitik* ('Machiavelli', Carr tells us, 'is the first important political realist'[2]), it is in the Italian city-states that we find the first routine use of double-entry book-keeping, of publicly traded state debt, of marine insurance, of sophisticated instruments of credit (such as the bill of exchange), of commercial and banking firms co-ordinating branch activity across the continent, and so on. Here too, the citizen militias gave way earliest to the mercenary armies that would later characterize European absolutism; and within the town walls, a population given over increasingly to commerce and manufacture elaborated new forms of urban class conflict.

The list reads so much like a catalogue of modern institutions that it is almost surprising to recall that the cultural self-definition of these polities was *backward*-looking: they identified themselves with the cities of Classical Antiquity, and their innovations were framed within a yearning 'to walk back into the pure radiance of the past'.[3] The similarities between the Italian and the Greek cities are indeed striking, by no means restricted to the Italian humanists' recovery of the Classical heritage. For the ancient cities too had developed a distinctive urban political culture and had explored a range of governmental forms – monarchy, oligarchy, tyranny, democracy – recognizable in the evolution of the Italian towns. Both systems had high rates of civic participation (linked originally in each case with a citizen militia), and both experimented with sortition and short terms of office as a means of maintaining the separation of private and public interests in the state.[4] In exalting the political community as the highest end of public morality, both elaborated secular ideologies which contrasted with the cosmological self-understanding of the hierarchical political formations which surrounded them. Both embraced and depended upon trading networks focused on maritime commerce, for which both developed extensive bodies of maritime law. Above all for our purposes, both constituted miniature states-systems.[5] The classical world had no precedent for standing diplomacy, but it appears to furnish a wealth of example and reflection – notably in the writings of Thucydides – upon the rights and wrongs of state behaviour, the emergent balances of geopolitical competition within a multipolar system, and the elaboration of diplomatic institutions for regulating interstate conflict in the face of threats from outside the system. It was, and remains, the best known historical site of a premodern discourse of *raison d'état*.

On the face of it, this paradoxical contrast may be a common enough feature of historical change. Marx referred to a 'process of world-historical necromancy':

> just when [people] appear to be engaged in the revolutionary transformation of themselves and their material surroundings, in the creation of something which does not yet exist, precisely in such epochs of revolutionary crisis they timidly conjure up the spirits of the past to help them; they borrow their names, slogans and costumes so as to stage the new world-historical scene in this venerable disguise and borrowed language.[6]

But for students of international relations, the dual identity of the Italian city-states – dawn of the modern, echo of the ancient world – necessarily bears an added significance. For it brings us face to face with that appearance of transhistorical continuity between states-systems of vastly differing social structure which realism draws upon to support its claims for the geopolitical realm as *sui generis*.

These realist historical credentials have led something of a charmed life within the discipline. They are rarely challenged – perhaps because the 'timelessness' of the Renaissance and Classical civilizations is taken so much for granted throughout the humanities. Shakespeare, wrote his friend Ben Jonson, 'was not of an age but for all time!' And what reader today could deny the same of Thucydides? Is not the arresting 'modernity' of his prose precisely evidence of a timeless logic

of interstate behaviour which forms the natural and distinctive starting point for IR theory? How else is it to be accounted for?

The ease with which these points follow on from each other perhaps
explains (and in turn is explained by) what seems at first a more puzzling
circumstance: namely, the paucity within IR of actual historical research into these premodern geopolitical systems. Behind the count-
less casual references to the Italian and Greek city-states, there lies
no corpus of historical analysis and debate within IR. (Elsewhere, of
course, there is plenty, but it is mostly not focused theoretically on
'the international question'.) A couple of dry, legalistic surveys by Wight,
the odd chapter or article here and there on Greek or Italian *political
theory*, two or three dusty volumes sleeping peacefully on library shelves
marked 'History of International Law' – is this really all there is?
Whatever other research has been done, it certainly keeps a very low
profile. This is not a live issue in IR theory. But it ought to be.

What if northern Italy did *not* see the genesis of the modern international system? What if Thucydides did *not* offer a balance of
power explanation of the Peloponnesian War? And what if the existence of an 'autonomous realm of the political', which indeed
characterizes all three cases – Classical, Renaissance and modern –
can be shown to have rested *not* on their shared 'external' identity
as states-systems but rather on an internal (and in each case different)
structural configuration of social relations? The answer is that this
may not be just a little local difficulty with dispensable historical
precedents: it may bear directly on the adequacy of the dominant
realist theory of the *modern* system. For it would show that this theory
lacks the historical definition to which it pretends. And ahistorical
theories in the social sciences tend to suffer two persistent and de-
bilitating liabilities. First, they have no means of testing whether
properties assumed to be universal are in fact specific to a particular
(usually contemporary) epoch. This blots with anachronisms their
image of the past. Second, without a historical depth of field there
is always the danger of posing as irreducible, essential starting points
aspects of the modern world which are themselves outcomes requiring explanation. Behind the veil of familiarity, the present too goes
unexplained. In the case of realism, historical examples work precisely to stress the irreducibility of its starting point (the autonomy
of the political), pre-empting further analysis by demonstrating its
elemental, transhistorical character. As Halliday has pointed out, it
is 'indeed paradoxical that a concept so central to the whole discipline
should escape explication as this one has'.[7] For what if the autonomy

of the political is itself a contingent historical development? Would that not mean that a crucial dimension of the modern system was opaque to realism? And would we not then stand in pressing need of an alternative explanation of the undoubted similarities between the Classical, Renaissance and modern systems?

The aim of this chapter, then, is partly to call the realist bluff by taking a closer look at these premodern geopolitical systems: can we trust the historical references, or are they hiding something? It will be argued in this connection that the historical terrain often regarded as the stronghold of realism is actually the site of its most spectacular failures.

The argument is set out in the following manner. First, the early development of the Italian city-state system is briefly reviewed, particular attention being given to the emergence of a distinct public political sphere. This, it is suggested, was crucially linked with the articulation of a discourse of *raison d'état*. The next section recalls Marx's discussion of the structural conditions of the rise of such a 'purely political state'; and the chapter then turns to consider how these conditions came to obtain in the Italian case – through processes extending deep into the feudal world surrounding the city-states. This makes it possible to assess broadly the supposed Italian origins of the modern system, before moving on to explore the structural basis of the 'purely political' sphere in Classical Athens. Here again, the emergence of a recognizable discourse of *raison d'état* is traced not to the multipolarity of the geopolitical order, but to the structural configuration of social relations organizing the material reproduction of the society – in particular the remarkable interdependence of democracy and slavery. This alternative analysis is then used to challenge the common association of Thucydides with the realist theory of the balance of power.

But the primary purpose is constructive. And it should perhaps be stressed again at the outset that the final destination of the argument is neither Italy nor Greece but rather our own modern international system whose actual historical identity is effaced by the too easy rehearsal of transhistorical similarities. For if the generic properties of states-systems will not suffice to explain the familiarity of Italy and Greece, then, as already suggested, they lose their credibility also as a starting point for understanding the modern world. For this reason, although the systematic treatment of the sovereign states-system is reserved for chapter 5, the perspectives used below to explore the premodern cases are, in the conclusion to this chapter, turned briefly on to the modern world in order to draw out their preliminary implications for IR theory in general. In short, it is not enough to perform the usual exposé and walk away. To secure the ground we must pursue our methodological critique into the sketching of an alternative historical explanation. We must give our own answer to the riddle of historical appearances. And it must be a better one.

Renaissance Italy

Political Development of the Commune

The independent development of the medieval towns of northern Italy, which in time produced the city-state system celebrated in IR, is conventionally dated from the repulse of two German imperial attempts to unify the peninsula under feudal monarchy. In 1160 the citizen militias of the Lombard League defeated the army of Frederick I (Barbarossa). In the following century his grandson returned to the attack, only to set in chain the events leading to the complete destruction of Hohenstaufen power in Italy. Both these campaigns assumed the form of the struggle between empire and papacy.[8] None the less, as Perry Anderson suggests, it was a cross-cutting dynamic, the precocious economic development of northern Italy, which proved decisive in their outcome.[9] Florence supplied not only troops for the papal cause: its merchants raised the enormous loans which funded the Angevin mercenary army that destroyed Frederick. In the decades which followed, French rule fractured in the south (the Sicilian Vespers of 1282), while the papacy first removed to Avignon (1309), returning in 1377 only to disable itself yet further by the Great Schism of the following year. Outside intervention and influence in northern Italy by no means ceased at this point, and the Ottoman threat in the east grew alarmingly in the following century; but with the drastic weakening of both papacy and empire in the peninsula, and France distracted by the Hundred Years' War, the region enjoyed a geopolitical seclusion that would last up until the French invasion of 1494. Thereafter, the substantive independence of the city-states was submerged again, first under French then Habsburg domination. It was the intervening 'Golden Age' (1378–1494) which saw the innovation, along with much else, of 'the system of organizing interstate relationship[s] which Europe later adopted'.[10]

The complex of political communities which achieved this had of course already undergone an extensive process of development by the time of the Great Schism. At the start of the thirteenth century there were some two to three hundred more or less independent Communes, towns which had shaken off episcopal authority (mostly in the seven decades up to 1150) and constituted themselves under the Consular system as self-governing merchant/landowning oligarchies.[11] Their numbers had already diminished considerably, as the combined effects of internal political instability, competition over rural hinterlands and trade routes, and the inability to meet the rising minimal military conditions of survival gave opportunity for expansion and absorption. The twelfth century in particular saw an accelerated process of combined external consolidation (the assertion of Communal authority in the *contado*, or rural hinterland) and evolution of internal political institutions.

Under these conditions the city-state system underwent not just a geopolitical reorganization but also a decline of the oligarchic Consular political form. The Consulates had proved unstable in part because the leading merchant families which composed both the commercial and the political elites carried their factional rivalry into the institutions of town government, already under pressure from the small-trader and artisanal class below. The measures taken by the citizens' assemblies to pre-empt the chronic risk involved in this arrangement constitute perhaps the single most remarkable – and certainly the most revealing – aspect of the political development of the Commune. Terms of office were shortened (sometimes to as little as two months as in the case of the *priori* making up the ruling council in Florence,[12] more usually to six months or a year) – with incumbents being ineligible (along with their entire families) for immediate re-election. The representative character of key elections was persistently diluted by adding in sortition rounds.[13] Legislative initiative was dispersed among a multitude of committees. And the highest legal and military offices – the *podesteria* (judicial authority) and *capitaneria* (army command) – were banned to native residents altogether: their terms usually restricted to six months, they were filled by candidates from outside who were rigorously vetted for remoteness of interest and blood, and then tightly sequestered for the length of their office in order to preserve their neutrality.[14]

In short, and albeit with considerable variation in detail and extent between individual towns, the Communes attempted to insulate government from the *private* power of individuals, to reconstitute the sphere of political life as an autonomous *public* realm, to separate out the state as an institution: the *podesta* 'was not a ruler, but rather he stood for the rule of law.'[15]

The public realm opened up by these developments was of course a restricted one. Citizenship did not extend to the *contado*, where a subject rural population was compelled to deliver monies, foodstuffs and military service to the Commune. The abolition of serfdom in the *contado* often signalled only the completion of Communal domination. Indeed, in some ways the towns were not so much anti-feudal as 'urban modalities of the general mechanism for surplus extraction typical of the age, directed against competing rural practitioners'.[16] But the distinctive institutional form of the Commune did none the less have significant external aspects. One of these is captured in Sereni's observation that 'Italian wars generally assumed the character of public wars, that is, of real conflicts between states, while private wars were still very frequent in the rest of Europe.'[17] What is a public war? Perhaps an acceptable definition would be: a war undertaken by or on behalf of a community, in which the goals pursued or threats responded to concern collective interests. In a public war, the corporate interests of the community (however these are ascertained) are assumed in principle to be the highest moral end. It is therefore legitimated by *raison d'état* in a way that private wars cannot be. And private warfare does not refer only to the prosecution of *défiance* by nobles. Any conflict formally undertaken in pursuit of individual material and political aggrandizement is a private war. In this sense, even wars between medieval monarchs remained private: their legitimation took the form of dynastic claims (often appealing also to religious sanction); and the feudal laws of war significantly pertained to the conduct of individuals rather than collectivities such as states.[18] This gives rise to something of a paradox. In the course of a riveting passage in *Renaissance Diplomacy*, Garrett Mattingly declares

> in Italy, power was temporal in the strictest sense of the term. It was naked and free, without even the most tenuous connection with eternity. ... [The Communes were] the first omnicompetent, amoral, sovereign states.[19]

By 'naked power' he refers mainly to the fact that the internal political constitution of the Commune was secular, wearing no sanction of religious legitimacy such as adorned the hierarchical structures of the surrounding feudal world. Mattingly is of course right to stress the permanent internal instability of the Communes; but the additional suggestion that brute force predominated in Italy as the irreplaceable support of illegitimacy is slightly misleading. Was noble power in the countryside any less brutal? And in one respect at least, was not the religious legitimation of feudal domination required precisely by its *private* character, which otherwise would indeed have appeared more 'naked' (in the sense of arbitrary and particularistic) than the internal political structures of the Commune? It is estimated that fully one third of the free residents of the Communes may have participated actively in the politics and administration of their towns each year – a proportion equivalent to that in Athens.[20] Perhaps, then, the real point is that the 'naked' power that requires no religious sanction may be despotic or usurpatious: or it may be *public power*, morally self-sufficient because it appeals to an arena, real or ideal, of common interests.[21] One index of this possibility in Italy is the vigorous attachment to the rule of law, which also had an external aspect: the cities agreed to continue observance of the municipal (cosmopolitan) law of the Empire even after imperial authority waned: 'When the Emperor was no longer recognized as superior, his place was taken by the law.'[22] We shall return to these themes below.

The standing embassies of later renown did not arise on a significant scale until the latter half of the fifteenth century, but organized diplomatic interaction between the Communes was continuous and intense from the start. So much so, indeed, that Waley suggests that 'the Commune of 1200 may be considered essentially the product of such [external] relations.'[23] In at least one sense this was often literally true: the military efforts required both to suppress feudal power in the *contado* and to secure new boundaries against attack from other Communes 'multiplied expenditure, hence revenue' and were 'the main force which matured the cities' fiscal institutions'.[24] But beyond this, the material and organizational reproduction of the Communes was carried on in significant part through their peacetime interaction by trade and joint political co-ordination. The growth of traffic between the cities called forth and was fostered by treaties extending reciprocal guarantees of the safety of communications, the civil rights of foreign merchants and arrangements for extradition. Cities negotiated about bilateral tariff concessions, the material facilities (such as warehouses) to be made available to each other's traders, the procedures for the settlement of private disputes, and so on. This in turn promoted an expansion of the apparatus of government in general, and in particular required an 'exact determination of the frontiers between the different states', leading often in turn to the appointment of 'magistrates charged with maintaining the boundaries'.[25] Thus, by a symbiotic process familiar to students of later absolutist Europe, the expanding scope of public organization within Communal territories, which produced a sharpening of the territorial form of the state, was increasingly both a function and a precondition of intercourse between Communes.[26]

By the start of the thirteenth century, the development of the public sphere was well advanced, and 'the *podesta* had become the rule rather than the exception.'[27] Yet it was from the beginning a precarious settlement. The town nobles continued their violent feuding from their towers or from the exile to which they were not infrequently despatched in large groups. The tensions between the nobles and the *popolo* could break out into open warfare. And to add to the manifold sources of inter-communal hostility, the peninsula as a whole was still (for the first half of the century) disturbed by the intervention of Emperor and Pope. Many Communes were increasingly obliged to place themselves under the military protection of local feudal lords. Even Florence, which retained its republican institutions well into the fifteenth Century, passed in and out of the protection of outside powers no less than three times between 1313 and 1343.[28] Elsewhere, the result was the rise to power of the *signori*. These new rulers were often feudal magnates whose access to rural military and agrarian resources had supplied the leverage at a moment of crisis to transform their tenure of *podesteria* or *capitaneria* into a permanent executive position.

The great republic of Milan fell to the Visconti just before the turn of the century,[29] and by the 1320s the *signori* held power throughout most of the system.[30] This development further hastened the territorial concentration of the city-states while at the same time arresting their political evolution. But it did not represent a straightforward reassertion of rural feudal power: the towns were now a curious amalgam of merchant and noble forms. As Salzer put it:

> in the *Signoria* the two political principles which had so long fought one another in Italy, Municipalism and Feudalism, [were] joined together.[31]

And to a greater or lesser extent, the *signori* found that they had to rule through republican institutions.[32] In the most remarkable instance of sustained political autonomy, the effective rule of Cosimo de Medici over Florence for three decades barely rippled the surface of republican government. The private economic power by which he maintained his influence in the committees provided the perfect counterpoint to the public sphere which he manipulated with such skill.[33]

Sources of Political Autonomy

The word 'autonomous' has been used above to describe the emergence of Communal political institutions. This is a loaded term in the literature of IR. There it is generally used to imply the possibility of studying the form and behaviour of the state *sui generis* and more or less in isolation from other social structures. What, however, is meant by it here? It may help in answering this question to compare Communal institutions with those characterizing the predominant, seigniorial form of political power in feudal Europe. For the most striking contrast is precisely that in the latter case economic activity and the exercise of political authority are *not* separated out. The heritable fief typically *combines* personal rights of appropriation over land and productive labour with extensive political jurisdiction. On the one hand, the fief is 'owed' to the liege lord not as a public office but as a personally contracted possession; on the other, it carries rights of economic exploitation which can be exercised only through mechanisms of political command and subordination – serfdom. There are thus no distinct 'political' and 'economic' realms. The emergence of a public political sphere is blocked by the particularist, private character of 'parcellized sovereignty'; and the 'purely economic' relationships which constitute the fabric of an 'economy' in the modern sense are precluded by the politically unfree status of rural labour.

There is also therefore no state in the modern sense. There is a degree of regulation of the noble class provided by royal suzerainty; and there are more or less concerted attempts to expand the scope of royal authority through the system of courts and the contesting of ecclesiastical prerogative. There are legal codes and attempts to consolidate centralized political rule. But 'there is as yet no political constitution as distinct from the actual material state or the other content of the life of the nation.'[34] Nothing could be more emblematic of this fusion than the role assumed by dynastic diplomacy as a mechanism of accumulation and expansion in the geopolitics of the age. This institution visibly depends for its operation upon the inseparability of personal property and political jurisdiction – depends, that is, on the non-existence of an autonomous state. Several other resultant peculiarities of feudal political power are frequently remarked – the recognition of private rights of warfare,[35] the absence of a distinct body of public international law, and so on.[36] One might add that in this period the very reference of the term 'the state' was different, denoting something closer to 'the civil state' later contrasted with 'the state of nature'. The modern sense, a public political organization contrasted with 'civil society', is a much later arrival again.

Marx was from the earliest in no doubt that the social transformations registered in the distance between these couplets – that is, the emergence and reproduction of the 'autonomous' state, on the one hand, and the 'non-political' civil society, on the other – had to be seen as structurally interdependent:

> The *establishment of the political state* and the dissolution of civil society into independent *individuals* – whose relations with one another depend on *law*, just as the relations of men in the system of estates and guilds depended on *privilege* – is accomplished by *one and the same act.*[37]

As Derek Sayer has argued, Marx's early writings repeatedly focus on the links between the dominant mechanisms of surplus appropriation characteristic of the new 'civil society' and this reconstitution of political power as public authority.[38] In particular, Marx stresses that so long as the material reproduction of a social order is organized through institutionalized political subjection, 'politics' cannot be disengaged from privilege. Under these conditions,

> the unity of the state, and also the consciousness, will and activity of this unity, the general power of the state, are likewise bound to appear as the *particular* affair of a ruler.[39]

It is only when 'the *political character of civil society*' is abolished (substituting non-political mechanisms of surplus appropriation) that politics can assume a general, autonomous form in the state, replacing the particularist private form of the estates. The overthrow of feudalism

> set free the political spirit, which had been, as it were, split up, partitioned and dispersed in the various blind alleys of feudal society. It gathered the dispersed parts of the political spirit, freed it from its intermixture with civil life, and established it as the sphere of the community, the *general* concern of the nation, ideally independent of those *particular* elements of civil life.[40]

Given the widespread assumption in IR (and elsewhere) that Marxism comprises a theory of civil society which is incapable of apprehending the state except in instrumentalist or reductionist terms, these passages are truly remarkable. For what is being discussed here except the very state autonomy which, generalized into a universal feature of political organization, forms the cornerstone of realist theory? 'The political spirit' can be nothing other than *raison d'état* (an idiom indeed foreign to the political discourses of feudalism). And these

phrases – 'the general power of the state ... the political state ... a
real state ... the state as such ... the state [as] a separate entity, beside
and outside civil society'⁴¹ – would not seem out of place on the lips
of E.H. Carr, Hans Morgenthau, or any other writer arguing for 'the
autonomy of the political'. The difference of course is that Marx does
not regard this autonomy as an attribute of institutions of rule *sui
generis*. Any exercise of government includes general social functions
and mobilizes collective powers; but the emergence of a 'purely
political' sphere is a historical development which rests upon a determinate structural configuration of social relations. Furthermore,
this is not to be understood simplistically as a causal autonomy of the
state as an organization. It does not follow that once a public political
sphere has emerged, some imputed universal properties of statehood
could then provide a self-sufficient basis of *substantive* explanation of
historical outcomes. On the contrary, this is a theory of 'the autonomy
of the political' which *begins* by grounding our analysis of the state
in a conception of the social totality.

Italy and Europe

Is this, then, what was happening inside the walls of the Italian towns
– and if so, does it not merely confirm the conventional image of
northern Italy as the advance guard of the emerging modern states-
system? This question requires that we supplement our account of
the internal characteristics of the Italian system with some observations on its external integration into the wider social formation.

The temporary *geopolitical* isolation of northern Italy from feudal
Europe in the late fourteenth and fifteenth centuries does not, of course,
mean that the development of the city-state system took place in a
vacuum. Rather the opposite is true. Any attempt to picture what
followed as the unfolding of 'a little world by itself', an independent
and self-contained system, would be drastically misleading.⁴² For the
city-states were at the very hub of the wheel of medieval medium-
and long-distance commerce. They virtually monopolized East–West
trade, in large part through their entrepôts in the eastern Mediterranean (Venice) and the Black Sea (Genoa). And these entrepôts were
not precarious footholds in a hostile, alien environment. In some cases
they were substantial territorial possessions in Asia Minor, continuously sanctioned by diplomatic recognition within a thriving east
Mediterranean states-system.⁴³

Venice had already been the principal conduit of western trade with Byzantium and the Levant in the ninth century.[44] (Formally still under Byzantine rule, it was far better placed to penetrate eastern trade than were its rivals[45]) It was, however, the Crusades, with the great opportunities they created for carrying and booty, which gave the cities their chance. After the First Crusade (1096), Genoa, which had led the way in providing direct naval assistance, acquired one-third of the city of Caesaria and the right to trade without duties and levies throughout the Crusader kingdoms.[46] In the century which followed, the Venetian colony of merchants in Constantinople grew to number some ten thousand individuals.[47] In the latter half of the twelfth century, however, this tremendously lucrative trade was beset with crisis.[48] The combination of increased competition among European carriers at Byzantium and Alexandria (forcing up supply prices) with persistent debasement of coinage by the European monarchs (reducing the value of sales) produced a gradual squeeze on profits. Meanwhile, Saladin restored Muslim control over Palestine and Syria – leaving only a narrow coastal strip to the Crusaders (dependent upon Italian naval support), and provoking a further reduction in trade due to papal bans on commercial intercourse between Christians and Muslims. Finally, the Venetian traders at Constantinople were suffering rising levels of violent resentment from their Byzantine competitors as (Greek) imperial protection weakened.

Relief came with the Fourth Crusade, culminating in the fall of Constantinople in 1204. For the leading Italian city-states, the spoils gained by their participation in this operation were nothing short of spectacular. Genoa founded the entrepôt city of Caffa on the Black Sea and was granted in addition 'vast neighbouring lands which were veritable colonies'.[49] Venice won (though, significantly, chose not to take possession of) three-eighths of the territory of the Byzantine Empire and secured not just monopoly rights but also the indirect rule of Constantinople for the next fifty years.[50] Venice and Genoa were to fight bitter naval wars over the next century for control of the eastern trade. But their prize was itself dependent upon a temporary and shifting geopolitical conjuncture. In the following (fourteenth) century, direct trading communication with the Far East was broken with the collapse of the Mongol Khanates. The diversion of this commerce into the hands of Muslim seafarers produced a further great increase in prices. And as the Ottomans extended their sway in Asia Minor (finally capturing Constantinople in 1453), their fiscal demands further depressed an East–West traffic which was already contracting due to the ravages of the Black Death (apparently brought from Caffa by Genoese sailors) and renewed papal restrictions on trade. A further, though temporary, challenge came from the Portuguese, with the opening up of the Cape sea-route to the East: 'In 1504 when the Venetian galleys arrived in Alexandria ... they found not a single sack of pepper waiting for them.'[51]

And yet the East–West trade was only one of four major axes on which the integration of the city-states into the wider European social formation turned. A second was their own production of manufactures – most saliently, textiles – for sale both in Northern Europe and in the East. By concentrating 'the thinly spread demand of an entire continent'[52] for certain goods, the cities secured the livelihood of their tens of thousands of artisans and labourers. And yet '[t]he Italians traded in other people's products at least as much as their own.'[53] And their industrial production itself remained to the end in the service of trade.[54] Thus, third, colonies of Italian merchants could be found in cities and town all over Europe and the Levant. Ralph Davis notes that '[i]n every considerable trading city south of the Baltic coastlands, Italian trading settlements had been established – and there were no corresponding northern settlements in Italy.'[55] These merchants were often factors, or branch agents, of companies based in Italy which co-ordinated a range of transactions in different parts of the continent. (By 1300 the sedentary merchant had come to predominate over his itinerant forebear.[56]) They represented a network of contacts through which large sums of money could be raised and financial credits transferred across long distances without requiring the physical movement of specie. The bill of exchange (which could be issued and redeemed in different currencies) was the expression of this facility through which 'to a large extent [they] dominated European trade'.[57] There was, fourth, an additional call on the liquidity available through these means: Italian merchants (especially Florentine) handled the financial transfers involved in the continent-wide activity of the Church, and they lent at interest on a large scale to monarchs – usually in connection with the latter's military purposes.

This last practice involved not inconsiderable risks. When Edward III of England defaulted on debts to the Bardi and Peruzzi companies which had been incurred in the course of his French wars, the collapse of those companies (which were exposed to the extent of fourteen times their share capital) so shook the prosperity of Florence that the town had difficulty maintaining its own military expenditure.[58] Holmes rightly notes the apparent paradox that the financial resources ... of two private Florentine companies could exercise a decisive influence in the policy of the King of England while, about the same time, the commune of Florence placed itself under the government of a rather obscure French soldier of fortune, Walter of Brienne.[39]

This is indeed a startling conjunction, and one, moreover, which is not much illuminated by considering the size of the political units involved. If it is true that 'in 1293 the maritime taxes of the single port of Genoa yielded 3½ times the entire royal revenues of the French monarchy',[60] then the geopolitical vulnerability of the city-states is not obviously explained by saying that they were 'small fry in the world of royal and seigniorial rivalries'.[61]

Any adequate historical explanation must begin instead with the way in which the actual political and geopolitical independence of the Italian city-states was articulated with the institutional separation of the processes of (agrarian) production and (urban) exchange within European feudalism[62] as a whole.

To the 'territorial states' of the north, land was (almost) everything: productive labour, the source of their wealth, was (legally) rooted in it; and the political and military command over this labour was the currency of seigniorial power. To the city-states their territorial base was (almost) nominal. Of the Venetian it was said: *Non arat, non seminat, non vendemiat*;[63] while Florence, in the words of a near contemporary, was 'powerful more by the advantage of its location, the capacities of its men, and the readiness of its money than by the extent of its dominion'.[64] This is not of course to say that the towns did not have to secure the military and strategic conditions of their survival; and this almost always necessitated local and foreign territorial expansion and, relatedly, the structural marriage of convenience embodied in the rise of the *signori*. But their real location, the site where they reproduced themselves, was athwart the flows of exchange which serviced European feudalism and which carried their citizens into every major town and court of the continent.

Insinuated thus into the pores of seigniorial power, Italian merchants could exercise considerable leverage based on their unique access to monetary flows[65] – quite apart from the importance of the commodities which they supplied to the north.[66] And this role was undoubtedly enhanced by juridical and political autonomy at the centres of mercantile accumulation. (Italy had its own cautionary examples of steep urban decline under the heavy hand of imperial or Angevin rule; and the Champagne fairs themselves met an unnatural end, strangled by the Dukes of Burgundy.[67])

But the same feudal separation of production and exchange which facilitated their penetration into the heartlands of seigniorial power, and allowed them to amass half the traffic of the continent under their control without any significant northward territorial expansion, also threatened to prevent the cities from consolidating themselves geopolitically. Like the circuits of mercantile capital with which they ringed Europe, the Italian cities remained crucially 'penned in the sphere of circulation',[68] relying heavily on external trade for their material reproduction – and in some cases circulating large sections of their population throughout the continent.[69] Thus although they were frequently at war, these wars were in general an adjunct to their commercial reproduction, fought to secure the conditions and expansion of trade. War was not, as it *was* for the feudal states, a primary mechanism of accumulation:

> The State eluded a comparable military definition, because competition in trade and manufactures – escorted and enforced by extra-economic coercion, the 'protection costs' of the age – had become an economic purpose of the community in its own right: markets and loans were more important than prisoners, plunder was secondary to engrossment.[70]

Moreover, because of this, because their extreme urban definition was precisely a measure of their necessary institutional subtraction from the rural feudalism which they serviced, territorial expansion was not a natural avenue of growth, and always carried the danger of providing geopolitical stability only at the expense of republican autonomy. In practice, predominantly urban social orders of this kind, cut off from the wider seigniorial political command over resources of productive and military manpower, were historically unstable as independent states. Purchasing the military services of local feudatories thus became the prelude to accepting the takeover of Communal institutions by a noble landed family.

What was in many ways an intriguingly similar drama was later played out in the United Provinces of the sixteenth century. There the parts of the Commune, the *podesta* and the *signor* were played by the Estates-General, the *Stadholder* and the House of Orange. In any fuller study, this would form an important additional case – not least because it provided both (in Grotius) the theory of an international rule of law and (somewhat later, in William of Orange) a candidate (already schooled in the autonomy of Dutch political institutions) fit to smooth a crucial episode in the consolidation of the institutional autonomy of the English state.

Returning, then, to the questions posed in the introduction to this chapter: was the Italian balance the origin of our own international system? Is it true, as Mattingly suggests, that 'Italy first found the system of organizing interstate relationship[s] which Europe later adopted, because Italy, towards the end of the Middle Ages, was already becoming what later all Europe became'?[71] Any such claims would need to be severely qualified. In particular, the appearance of continuity with later Europe is in many respects an optical illusion. It is misleading to picture the modern states-system beginning in Italy and then, through the collapse of the local balance of power, drawing in other states and thus becoming generalized to Europe as a whole, whence it later spread to cover the globe. Such an image is inadequate even on straightforward empirical grounds. There is an important 150-year gap between the resumption of major foreign intervention in Italy (1494 – which Dehio marks as the start of the Europe-wide system) and the eventual construction of multilateral standing diplomacy at Westphalia in 1648. Closer inspection of this intervening period shows not only a fitful and restricted take-up of the Italian methods, but also a significant *regression* in the evolution of the diplomatic system in the ninety years leading up to Westphalia.[72] In the 'international' sphere, as in the development of its distinctive internal constitution, 'the city-state proved a dead-end rather than the direct antecedent of the nation-state'.[73]

This conclusion becomes inescapable when we turn to the structural and historical conditions of the Italian episode. The city-states indeed innovated 'purely political' geopolitical networks (culminating in standing diplomacy) just as they innovated many 'purely economic' ones (in the financial and commercial fields). The conditions of each were the same: a radical institutional separation of politics and economics premissed upon a form of material reproduction dominated by exchange relations, itself contingent upon a structural location within feudal Europe which enabled the cornering of such flows sufficient to support them. The very specificity of this role meant that it could not be generalized to Europe as a whole. To rework Mattingly's formulation: for the cities to look like what all Europe would later become, they had to be released from the grip of seigniorial and Church power. But there was a clear limit to how many Venices and Florences there was room for within Christendom. For Europe to undergo *its* transformation, Christendom had to be *destroyed*. This process would reach its climax in the century and a half which followed, producing a transformative crisis too in the underlying structural conditions of existing diplomatic institutions.[74] This is the unremarked historical content of the 150-year gap noted above in the continuity of diplomatic evolution. And it was not to be the work of merchant capital.

Classical Greece

Peculiarities of the Greeks

The perception of the Classical Greek city-state system within IR has been a somewhat confused and contradictory one. On the one hand, the causes and prosecution of the Peloponnesian War are referred to as a *locus classicus* of the dynamics of the balance of power. Thucydides is credited with being 'the first scientific student of international relations',[75] 'an early student of decision-making'[76] and the father of realism – the latter often on account of his celebrated judgement that 'what made war inevitable was the growth of Athenian power and the fear which this caused in Sparta.'[77] Furthermore, Thucydides' portrayals of public debates and diplomatic exchanges – most famously the Melian Dialogue[78] – pursue with a startling faithfulness the logic of *realpolitik* familiar from the modern realist theory of the states-system. So much so that in the Melian Dialogue itself – sometimes invoked as the prototypical contest of realism and idealism – both sides accept explicitly from the start that the issue will turn not on the moral claims but rather on the *public interests* of the parties involved.

On the other hand, the exemplary status of the Greeks suffers a dramatic downgrading at the hands of writers seeking to draw out their 'modern' character in greater historical detail. Wight concludes bluntly:

> Just as they had no diplomatic system and no public international law, so they had no sense of an equilibrium being the foundation and as it were the constitution of international society.[79]

To the evident disappointment of the English School, '[t]here was no Greek Grotius.'[80] Others too have been puzzled by a 'virtual absence of active theorizing about interstate relations' and have been led to speculate about treatises lost to posterity or the exhaustion of the collective Greek mind following its exertions in other areas.[81] But the confusion is after all grounded in a genuine paradox. Purnell suggests that the lack of a developed theory of interstate relations is partly the result of a 'habit of referring to actual city-states as a body of people rather than a named political unit'. This, he argues, 'limited the degree to which they could theorize about relations between states as such'.[82]

But this apparent terminological blockage reflected not a theoretical incapacity but rather a widely recognized institutional reality: in classical Greece there *were* no 'states as such'. Perry Anderson says of Athens:

> There was scarcely any separate or professional state apparatus in the city, whose political structure was essentially defined by its rejection of specialized bodies of officials – civilian or military – apart from the ordinary citizenry: Athenian democracy signified, precisely, the refusal of any such division between 'state' and 'society'.[83]

Realpolitik without states? Whence then derives that public discourse of *raison d'état* which is heard so clearly in the pages of *The History of the Peloponnesian War*? And how is it that the Greek *polis*, which in its underlying character could hardly have been more different from the Italian city-state of the Middle Ages, none the less bears such a striking resemblance to it? If we can answer these questions we will begin to penetrate the riddle of appearances on which the transhistorical claims of realism are founded.

The comparison of the Italians with the ancient Greeks has of course been run many times,[84] and the first and most emphatic contrast to emerge concerns the absence in Greece of the role played by trade in medieval Italy. Not that trade was unimportant: among the key mechanisms of Athenian imperial power were the enforced use by subject cities of Athenian currency, and the maintenance of entrepôt.[85] But manufactures for the most part 'had a purely internal significance, not connected with inter-state affairs';[86] and even if one includes the corn trade, which seems to have accounted for the bulk of mercantile activity, 'the scale and total volume were small ... even of the most highly urbanized communities like Athens.'[87] Moreover, the traders and seafarers themselves were for the most part not citizens but *metics*, or foreigners, often granted considerable rights of passage and settlement but generally excluded from both voting and land-ownership.[88] Mercantile and craft activity was held in low regard 'not unconnected with the servile status or ex-servile status of many of the practitioners of retail trades'.[89] Plato's ideal state of *The Laws* would have proscribed the involvement of citizens in trade, and Sparta actually did so, delegating its craft production and trading to the partly subject *poleis* of the *perioeci*.[90]

Unlike the Italian republics then, the classical city-states remained 'in origin and principle, urban congeries of landowners'[91] – forming paradoxically an urban civilization without an urban economy. The material and institutional conditions of this development derived not from tapping the flows of inter-regional exchange as in Italy, but rather from the hyper-exploitation of captive labour: slavery. Considerable disagreement persists as to the quantitative and qualitative weight of slave labour in Greece. While Perry Anderson suggests that slaves outnumbered the free in Periclean Athens by 3:2,[92] it is also the case that the heaviest concentrations were in mining and domestic service, while in agriculture freemen were more numerous.[93] Hence '[t]he view of Athens as a community of leisured citizens whose slaves greatly outnumbered the free is against the evidence.'[94] This, however, is not quite the point. Slavery 'released from any economic concern, or even activity, the men who gave political leadership to the state, and, in large measure, the intellectual leadership as well';[95] but crucially, it did so in a way which did not require the *political* subjection of labouring fellow-citizens, whatever polarization of wealth might occur among them. Thus slavery was not just a source of material surpluses; by providing a continuing supply of cheap labour it acted also as a valve reducing the pressure on the economic independence of the smallholding class which was the precondition of political democracy. Slavery and democracy had in fact grown up together following the abolition of debt peonage by the reforming tyrannies of the sixth century BC. Fittingly enough, it seems that the first political democracy, Chios, was also the first significant importer of slaves.[96] And '[t]he full exploitation of slaves in Hellenic territory fell in the blossom-time of democracy.'[97]

One has only to compare the Funeral Oration of Pericles with the speech of the Venetian Doge on the resources of *his* city in 1421 (even granted the different occasions) to sense the enormous cultural gulf between the two civilizations, reflecting in turn the contrasted structural bases of their pre-eminence. Pericles' speech is a eulogy of public political institutions, while 'the most beautiful garden of Venice'[98] is the 2,800,000 ducats of annual trade with Lombardy.[99] These fundamental differences can be elaborated to explore a range of sharp discontinuities between the Greek and medieval Italian cities: the *polis* knew nothing of the structural antagonism of town and country, pursued a militarist logic of accumulation alien to Italy, and so on.[100]

Where the real institutional similarities none the less persist is in the forms of political organization. Pericles lays great stress on the rule of law and the juridical equality which it prescribes for the citizen body as an index of the achievement of Athens.[101] He expressed pride in the fact that his political influence was mediated by the Assembly, and not exercised by virtue of any formal executive authority.[102] And while the citizen-wide eligibility for office did not prevent political power from being largely the vocation of a wealthy, leisured minority, the latter were 'increasingly servants of the state, instruments of the law, and not arbitrary wielders of power'.[103] The language in which they addressed the Assembly was wholly of a piece with this:

> The interests of the state were always justification enough, whether of war or of diplomacy and negotiation or of capitulation (if necessary even to the Persians). The choice of instruments in any given situation was arguable only on the question of tactics, pragmatically but not morally. [104]

Again and again Thucydides gives witness of this in set-piece debates – for example, the Mytilenian Debate on the efficacy of mass capital punishment, where Cleon's opening hard line is countered not by moral objection but by Diodotus' subtler expediency.[105] But what is this 'state' whose interests are invoked as paramount? As we have already noted, it does not have any existence other than the political self-organization of the citizenry.[106] It has no bureaucratic apparatus to which the decision-making authority of the populace is formally alienated and which might provide a basis of 'independent' interests and capacities. It is anything *but* autonomous in this restricted empirical sense. And yet it talks like a state! This suggests that the underlying consitituents of *raison d'état* may lie elsewhere – not in the existence of a separate state organization but in a particular social relation among the population.

In Athens this was transparently so. In every sense, the democracy depended upon the institutional exclusion from the political sphere of those social relationships of juridical inequality (namely slavery and the *metic* status of trade) by which the security of smallholders in the face of large landed and commercial wealth was maintained. Thus, from the point of view of the population as a whole, 'civil society was the *slave* of political society.'[107] Among the citizen body, however, the effect was to 'set free the political spirit':

> in Greece, the *res publica* is the real private affair of the citizens, their real content ... the political state *qua* political state, being the true and only content of the life and will of the citizens.[108]

For the citizenry, the political realm was, whatever divisions of wealth it encompassed, objectively the realm of their deeper common interest – truly a public sphere, albeit one whose structural conditions rendered it incapable of extension beyond a minority of the population. Within this sphere, a discourse of *raison d'état* could flourish because the formal equality of its members made it possible for issues

to appear in their 'purely political' technical aspect. (This is not of
course to imply substantive unity within Greek democratic assemblies, which were, on the contrary, generally riven with the most
vigorous factional strife – as indeed is the public sphere in 'open'
societies today; the point is the existence of a public sphere at all.)
But the referent and ground of this discourse was not a bureaucratic
state organization; it was the nexus of internal and external social
relations which produced and reproduced their ascendancy in the
role of a 'purely political' elite. At the end of our long trail back
through history in pursuit of the elemental category of realist theory,
we have arrived at an 'autonomy of the political' (a separating out
of a distinct sphere of 'the political') without a state.

Excursus: Causes of the Peloponnesian War

Before examining the implications of this for our understanding of
the *modern* state, we might take this opportunity to assess briefly
the claim that Thucydides provides a realist explanation of the
Peloponnesian War in terms of the balance of power.

As Doyle has argued, the Delian and Peloponnesian Leagues ranged
against each other differed fundamentally in both the political com-
plexion of the *poleis* involved and the mechanisms of interstate control
which held them together. Athens had assumed leadership of the Delian
League in 487 BC, determined to press forward the expulsion of the
Persians following the naval victory at Salamis and the freeing of
Ionia. In this it was beckoned on not only by the opportunities for
plunder, enslavement and colonization which attended each engagement; it also sought to secure the sea-routes for the corn imports from
the Black Sea on which it was becoming increasingly dependent.
(Athenian leadership took over from that of Sparta, which, by contrast, supplied most of its cereal needs from domestic production,
and, for reasons detailed below, could ill afford large and prolonged
military deployment abroad.[109]) The League began as a voluntary
association to which each *polis* supplied an agreed tribute of ships and
men or money. It was transformed into an empire as the Athenians
forcibly prevented secession (beginning with Naxos in 469 BC), transferred the treasury from Delos to Athens (454), suppressed independent naval activity and assumed an ever closer supervision of the
payment of the tribute. In its most developed form, this was accompanied by the arrogation to Athenian courts of all capital trials in
member cities as well as the proliferation of Athenian currency minted

from the silver mines at Laurium, and the maintenance of the port of Piraeus as a compulsory entrepôt for all Greek imports of corn from southern Russia. The exercise of Athenian power facilitated by these arrangements took three principal forms: an effective naval monopoly permitting (in a predominantly coastal civilization) direct military sanctions against recalcitrant *poleis*; a political hegemony over allied democratic factions dependent on Athenian support against oligarchic revanchism; and a commercial supremacy which distributed the benefits of reduced piracy and a guaranteed currency while concentrating regulative authority. (Hopper observes that Athens 'learnt to use [its] control over corn and ship timber as instruments of domination over other states'. At the same time it could 'virtually close, for an individual, the majority of the Greek ports of importance in the eastern Mediterranean'.[110])

It was otherwise in the Peloponnesian League, for reasons closely connected with the internal peculiarities of the Spartan *polis*. After a precocious early political development in the Archaic period, the evolution of the Spartan *polis* had arrested in a rigid oligarchic form which it was to retain for over three hundred years. This was largely due to the fact that, whereas enslaved communities were normally dispersed on capture through the fully commodified slavery practised by *poleis* such as Athens, the Spartans had opted to exploit their subject populations in Laconia and Messenia *in situ*. The continuous occupation of these areas placed extreme military demands on the citizenry who organized themselves into a permanently mobilized army – a development finalized following the Second Messenian War of the third quarter of the seventh century. Thus, enigmatically, Sparta's 'great power' role arose out of its internal instability and remained connected with it:

> Her first and only unwavering concern was peace at home, in the Peloponnese. This she never fully achieved, but she came near enough through the instrumentality of the Peloponnesian League.[111]

This inward orientation of the Spartans' policy, for which they were roundly criticized by their allies,[112] is witnessed also by the fact that the League was not an empire, an interstate and 'transnational' mechanism for surplus accumulation at the metropole.[113] Thucydides says that

> The Spartans did not make their allies pay tribute, but saw to it that they were governed by oligarchies who would work in the Spartan interest.[114]

Nor was this interest pursued through the imposition of preferential trading arrangements. On the contrary, the oligarchies such as Sparta 'sought to avoid commercial contact in order to prevent the mobilization of their democratically inclined middle and lower classes'.[115] Spartan military prowess, coupled with a fear of being undermined *domestically* by the influence of the politically more advanced *poleis* to the east, were the principal forces which held the league of oligarchies together and made it the natural pole of attraction for Athens's other rivals too. The latter knew well how to play on the underlying conflict of social systems. '[Y]our whole way of life is out of date when compared to theirs', declared the Corinthian delegates, goading the Spartan Assembly into war; 'Athens, because of the very variety of her experience, is a far more modern state than you are'.[116] This was no revelation. Sparta found it difficult enough to live with Athens even when the latter was providing friendly military assistance: the Athenian army sent in response to Spartan requests for aid in putting down the helot revolt of 464 was sent home early for fear they might 'become the sponsors of some revolutionary policy'.[117]

What then was 'the real reason for the war'? Was it the perceived tipping of the military and geopolitical scales between the two alliances threatened by the Athenian takeovers in Corcyra and Potidaea?[118] Or do these incidents, however central to the mechanisms of escalation, belong rather among those factors by which 'the real reason' is 'most likely to be disguised'? Was it the wider conflict of social systems which generated incompatible external needs?

> Athens was securing her position in many of the subject cities by supporting democrats ... against former governing classes. ... Conversely, there were unprivileged classes in some mainland states who looked longingly towards Athens. It was this which made it difficult for the two power-blocs, representing different social systems, to lie down together.[119]

Or can it be grasped only by Thucydides' most comprehensive category of historical explanation, the 'uneven development' of Greece as a whole, as a result of which 'up to the present day much of Hellas still follows the old way of life',[120] with all the strains and intercommunal tensions which followed from this?

Whatever the answer, one thing at least must be allowed: when Thucydides describes 'the real reason' as 'the growth of Athenian power', he does not, *could* not, mean geopolitical power on the modern realist definition – the fungible, strictly interstate, transhistorically generic medium of the balance of power. For on his own account, the Athenian threat comprised qualitatively distinct forms of influence and control which Sparta could not reproduce, even in smaller

quantities.[121] Moreover, its external geopolitical advance was inseparable from the sociopolitical vulnerability which it compounded within
the Spartan *polis*. In other words, we find here neither a common
structural definition to the forms of geopolitical power exercised by
the two alliances, nor a distinct terrain of interstate politics whose
dynamics could be analysed *sui generis*. Given this, it becomes difficult
to see what the balance of power *as an explanatory tool* (rather than as
a piece of descriptive shorthand) could refer to except purely military
logics of escalation. And no one, least of all Thucydides, would reduce
the causes of the Peloponnesian War to those.

Restored to its original context, Thucydides' famous one-liner is
emphatically *not* an instance of a substantive realist explanation. This
ought to be evident from the fact that it occurs in Book I of his *History*
as the *preface* to actual historical explanation, not at the end as a
summary of its content. And in any case, when the meaning of 'power'
is fleshed out, it violates several of the key premises of realist method.
A balance of power explanation here is either substantively incorrect
or a mere banality – a double failure which, as has been argued in
chapter 1, is the recurrent fate of realism as a social theory. Despite
the chorus of assent, there is in fact no warrant to conclude that
'Thucydides belongs to the realists'.[122]

The Structural Basis of *Raison d'Etat*

The Greek and Italian city-state systems were both, in their different
ways, 'one-off' anomalies in the run of European history – incapable,
despite their tremendous political and cultural creativity, of being
generalized into a wider system. If the Commune was, as Waley
suggests, 'a dead-end', the *polis*

> required so rare a combination of material and institutional circumstances
> that it ... could be approximated only for a very brief period of time; ...
> it had a past, a fleeting present and no future.[123]

Why then do they appear so familiar to the modern international
system which, by contrast, has achieved a fully global reach? This
question is perhaps best approached via Marx's analysis, discussed
above, of the structural conditions of the capitalist 'purely political'
state.

It will be recalled how Marx (in Volume III of *Capital*) located the
cutting edge of historical materialism as a method in historical
sociology:

> The specific economic form, in which unpaid surplus-labour is pumped
> out of direct producers, determines the relationship of rulers and ruled ...
> It is always the direct relationship of the owners of the conditions of pro-
> duction to the direct producers ... which reveals the innermost secret, the
> hidden basis of the entire social structure, and with it the political form
> of the relation of sovereignty and dependence, in short, the corresponding
> specific form of the state.[124]

Capitalism is unique as a mode of production in that this relationship
assumes a 'purely economic' form. That is to say, the 'specific economic form' is profit appropriated through a series of relations of
exchange, rather than tribute (in money or kind) extracted through
direct political relations of domination. The commodification of labour-
power which lies at the heart of this sudden and unprecedented ubiquity
of exchange relations ('the market') does not cancel the actual subjection of the direct producer. Rather it reconstitutes it, through the
structured inequality of the labour contract, within a privatized realm
of production where it is maintained via the direct material dependence of a free (propertyless and untied) workforce. We should therefore be careful not to mistake the formal separation of politics and
economics (or state and civil society) under capitalism for a substantive evacuation of relations of domination from the realm of production.[125] Nevertheless, because this 'strategic relationship'[126] is held in
place by private 'economic' sanctions (unemployment) rather than by
the exercise of jurisdiction (coercively upheld legal rights of exploitation as under feudalism), *political* inequality is not inscribed in the
relations of production – whereas it is for all precapitalist modes of
production.[127] This is why the realm of 'the political' emerges both
as institutionally discrete and as potentially the domain of universal
interests. In *The German Ideology*, Marx summarized this in an epi-
grammatic punning formula: 'the modern state ... is based on *freedom
of labour*'.[128] Once again, the formal separation should not confuse us
– this time into thinking that this 'purely political' 'autonomous' state
is a self-sufficient, transhistorically viable form of rule. It is not:

> The abstraction of the *state as such* belongs only to modern times, because
> the abstraction of private life belongs only to modern times. The abstrac-
> tion of the *political state* is a modern product.[129]

But if modern state autonomy is structurally specific to capitalism,
what does it retain in common with Renaissance Italy and Classical
Greece? Much and little. As we have seen, in all three cases, the
opening out of a public sphere rests upon a formal political equality
among the citizen body. In each case too, the condition of this formal

equality is the exclusion from the mutual relations of the citizenry of political mechanisms of surplus appropriation. It is this which allows the emergence of institiutions of political governance which are *both* potentially autonomous of factional interest ('purely political') *and yet* uniquely an expression of the structural and historical identity of the society whose determinate conditions of reproduction they can have no higher aim than to secure and promote. As the Athenians accurately put it: 'The law is king'[130] – meaning both that *law* rules and that *the laws* (the constitution) are the highest moral end of public life. The Italians averred the same when they upheld the municipal law of the Empire even after the repulse of Hohenstaufen power from the peninsula. But how is it that in each of our three cases, political mechanisms of surplus appropriation, which are unquestionably the dominant form in human history, are excluded? Here we find a crucial difference: for capitalism is the only case in which this condition of the emergence of a discrete sphere of 'the political' is actually *internal* to the mode of production.

In capitalism the domain of formal political equality does not need to be a segregated realm of privilege resting upon surplus extraction elsewhere in the wider social formation. Or, at any rate, this 'elsewhere' is but another dimension of the lives of the same individuals: so far as the direct producer is concerned, the capitalist labour contract is free and equal on the outside but unfree and unequal within. (Marx's best-known formulation of this is his contrast of the heaven of political citizenship with the earth of capitalist socio-economic relations.[131]) To call the outside 'public/political' and the inside 'private/economic/civil' obscures as much as it reveals about the character and interconnection of the social relations involved. As Ellen Wood points out,

> the differentiation of the economic and the political in capitalism is, more precisely, a differentiation of political functions themselves and their separate allocation to the private economic sphere and the public sphere of the state. This allocation reflects the separation of political functions immediately concerned with the extraction and appropriation of surplus labour from those with a more general communal purpose. ... the differentiation of the economic is in fact a differentiation within the political sphere.[132]

This is indeed more accurate than the designation above of the capitalist mechanism of surplus appropriation as 'purely economic'. For the latter is always in danger of lending credence to the misleading definition of capitalism solely in terms of the complex of exchange relations which it presents to public view.[133] None the less, once these limitations to any discussion of a 'purely political' realm are accepted, it remains valid and instructive to note how the conditions of the emergence of the latter in Renaissance Italy and Classical Greece differed from those obtaining in modern capitalist societies.

As already suggested, in both earlier cases these conditions arose externally to the political community involved. This is most obviously the case with the Italian Commune, where interregional trade provided the all-important supplement to local agrarian surpluses. The freedoms of the Commune depended on the wider unfreedom of agrarian labour in Europe and the East; for, as Marx noted, the targets of interregional mercantile activities in the precapitalist period are the surpluses already appropriated and held by superordinate groups in the foreign societies between which the traders' activities mediate.[134] (What was specific to the city-states was the additional, geopolitical dimension which they lent to this structural separation of production and exchange.) Unlike the *polis*, the Italian city-state evolved a real urban economy, but an unrepeatable one resting on its location within the wider agrarian formation. Its political antagonism towards the feudal countryside thus did not reflect any overall transformative capacity comparable to that of its capitalist successor. But in Greece, too, it was the admixture of slavery alongside (but institutionally outside) the dominant mode of production which provided the basis for 'the separation of political functions immediately concerned with the extraction and appropriation of surplus labour from those with a more general communal purpose'.[135] Greece, too, was 'freakish' in this regard; and this makes it apparent that in both cases the external conditions enabling the emergence of a distinct political sphere *themselves* set internal *structural* limits to its expansion and hence generalizability.[136] In Italy the public sphere was bordered horizontally by (and depended upon) the surrounding feudal rural institutions; in Greece, its delineation was the vertical one of citizenship versus slavery. And because in both cases the city was the locus and mechanism of the political sphere, the differences between them (and those which set the modern world apart again) can be expressed by tracing the modulation in the overall relationship of town and country, as indeed Marx indicated in the *Grundrissse*:

> Ancient classical history is the history of cities, but cities based on landownership and agriculture... the Middle Ages... starts with the countryside as the locus of history, whose further development then proceeds through the opposition of town and country; modern (history) is the urbanization of the countryside, not, as among the ancients, the ruralization of the city.[137]

Implications for Contemporary IR Theory

We cannot leave this discussion without suggesting briefly what lines of further research are indicated for theories of the international system. Two related avenues suggest themselves immediately: extending the critique of the realist theory of the state to cover its conception of the states-system; and demystifying the institutional forms of contemporary international power. A single example may serve to illuminate what might be involved in both directions.

The twentieth century has witnessed, among many other things, both the end of colonialism *and* a significant contraction of the developed, privileged core of the world economy. (Hobsbawm, reckoning the latter as a proportion of the world's population, has estimated a decline from 33 per cent to 15 per cent between 1900 and 1990.[138]) At the very least it will be accepted that the achievement of formal sovereign equality between states has streaked far ahead of any prospect of material equality between populations – even in the provision of basic human needs. The United Nations as an organization is emblematic of this paradox. Is then the sovereign equality which it proclaims an indictment of the hollowness of formal political rights, or is it a sign of hope – a potential lever of universal future advances?[139] Ultimately, of course, this question will admit only of historical answers. But our discussion above does enable us to go beyond the despairing cynicism or rootless utopianism which it usually provokes. For we can see that sovereign equality and the right of self-determination are attended by the same combination of genuine, hard-won achievement and cruel ironies of dispossession which has dogged the struggle for the juridical equality and political freedom of the individual within the liberal democratic state.

This is because the two realms (domestic and international) manifest common structural properties given by their shared capitalist identity: in the international sphere, too, the absolute character of the political right of self-determination (like the freedom of labour/the individual) may be seen to hinge precisely upon its substantive permeability by other, 'non-political' mechanisms of surplus appropriation. Capitalism is the only historical system which permits the exploitation of productive labour under an alien jurisdiction. But, as we have already seen, the 'privatizing' of surplus appropriation which allows this is at the same time the 'abstracting' of the state as a 'purely political' public institution. The possibility of an international economy is thus structurally interdependent with the possibility of a sovereign states-system. At the institutional level, however, this same interdependence manifests itself precisely as a *separating out* of international politics and international economics.[140]

The community of nations, too, thus has its public 'heaven' (the sovereign states-system) and its private 'earth' (the transnational global economy). To put it in these terms is not to indicate a ready-made causal model capable of automatically producing explanations of historical outcomes. The point is not that 'earth determines heaven' in the manner of the vulgar Marxist formulations which have for so long been the butt of easy criticism. It is that these institutional realms are no more capable of being understood separately from each other than are their equivalents 'within' the state, discussed in the body of this chapter above. Thus if we set out to construct a theory of international politics, it is futile to proceed from the realist idea of a generic states-system (studied by IR) on the one hand, and a global economy of market relations (studied by economics) on the other – the two spheres reciprocally linked by a set of causal relationships constituting the further field of international political economy. Rather, at this level, too, we must explore what is involved in seeing the essence of capitalism not as the separation of politics and economics which it presents to view, but as 'a differentiation within the political sphere'.

It should be added that to speak of a capitalist states-system is not to foreclose the associated historical debates concerning the dynamics and agency of socio-political development and transformation, either in early modern Europe or elsewhere. On the contrary, even in England, the social relations we have been discussing did not emerge suddenly and fully-fledged but rather evolved, often bloodily, in the course of several centuries. And if it makes sense to describe the modern international system as capitalist, this is not because all its members are assumed to have followed the same path; it is because its dominant institutions have been shaped by liberal states in a way that facilitates the international exercise of capitalist social power. To explore theoretically the capitalist character of this system is indeed to trace the specificity of the dominant modern form of international power. But the contingent historical processes by which this sovereign states-system came into being, and by which it continues to develop and to be reproduced by real living individuals, remain to be recounted and explained. History (hence the need for historical explanation) does not end. In this respect, the conclusions reached here do nothing more than probe the broadest contours of an alternative, non-realist terrain of IR theory.

On the other hand, even at this range they may throw some light on the paradox of universal sovereign equality overseeing a global deepening of material inequality – the paradox summed up in the United Nations Organization. For they suggest that to regard the UN either as a failure for not actualizing substantive international rights (sometimes known as social and economic rights), or as in principle limited only by the collective will of its members in its potential as an agent of universal interests, is implicitly to misread the specificity of political institutions under capitalism. For the very possibility of sovereign equality is, as we have seen, dependent on the abstraction of the purely political states-system which creates the realm of private transnational power (the world market) in which, in turn, the material inequality is reproduced.

Thus even if, for the sake of argument, all the world's governments were political democracies and the UN constituted a world assembly wielding executive authority determined by majority voting, there is no special reason to believe that it would become the irresistible protagonist of 'economic rights', if this means instituting a planned development which suppresses the complex operation of the world market. This kind of thinking once promoted the delusion (on both right and left) that capitalism would be overwhelmed by universal suffrage.

This does not mean that progressive international political or redistributive advances cannot be achieved via the UN – any more than one would wish undone the political and material benefits of social democracy in Western Europe. But if our historical review teaches us anything, it is that democracy, slogan of our epoch, has no determinate content until its structural conditions are specified. Its historical definition always requires that we extend our focus beyond the self-definition of the political realm. In the case of our other historical examples, this revealed an insurmountable dependence upon forms of political unfreedom elsewhere in the social formation. In the case of the modern international system, *sovereign* equality may be seen to rest on conditions ('economic' unfreedoms) which set internal limits that capitalism is structurally incapable of transcending.[141] Paradoxical this may seem; inexplicable it is not:

> The representative system is a very specific product of modern bourgeois society which is as inseparable from the latter as is the isolated individual of modern times.[142]

And this, it should be clear, is not a conspiracy theory, or an 'economic reductionism': it is a straightforward argument about the determinacy and effectivity of social structure.

Conclusion

At first sight, the remarkable institutional similarities between the Classical, Renaissance and modern states-systems do indeed seem to offer the basis for a transhistorical theory of states-systems *sui generis*, which can be elaborated fully at the interstate level in terms of the distinctive discourse of *raison d'état* common to all three. It is no wonder therefore that many realists look to Italy as the dawn of the modern system and to Classical Greece as evidence of the timelessness of those properties which they single out as *sui generis* and hence the starting point of their theory of the modern states-system. On closer inspection, however, this transhistorical continuity resolves into a gigantic optical illusion. For it becomes apparent, first, that in reality the three systems are utterly different in character; second, that in no case (least of all the causes of the Peloponnesian War) can an adequate explanation of actual historical outcomes be derived solely at the interstate level; and, third, that the very appearance of a self-sufficient purely political realm *itself* rests upon an *internal* (and in each case different) structural configuration of social relations. Once these *differentia specifica* are isolated, they provide an alternative and surer starting point from which to explore the historical character of the geopolitical systems concerned.

Dispelling an optical illusion is not always a straightforward affair, for it is necessary not only to show how reality has been distorted but also to explain why the illusion recurrently arises. And the task is still not complete until an alternative explanation is fully elaborated which can be seen to illuminate more about the social processes and outcomes under view. But that even the preliminary conclusions reached here constitute an advance on realism is surely not to be doubted. For realism is not only incapable of identifying, let alone explaining, the optical illusion: it positively embraces it, and elevates it to the level of a general theory embodying the acknowledged common sense of the age. This self-confidence lends realism a resilience far greater than its intellectual credentials could warrant. But then, IR would hardly be the first discipline in which basic theoretical advances have needed to be made in the face of common sense.

4

Trade and Expansion in Early Modern Europe

The construction of the 'early modern' intercontinental empires was the first great thrust of a geographical expansion of European power which led eventually to the emergence of our modern nation-state system. The rapid growth of trade which they promoted (though itself dwarfed by what was to follow in the nineteenth century) established circuits of exchange which ringed the globe for the first time in history, presaging the scope of the modern international economy. It is not surprising then that for all three branches of IR theory which invoke historical perspectives to validate their image of the *modern* international system, these early empires are associated with decisive turning points in the emergence of the world of today.

For realism, the empires arise as the inevitable geographical extension of the European balance of power, interstate competition in Europe spilling over into the New World and the Far East almost as soon as these peripheral theatres became available. The *annus mirabilis* on this view is 1713, when the Treaty of Utrecht settled the war of Spanish Succession by (among other things) a redistribution of colonial and other territories, for the first time formally designed to establish and guarantee a balance of power among the European states. For the English School, Francisco de Vitoria, arguing the legal rights of heathen Amerindians against Christian conquerors, was perhaps the first theorist of the emerging international society – in both its narrowly legal and broader philosophical senses. Finally, for the World Systems Theory of Immanuel Wallerstein, European expansion in the long sixteenth century was, so to speak, the Big Bang which created the expanding universe of the capitalist world economy (CWE).[1]

So whatever else they may disagree about, realism, the English School and World Systems Theory apparently concur on two points, one methodological and the other historical. First, all agree that the modern international system is best conceptualized as a single whole, differing only on whether its essential unity comprises overarching dynamics of a politico-military (states-system), cultural/legal (international society) or economic (CWE) kind. Second, all agree that the core institutional mechanism regulating the system as a whole (respectively, the balance of power, the secular doctrine of statehood/ sovereignty, the world market) was consolidated in this period.

In short, irrespective of differing emphases, an underlying consensus synchronizes the institutional modernity of the international system with its geographical expansion. Is this correct? In the case of the modern world economy, such a claim is not only empirically controversial,[2] it is also heavily loaded with theoretical implications. Let us suppose for a moment what historical inquiry alone can confirm or refute: namely that the 'international economy' of the absolutist empires is *not* structurally commensurate with the modern world economy. What would be the consequences for thinking about today's global political economy? Negatively, it would seem to follow that any attempt to assimilate its basic structural character to economic relations prevailing by the end of the long sixteenth century – for example, by describing both as capitalist – is either missing something important about the modern world economy, or else is reading back modern conditions into an earlier social system. Both these charges have been levelled against World Systems Theory.

If this diagnosis of World Systems Theory is correct, the very form of the deficiency it identifies would point to a remedy. For if it could be argued that the early modern expansion of Europe was not capitalist, then the epoch of absolutism, brief and transitional as it is, provides a last fleeting chance before the onrush of capitalist industrialization to mount a *comparative* historical analysis – to set the contemporary world economy into relief against the backdrop of an earlier and different kind of 'international economy'. Since this would focus precisely the *differentia specifica*, it would also provide us with theoretical categories to develop a historical and structural definition of the modern world economy.

Moreover, this is a historical period rich in example and counterexample. For one of the first results of a closer examination of the absolutist empires is that the image of a composite intercontinental economy immediately breaks down into a more variegated pattern. In fact we need to speak of (at least) four waves of European expansion in this period, each associated with different institutional mechanisms of mercantile extraction and metropolitan accumulation. Thus the Portuguese established a seaborne trading empire in the Far East unaccompanied (in this period) by any extensive settlement or territorial consolidation. By contrast, the Spanish *conquistadores* installed themselves in the Americas as a semi-feudal ruling elite, directly exploiting the labour of subject populations. Further north, the English (and French) also settled permanently – but they did not (or could not) incorporate indigenous labour. Finally, although the Dutch Empire did not spawn settler-colonies of this kind, its regional power became more and more territorially defined as it sought to tighten its grip on production and supply. And there were, of course, overlaps: the Portuguese claimed a vast territorial empire in Brazil; the Dutch sought to plant settler-colonies in North America; and the English eventually ran the entire gamut of forms. This deepening historical complexity might be thought to render impracticable the structural comparison advocated above. However, it may be the case that the institutional differentiation and its broad association with different 'national' metropoles actually assists our overall project of clarification. For it means that we have not one but four premodern variations of 'international trade' to compare with our own, each constituted as a distinct historical structure of social relations embodying processes of 'international' accumulation.

Such a full comparative and theoretical exercise lies beyond the scope of this book – though arguably it remains necessary to any adequate historicizing of the disciplines of IR and international political economy. Moreover, it would also contribute strongly to any narrative of the international processes involved in the historical emergence of capitalism. For in the brief intimations which Marx gives of the latter, the cumulative development of these empires is central to what might be termed the process of 'international primitive accumulation':[3]

> The different moments of primitive accumulation can be assigned in particular to Spain, Portugal, Holland, France and England, in more or less chronological order. These different moments are systematically combined together at the end of the seventeenth century in England.[4]

Our task here, however, is a far more modest one. In this chapter, we shall explore aspects of the Portuguese and Spanish empires in order to develop further the central claim of the book: namely, that geopolitical systems and processes cannot be adequately understood until their analysis is integrated into that of the wider social structures which constitute them. In particular, it will be suggested that both the financial mechanisms and the territorial form of the Portuguese Empire in the East showed features which derive from the different character of trade associated with precapitalist social structures. Meanwhile, in the Spanish case we shall use similar arguments to illuminate the momentum, form and orientation of the geopolitical expansion which engulfed the New World in the West.

India Portuguesa

Portuguese Expansion

The story of Portuguese naval expansion in the fifteenth and sixteenth centuries is that of the first early modern wave of Europe's expansion. To its epic poet, however, who sang the heroism of Vasco da Gama,

> It is the story too of a line of kings who kept ever advancing the boundaries of faith and empire, spreading havoc among the infidels of Africa and Asia and achieving immortality through their illustrious exploits.[5]

And once we pass behind the reflected glare of modern mythology – Henry 'the Navigator' received his sobriquet from a nineteenth-century English biographer[6] – it is these feudal, militaristic, crusading strains which sound loudest.

The first advance beyond the shores of Europe was the capture of Ceuta from the Moors in 1415 – 'itself conceived as part of a crusade which might one day encircle the earth and take Islam in the rear'.[7] Ceuta was an important port and terminus of caravan trade on the Moroccan coast. It was a point of transshipment for the West African gold which at this time provided some two-thirds of the bullion circulating in the western hemisphere.[8] The fall of Ceuta, by depressing the trans-Saharan gold trade, provided an additional pressure to make direct contact with the Guinean source. And this was indeed one of the leading goals of the annual voyages of exploration down the West African coastline instituted by Henry in 1421. Henry himself, however, scaled down his financial contributions after being routed by the Moors at Tangiers in 1437. And after his death in 1460, North African crusading again diverted resources from the project of discovery.[9] In the reign of Manoel I (1495–1521), these efforts continued to preempt a fuller commitment to more distant – and more profitable – imperial activities. And Alfonso de Albuquerque himself, under whose vice-regal leadership (1509–15) the empire was largely constructed, held on to the end to dreams of an anti-Ottoman alliance with Persia, and a scheme to starve out Egypt by persuading Abyssinian allies to divert the waters of the Nile.[10] Thus, as Parry suggests, weighing the overall relationship between the spread of the Renaissance and the sudden, dramatic expansion of European geographical horizons,

> However Renaissance be defined, the Reconnaissance ... began independently and with medieval motives and assumptions.[11]

The 'medieval' Portuguese were, however, unusual in at least one regard. For a combination of reasons (which included domestic labour shortages after the Black Death and the decimation of the 'old nobility' following the war with Castile in 1385)[12] the ideological denigration of mercantile activities which held sway throughout much of feudal Europe exercised no veto over the Portuguese aristocracy. Prince Henry himself drew funds simultaneously from his feudal lands, his stewardship of the crusading Order of Christ and his many trading interests – which included slaving, fishing, the importation of dyes and sugar, and the control of domestic soap production. And later on, the 'mixed social origins of the investors and directors were reproduced among those who actually navigated and commanded trading posts'.[13] Whether this circumstance indicates the political strength of urban trading and shipping interests, or precisely the weakness of the indigenous commercial bourgeoisie (hemmed in on its other flank by thriving Italian financial communities in Lisbon and Oporto), is a matter of some scholarly debate.[14] Indeed, in the more highly charged idiom of the time it was also debated by contemporaries: Dom Manoel styled himself 'Lord of the Conquest, Navigation and Commerce of Ethiopia, Arabia, Persia and India'; but Francis I, his French neighbour, dubbed him simply 'the grocer king'.[15] Without entering too far into this debate, two striking circumstances would seem to tell against the claims that have been made for the 'modernity' of Portugal. First, the noble domination of much trade and indeed industry (which was exercised through the farming out of royal monopolies) did not affect the denigration of non-noble merchants. As the mercers of Lisbon complained as late as 1689: 'in the conceit of the Portuguese, a merchant is no better than a fish-porter.'[16] The same was true, equally surprisingly, of 'the contempt and dislike with which the mariner's calling was for so long regarded'.[17] Indeed, it was not until the eighteenth century that professional (non-noble) seamen came to replace the *fidalgos* as captains of the ships plying the *carreira da India*.[18] Thus if the Portuguese nobility took to trade and the high seas, this signalled more the rampage of an unchecked feudal estate than its enlightened fusion with a rising commercial bourgeoisie. But second, if the exploring Portuguese were the first of the moderns, how are we to explain the trajectory of their subsequent political and cultural development, in which precisely the failure to develop 'modern' institutions and sensibilities earned them the epithet 'the kaffirs of Europe'?

In September 1499, Vasco da Gama arrived back in Lisbon with the first cargo of eastern spices to reach Europe via the Cape. Within six months, a second fleet had departed. Its experience was to confirm the impression of da Gama's voyage – namely that a peaceful takeover of the Indian Ocean spice trade was inhibited by two principal factors: the unwillingness of local rulers to antagonize the Muslim mercantile interests already entrenched in the region, and the inability of the Portuguese to provide European commodities (for the purpose of entering the trade by exchange and barter) able to match the quality of what was already available in the East. (Da Gama's gifts to the Samorin of Calicut had provoked open laughter when unveiled.[19]) For this reason, the third trip (1502) comprised a heavily armed fleet of fourteen sail which exacted tribute in West Africa (Kilwa), bombarded Calicut from the sea and sank an Arab fleet which offered resistance.

The next step might have been to secure port facilities for the permanent stationing of a fleet to protect Portuguese shipping, thus exploiting the concessions already obtained. The Portuguese, however, had grander designs. Tracking the flows of East–West trade, they perceived that three choke-points, corresponding to the three northern exits from the Indian Ocean, formed natural entrepôts in the overall circulation. In the west, the island of Ormuz in the mouth of the Gulf, and the port of Aden at the southern tip of the Red Sea, governed the approaches to Europe. In the east, the straits overlooked by Malacca formed the gateway to China. Hence Alfonso de Albuquerque's anticipation of the low overhead costs of an eastern trading empire: 'four good fortresses and a large, well-armed fleet manned by 3,000 European-born Portuguese'.[20]

In six short years, mostly under Albuquerque's energetic leadership, much of this was achieved. Having taken Goa in 1510, the Portuguese captured Malacca in 1511 and Ormuz in 1515. Major naval battles at opposite ends of the Indian Ocean, where European gunnery destroyed Egyptian/Gujarati (Diu, 1509) and Javan (Malacca, 1513) war fleets, settled the dominance of Portuguese sea power. During this time the Portuguese suffered only one enduring setback, the failure to take Aden in 1513 – a goal which, for various reasons, they would never achieve. For the rest, however, they remained undefeated at sea until two routs by Chinese coastguard fleets (1521 and 1522) finally set the eastern bounds of their naval dominion.

The rapidity of this expansion requires some explanation. Boxer cites three factors over and above the widely remarked technological superiority of European warships.[21] First, he stresses the considerable determination of the Portuguese forces, whose capture of Goa, Malacca and Ormuz was achieved in each case only after having suffered an initial repulse. Second, the strongest Asian polities at this time were land powers, whose rulers were neither threatened by nor much interested in the Portuguese advance. Third, the Portuguese were able, by alliance and diplomatic manoeuvre, to exploit the frequent disunity within and between the coastal trading polities in order to assist their military operations. It might also be added that the technological inferiority of the Asian warships is perhaps itself to be explained by the institutional character of the Muslim trading system, which, as Curtin puts it, 'operated with comparatively low protection costs':[22] heavily armed merchantmen were not necessary to ply an open trade and hence were not available to defend it from external aggression. Finally, it should be remembered that Portuguese power, though of vast geographical extent, was almost exclusively naval, 'rarely able, even when [it] wished, to take the initiative outside the tiny fortress areas under [its] control'.[23]

The imperial organization constructed in the aftermath of these successes rested upon two central institutions: the royal monopoly and the *cartaz* system. The first of these was managed by the *Casa da India*, the royal trading firm based in Lisbon itself, which monopolized trade in the most important Asian imports – especially pepper. The 896 vessels which embarked for the East between 1500 and 1634 were built, owned and managed on behalf of the Crown.[24] Of these, just over half, 470, made it back to Lisbon.[25] For the rest, 28 per cent were lost at sea, while the remainder stayed on in the Indian Ocean.[26] In the 1560s this trade accounted for roughly half of the spices imported into Europe from the East.[27] For reasons discussed below, this Portuguese share soon diminished as a proportion of the whole – even before the Portuguese were dislodged by the Dutch. Over the same period, however, (the latter half of the sixteenth century), Asian production and European demand for spices doubled, while prices may have increased threefold.[28] Thus, the channelling of the maritime India trade through the *Casa da India* in Lisbon was a source of considerable profit for the Crown. Indeed, Wallerstein suggests that as early as 1506 the Crown drew over half its revenue from its monopoly of trades in West African gold and eastern spices.[29]

The second great institution of Portuguese imperial power, the *Estado da India*, was also based in Lisbon. In practice, however, its operational and administrative centre was in the port of Goa on the western coast of India. For this was the (geographically) vast apparatus of protection by which the Portuguese sought not only to secure the passage of the East Indiamen, but also to tax all interport mercantile traffic throughout the Indian Ocean. Under this system, freedom from Portuguese molestation was purchased in the form of a certificate (*cartaz*) which, though itself moderately priced, required that ships use Portuguese entrepôts, where a 6 per cent tax was levied on goods unloaded. The turnover of the *Estado* was even greater than that of the *Casa da India*, including as it did both the receipts from protection and the expenses of the Portuguese fleets and garrisons throughout the empire. But rarely did this coercive infrastructure yield a profit for the Crown; on the contrary, over the long run it acted as a net drain on official resources. Not unlike the Spanish Crown, which declared bankruptcy at the very point when silver imports from its American territories reached their highest levels, the Portugese authorities proved strangely unable to benefit from their unique good fortune:

> Despite the wide-ranging nature of the Crown's fiscal arm, successive Portuguese rulers were never able to enjoy an excess of income over expenditure for any length of time. ... For most of the 16th century, the Crown operated to a large extent with money borrowed on onerous terms from merchant bankers against the security of future pepper imports.[30]

Structural Features of Precapitalist Trade

What was going wrong? To answer this question, we need to enhance our analysis in two ways. First, we must map the overall structural character of this form of trading empire: where and how were the surpluses which were skimmed off as trading profit generated? By what mercantile and other mechanisms were these surpluses brought into circulation and both redistributed socially and relayed geographically? What were the wider conditions needing to be satisfied in order for these mechanisms to operate effectively? Second, having explored its formal structural properties, we need to reconstruct its actual historical insertion into the living social world of the sixteenth century. How was the attempt to consolidate such a system affected by the limited resources of Portugal, the nature and dynamics at that period of the societies of the Indian Ocean littoral, the lie of land and sea requiring territorial forms of control, the developing state of naval technology and nautical knowledge, and so on?

Taking these in order, it is generally agreed that the Portuguese empire, when compared with prior European or Asian trade networks, does not stand out by virtue of any significant technical, organizational or other institutional innovation. Parry avers that

> all the types of settlement which the Portuguese and other Europeans were to establish in the East in the sixteenth and seventeenth centuries had their precedents in Italian settlements in the later Middle Ages in the Mediterranean and the Black Sea.[31]

And J.C. van Leur suggests that the Empire 'did not introduce a single new economic element into the commerce of Asia'.[32] Moreover, 'it is central to the understanding of the situation that the Portuguese did not create the trade'[33] of the Indian Ocean. Rather they captured it (or a part of it) and sought to use it as a complex intercontinental mechanism of surplus appropriation.

What, then, was this pre-existing institutional pattern of mercantile activity which came to be reproduced across the vast canvas of *India Portuguesa*? This question brings us to that great enigma of early modern Europe: 'merchant capital'. The scare-quotes are important, for it can be argued that the historical practices denoted by this term in the work of Wallerstein, the Dobb–Sweezy debate, and indeed in Marx's writings too, reflect precisely the distinctive character of *precapitalist* markets and exchange relations. Thus, Eric Wolf cuts through much unnecessary confusion when he asserts baldly:

> There is no such thing as mercantile or merchant capitalism. ... There is only mercantile wealth. Capitalism, to be capitalism, must be capitalism-in-production.[34]

This is, of course, a definitional insistence, and its justification, as Dobb who shared this perspective recognized, 'must ultimately rest on its successful employment in illuminating the actual process of historical development'.[35] For the moment, however, these points are raised simply to assist in a clearer presentation of the discussion which follows.

With these caveats in mind, let us proceed to examine the character of 'merchant capital'. Marx observes in chapter XX of Volume III of *Capital* that

Prima facie, a pure and independent commercial profit seems impossible so long as products are sold at their value.[36]

And since, in the carrying trade particularly, mercantile profits appear at the end of a series of transactions which mediate the circulation of commodities without visibly adding to their value, the association of commerce with swindling is natural enough. Luther protested that

> princes should punish such unjust bargains with due rigour and take care that their subjects shall not be so outrageously abused by merchants [who] ... daily rob the whole world ... and steal with greater assurance than all others.[37]

Nor was the calmer analysis provided by the fourteenth-century Muslim 'sociologist' Ibn Khaldun any more reassuring on this score:

> commerce is the search for gain by increasing the initial fund when one buys commodities at a favourable price and resells them at a higher price. ... This increase is called profit. This profit is obtained by storing the commodity and awaiting a fluctuation in the tendency of the market to rise, which produces a great profit; or by transporting the commodity mentioned to another region where the demand for it is stronger, which also produces a great profit.[38]

Speculation and the manipulation of market imperfections – was this the worm-eaten core of premodern mercantile practice? Certainly the Dutch would later find in pepper the perfect commodity for both of these: available only from remote sources, a high value/weight ratio, minutely and easily divisible, and able to be stored for long periods at low cost. The temptations were irresistible, and some cargoes of pepper are known to have been detained in storage for over thirty years, awaiting *le moment juste*.[39]

At the same time, however, the Dutch were also plying and dominating an *open* trade, partly in bulky, perishable staples, across the Baltic, which offered less spectacular opportunities for artificial profits. By the mid seventeenth century, the Dutch 'carried perhaps ten times as much out of the Baltic as any competitor'.[40] And yet this was not a militarily enforced monopoly. Dutch commercial supremacy here rested on a real competitive edge resulting largely from 'cheap freights and the control of a sufficient supply of silver for export'. As a result, 'Dutch merchants could sell Baltic goods in *England* more cheaply than English merchants could.'[41]

The real point about precapitalist markets, then, is not that they were protected, artificial monopolies – though many of them were.

Instead, it concerns the underlying structural reason for this latter circumstance: the mechanism of mercantile surplus accumulation which was being fought over lay in control of the circulation of commodities (not their production); and competition of all kinds – military, technological, organizational – therefore concentrated in that realm. In a dramatic illustration of this, Louis XIV's finance minister, Colbert, suggested in 1669 that France could secure dominance of the trade of Europe by capturing the Dutch share of the 20,000 ships in which it was carried.[42] The plan ended in defeat. But if it seems outlandish, it should be remembered that at this very time others were pursuing similar policies with great success: 'enormous numbers [of Dutch vessels] were captured by the English during their three wars with the Dutch between 1652 and 1673, largely restocking the English merchant fleet.'[43] Of course, if control over the processes of circulation, or an acceptable share of them, could be achieved by non-military means, thus lowering protection costs, so much the better.

The *source* of the wealth which the merchants sought to tap was in the hands of the surplus-takers, the land-owners who continued to command the vast bulk of material production. If the merchants themselves became involved in production – say urban craft production – they did so in order to accelerate the wheels of circulation and not to gain an income from the direct competitive exploitation of productive labour. Why is this distinction so important?

This question needs to be addressed in greater historical and theoretical depth. For the moment, however, some brief indications must suffice to point up the specificity of premodern trade in comparison with its equivalent today. And perhaps the most useful starting point is Marx's suggestion that

> In the precapitalist stages of society commerce ruled industry. In modern society the reverse is true.[44]

The first half of this we have already noted above. From the point of view of mercantile accumulation, urban (and, increasingly, rural) manufactures were promoted in order to fuel trade. They were one among a number of weapons used in the struggle for control of lucrative exchange relations. But what does it mean to say that today industry rules commerce? In the premodern era, trade comprised a process in which producers could exchange surpluses, but in which the contingent relation of prices to the costs of production (a relation muddied by the non-commodified status of labour exploited outsided the market) was governed above all by factors affecting circulation, where the mechanisms of mercantile profit therefore lay. Not so today: for trade now is predominantly the realm in which surpluses generated by the competitive exploitation of commodified labour in the sphere of production are realized as exchange-value. Hence

> the production process has ... absorbed circulation as a mere phase of production ... The production process rests wholly upon circulation, and circulation is a mere transitional phase of production.[45]

There is a great deal more than this to be said. But the key point is that what we have here are not simply two different alignments of production and exchange relations within an overall political economy which remains unaltered but for a shift of quantitative weight between pre-existing commercial and industrial sectors. Rather, we have two dramatically different kinds of market – different with regard to their mechanisms of accumulation, their conditions of reproduction, their dynamic structural properties, their articulation within the wider social formation, and the determinate forms of social power which they promote. For the category 'the market' (hence also 'the world market'), whatever general features it might correctly identify, is, just like 'the state' (and 'the states-system'), a hopelessly blunt instrument of social explanation until it is sharpened up by historical and structural definition.

One further observation may be made before we continue. The distinction roughly sketched above between capitalist and precapitalist markets may or may not be a useful one: that remains to be tested by deploying it in the construction of actual historical explanations. But, reverting to our earlier discussion of definitions, it is not one that is available as a theoretical tool (or therefore visible as a historical contrast or discontinuity) so long as we operate with a market definition of capitalism.[46] For if capitalism is understood as rational calculative activity with regard to 'the market' (Weber) or production oriented to 'the market' (as in the work of Wallerstein) without specifying what *kind* of market, then its historical specificity (as opposed to its quantitative weight within a given society) is simply not an issue. Throughout history there have always been markets and, by dint of urban consumption, there has always been market-oriented production. Weber recognized this and happily wrote of capitalist interests in imperial Rome.[47] But then, for Weber, the concept of capitalism was not primary in the definition of modernity.

The Mercantile Practice of the Portuguese

Since mercantile profits depended upon control of the processes of circulation, it was imperative that the Portuguese should keep as tight a grip as possible on these in order to exploit the India trade to the full. This involved a number of preconditions, perhaps the most basic of which was the preservation of the secrecy of the Cape route itself. For, as Curtin notes, 'the 'maritime revolution' of the fifteenth and sixteenth centuries was not so much a revolution in ship design as the discovery of the world wind system'.[48] In the age of sail, therefore, the knowledge that there existed a sea-route to the East did not open the field to all comers, and the Aviz dynasty decreed the death penalty for persons found smuggling charts to foreign rivals.[49]

The Portuguese were also fortunate after 1479 in not having to face Castilian military competition for (and privateering raids upon) their West African trade. In that year the Treaty of Alcacovas which ended the Castilian War of Succession legitimized 'the Portuguese monopoly of fishing, trade and navigation along the whole West African coast'.[50] The Treaty no doubt fortified the Spanish pursuit of westward exploration;[51] furthermore, it afforded the Portuguese almost a century free from serious European naval competition in the Indian Ocean.[52]

But armed rivalry, as it turned out, was among the least of Portugal's problems. More damaging was the inability of the Crown to finance the spice trade which it controlled. Although the prospect of huge windfall profits was real enough,[53] neither the monarchy nor any indigenous commercial interests had the resources either to underwrite the outgoing voyages or to buy the cargoes on their return. Hence, attempts to exclude foreign investment were abandoned after 1505:

> The Crown undertook all subsequent voyages, but sold the entire cargoes in Lisbon to merchant syndicates, mostly Italian and German, who shipped the goods to Antwerp and distributed them there. Frequently, the Crown sold cargoes in advance, while they were still at sea, or borrowed on the security of future cargoes, so that in effect the foreigners provided most of the capital, and both as creditors and as middlemen absorbed most of the profit.[54]

Part of the problem here was that the circulation of the India trade was only half done when the cargoes arrived at Lisbon. Nine-tenths of the consumers lived in northern Europe.[55] And it was under foreign ownership that the pepper and spices were carried to the central

entrepôt of Antwerp where they finally entered the capillaries of
internal trade.

> the wealthy merchant houses seek to buy up large lots and form consortia
> with the aim of maximizing profits on the resale and distribution of the
> pepper over Europe. The constellations of interested parties are in con-
> tinuous flux, and the pepper never stops being manipulated.[56]

The Crown tried between 1508 and 1549 to extend its control of
circulation northwards by maintaining its own agency in Antwerp.
Not only was this body unable to compete with its commercial rivals;
by the last quarter of the sixteenth century it was 'foreign pepper
contractors [who were being] allowed to station their own representa-
tives at Goa and Cochin, in order to supervise the purchase and
shipment of the spices for which they had contracted'.[57] Braudel notes
that the impact of the Portuguese trade is visible in the considerable
diversion of German silver and Hungarian copper production away
from its erstwhile Venetian destination and towards Antwerp. For
copper, in the six years after 1502–1503, he cites a rise from 24 per
cent to 49 per cent, leaving Venice with a mere 13 per cent.[58] One
wonders how much of this actually made it back to Lisbon, and how
much was siphoned off along the way. Certainly, the fact that 'the
West was being drained of its silver for the benefit of the Portuguese
trade circuit'[59] did not entail either that the West was becoming
proportionately poorer, or Portugal proportionately richer, as a
result.[60]

By one means or another, then, commercial agents downstream
in the flow of the India trade were able to reach back and exploit
mechanisms of mercantile profit located at earlier points in the process of circulation. This must have been galling to the 'Lord of Conquest, Navigation and Commerce'. But the circuit was hardly more
secure if he looked upstream to the Indian Ocean itself. Only two
of the three key entrepôts had been captured, and the Red Sea spice
route overlooked by Aden remained open. This, coupled with the fact
that the Portuguese were never able to monopolize the purchase of
spices, but chaffered at the markets of Malabar alongside Indian
merchants, was a severe limitation:

> In the middle years of the sixteenth century, the volume of the Levant trade
> was as great as it had ever been, and at least as great as that which the
> Portuguese carried around the Cape.[61]

A failed monopsony in Asia thus reinforced the failure to achieve a
monopoly in Europe.

That said, the mercantile ingenuity of the Portuguese must also be recognized. For they succeeded, intermittently at least, in harnessing their participation in the interport trade of Asia as a means of driving the overall process of intercontinental accumulation. Indeed, without this 'country trade' it would have been impossible for them to conduct East–West trade on the scale that they did. The reasons for this were simple: Portugal was not a productive centre, Europe as a whole did not provide suitable commodities on an adequate scale, and sufficient quantities of bullion were not available to the Crown. Thus it was by breaking into the Asian circulation of indigenous commodities as carriers that the Portuguese came by the use-values which could be bartered for spices and the surplus exchange-value which made up the deficit of payment from Europe.

The primary circuit in what developed into 'a whole network of ancillary trades'[62] playing this role was the Portuguese export of Indian cotton goods to Indonesia where they were accepted in exchange for spices, and to East Africa where they earned gold and ivory. In the last quarter of the sixteenth century, the voyages from Goa supplying Portuguese Macao (on the Chinese coast) were extended to take in the Sino-Japanese trade in silks and bullion forbidden to Chinese vessels by imperial decree. Since Chinese silks were paid for in Japanese silver, the value of which was markedly higher in China, enormous windfall profits in gold were made on the return run from Nagasaki. In addition, most of the spices purchased by the Portuguese were resold in Asia.[63] Thus after about 1547:

> the greater part of the gold required by the Portuguese for their purchases in Malabar was obtained from south-east Africa, Sumatra and China.[64]

Since the Crown owned in principle almost the entire Portuguese operation, under ideal conditions this articulation of regional and East–West exchange relations should have been worked as a gigantic geo-commercial machine relaying enormous surpluses to Lisbon at diminishing cost. But by any comparison with this potential, the royal returns, though handsome enough, were small. Indeed, the passage to and from the Lisbon metropole 'formed the weakest link in the chain of empire'.[65]

This striking outcome – an imperial structure partly cut adrift from the originating centre which yet retains offical control and ownership – might be seen as an extreme instance of the special vulnerability to smuggling, contraband and embezzlement of any commercial network in which the sources of profit lie exclusively in the control of circulation – in other words, of any precapitalist network. But it needs also to be understood in relation to the distinctive institutional forms of Portuguese royal power. We noted earlier that the strong noble presence in Portuguese trade and industry took the form of grants of royal monopolies to individuals. This in itself was distinctive in an age when monarchs elsewhere guarded their monopolies jealously. But it did not end there:

> Perhaps more than in any other country, it was a long-established practice ... for the Crown ... to farm out the smallest public offices which might be expected to produce any revenue.[66]

This device characterized Portuguese overseas expansion too. Whether it was the governorship of a lucrative entrepôt, the captaincy of a round trip in the *carreira* or the Goa–Nagasaki route, rights to exploit teak forests in India or one of the plethora of lesser administrative posts, offices were contracted out, either as remuneration or into the hands of the highest bidder. These bidders might be individuals or syndicates, and subcontracting was routine in the more complex branches of imperial activity.

However, it was the conjunction of this commercializing of office with another factor which transformed an administrative gamble into the world-wide carnival of corruption known to later historians. Unable to pay adequate wages to the roughly 2,400 men sent annually to the East during the sixteenth century, the Crown conceded a limited right of individual employees to trade on their own account. For the crew of the Indiamen this meant the 'liberty-chests' – part of the storage capacity of the vessel given over to their private use. For officials stationed in the East it could mean anything from limited private deals on the side to a purchase of the temporary right to engross all trade under the control of their office to their own private profit. For the system as a whole, however, this 'spoils system' merely ensured that the Empire was staffed from top to bottom by men with a powerful and mutual interest in defrauding the Crown. And the resultant internal haemorrhage sharply reduced the flow of surpluses reaching the metropole.[67]

Given its unprecedented geographical extent, *India Portuguesa* was a remarkably flimsy empire in many respects:

> it is probable that had the Portuguese abandoned their Indian empire at the end of the sixteenth century, they would have left even less trace than did the Greeks, Scythians, and Parthians.[68]

But precisely this territorial profile – long lines of communication linking distant points rather than borders enclosing areas of rule – was the signature of the precapitalist trading-post empire *pur et dur*. (Thus did Venice and Genoa throw out their strings of military bases along the Mediterranean littoral, in order to compete by force over the sea-lanes of the Levant trade.) As with any territorial strategy, its shape and orientation followed the particular social relations it sought to affect: the stuff of Portuguese imperial power was the control over the mercantile mechanisms of surplus appropriation available in the circulation of commodities, not an extension of command over the actual generation of those surpluses in the exploitation of productive labour. Its superficiality of impact and its huge geographical scale can therefore both be illuminated by an understanding of its structural identity.

New Spain

On the face of it, the Spanish Empire in the Indies could hardly form a starker contrast with its Portuguese contemporary in the East. The latter was a naval empire *par excellence*, the former a territorial dominion. The Portuguese found and penetrated an existing mercantile system, without (in our period) exercising extensive political rule over subject populations; the Spaniards found no maritime commerce but subdued and ransacked two enormous empires, subsequently installing themselves as a ruling elite living off the labour of the surviving population. *India Portuguesa* was carved out and operated under the jealous leadership of a grasping aristocracy; America was captured by 'dispossessed Spaniards of all conditions ... mostly of low extraction'.[69] Clearly, these two fronts of sixteenth-century European expansion, though both commanded from the Iberian peninsula, were advancing according to very different dynamics, over very different terrains of operation, and were consolidating themselves by very different mechanisms of control.

Moreover, one of the key differences, Spanish exploitation of indigenous labour, enables us to explore further the theme of capitalist and precapitalist 'international economies'. For by the end of the century, the Spaniards had not just substituted themselves for the Aztec and Inca elites, taking over the existing structures of surplus extraction and appropriation; under the combined pressures of demographic collapse, rising demand for labour in the mines, and an absolutizing monarchy, they had reconstituted the remaining population into a new society, New Spain, a tributary social formation

organized around the production of bullion and its relay, via a controlled series of exchange relations, to the Castilian metropole.

Social Forms and Structural Dynamics
of Castilian Expansion

It is a truism that the Spanish assault on the Americas proceeded
under the momentum and using the techniques of the recently completed *Reconquista*. Thus, Claudio Sanchez-Albornoz describes it as
'the most immense result of the peninsular activism created by Spain's
centuries-long struggle with Islam'.[70] And James Lang suggests that

> The extension of royal power to the vast area of two continents was a
> monumental task. But it was not a new task nor even a bold new policy.[71]

Both the structural continuities and the dynamic links between the
Old World and New Spain are indeed vital to any historical understanding of the Spanish moment of European expansion. To render
them visible, however, we must revive some of the anterior theoretical
and historical questions which truisms, by their nature, typically
abbreviate: What does it *mean* to speak of a 'momentum' of territorial
expansion? How did such a momentum, associated above all with
seven hundred years of land warfare, suddenly come to spill over
across two thousand miles of uncharted ocean? And how were the
institutional forms of Castilian power expressed at the new level of
an intercontinental system of control as opposed to their earlier
innovation within the expanding territorial unity of the Iberian
kingdom?

As Perry Anderson points out, the eighth-century Muslim conquest of Iberia interrupted the slow fusion of Germanic and Roman
social forms which elsewhere characterized the emergence of European feudalism. Instead, the seven centuries' struggle with the Moors
'was the fundamental determinant of the forms of Spanish feudalism'.[72] This *Reconquista* was a temporally uneven and regionally differentiated historical process: different areas were recovered at different
speeds, were absorbed in different ways and with differing consequences for the development of the expanding whole. Moreover, its
pace was affected also by developments within the world of Muslim
Spain – notably the break-up of the caliphate of Cordoba (from 1031)
into twenty to thirty competing *taifas* (successor states), and the
Almoravid and Almohad Berber *jihads* (*c.* 1036 and *c.* 1135) which
temporarily threw the Christians back onto the defensive.[73]

During the 'slow reconquest' of the tenth and eleventh centuries, the peasants' haven of a no-man's-land on the moving frontier had undercut the consolidation of seigniorial relations further north, thus simultaneously elevating the organizing military role of the monarchy and inhibiting the political consolidation of a landed feudal nobility.[74] Instead, an urban class of commoner knights (the *caballeros villanos*), drawn from the free smallholders who settled the land, were used to staff the frontier towns and fuel the waves of military advance. The recruitment of this class was organized through the granting of fiscal privilege and the reservation of municipal office. Furthermore, 'apart from stock-raising, these towns in the twelfth and thirteenth centuries lived chiefly from booty in the form of cattle, slaves, moveables and even foodstuffs.'[75] Thus the structural relation of town and country was very different to that which characterized the material reproduction of feudalism, either in central and western Europe or in northern Italy. The Christian towns of central Spain did not arise as centres of trade and craft production dominated by a commercial class distinct from surrounding hierarchies of feudal rural power. They were 'military and religious centres'[76] – comprising indeed the bulk of the population[77] – whose internal organization co-ordinated both the intra-Castilian relations of authority, and the marshalling of resources for further campaigns against the Moors.[78]

Thus the material and political reproduction of the Castilian social order was organized around permanent military mobilization, continuous plunder (whether direct, in the form of marauding raids, or indirect, as in the case of the 'heavy annual tribute' extracted from the Caliphate from the eleventh century onwards[79]) and the task of incorporating and settling new lands inhabited by non-Christian populations. Indeed the very name 'Castile' witnesses to the distinctive, militaristic origins of this polity: a buffer state erected by the Kingdom of Leon in the ninth century, fronted by a line of castles built as a forward defence against Moorish raids on the newly recaptured plains of Asturia.[80] On the one hand, this entailed that the final closing of the frontier – or even a long pause in the *Reconquista* – would threaten social disorder, and require fundamental changes in the structure of Castilian society.[81] On the other, it meant that the *conquistadores* who landed in the Americas were equipped with a formidable repertoire of institutional devices and forms by which to imagine, organize and legitimate their conquest and plunder. Thus the *capitulaciones* which apportioned in advance the respective rights of king and *conquistador* over any human and material resources captured in the Americas echoed the 'practice of the Crown to make contracts with leaders of military expeditions against the Moors'.[82] The *encomienda* system by which, following the opening round of slaughter and looting, the Spaniards institutionalized their command over native labour was adapted from institutions developed earlier by the Crown to allocate newly reconquered Moorish territories.[83] And the distinctive role of the Castilian town – both as the garrison planted in an alien countryside and as a co-ordinating grid of intra-Spanish relations of authority and appropriation – was also carried over.[84] As in medieval Spain,

> Towns in Spanish America did not 'emerge'. They were planned in accordance with a definite ritual. ... An instrument of domination, the Spanish town was planned to control the countryside.[85]

When Cortés arrived on the mainland in 1519 with 600 men in search of the Aztec capital, almost his first action was to found a new town, Vera Cruz, and formally to appoint himself and his men to municipal offices. This, clearly, was not a piece of innocent town planning. It was a deliberate political act which served formally to redefine the legal status of his expedition, repudiating the authority of the colony of Hispaniola and invoking direct allegiance to the Castilian monarch.[86] This was to become a routine device,[87] its real purpose underlined by the fact that permanent settlement did not result. On the contrary, the new towns were routinely *depopulated* as soon as further prospects of plunder beckoned.[88]

As already suggested, the *Reconquista* was an uneven process. By contrast to the slow build-up described above, the 'quick reconquest' in the first half of the thirteenth century saw the Moors expelled from the Algarve by the Portuguese, while the Aragonese captured Valencia and the Castilians overran Extremadura, Andalusia and Murcia, leaving Granada the last Moorish kingdom on the peninsula. In Portugal this swift conclusion allowed the leading military institutions, the monarchy and the Church, to block off the emergence of a strong nobility for over a century.[89] In Castile, however, the very scale of the new territories to be digested obliged Ferdinand III to parcel out huge estates to aristocratic supporters.[90] Had Castile bitten off more than it could chew? Certainly, after 1270 the *Reconquista* slowed to a halt which lasted two hundred years; and Castile entered the general crisis of the fourteenth century already riven by the revolts and dynastic struggles of an overmighty magnate class.[91]

A further consequence of this penultimate wave of expansion was the rapid growth of wool production enabled by the incorporation of Andalusia, an industry which came to absorb much of the demobilized class of *caballeros villanos*:

> For the first time sheep owners could move their flocks with real safety along the great *canadas* (sheep walks), which extended the length of Spain from the summer pastures in the northern mountains to the winter grazing grounds in the Guadalquivir valley.[92]

This development, combined with the introduction[93] of the *merino* sheep, was full of consequences for the future. Apart from ensuring in Castile 'the triumph of a pastoral economy',[94] it linked Spain with Italy, both as a raw materials producer and as a luxury market. In addition, the making over of arable soil to pasturage began to displace agrarian labour on a scale later reflected in the disproportionate demographic contribution made by Andalusia to New World settlement.[95] It was a pattern of agrarian change which would recur in Mexico.[96]

A Systemic Pressure?

Cortés and his followers also brought with them that 'wolfish greed for gold'[97] for which the *conquistadores* have been famed: 'I came here to get gold, not to till the soil like a peasant.'[98] How are we to explain this obsession which almost brought Columbus's first voyage to grief,[99] and which soon manifested itself as the overriding pressure leading to the extermination of the unhappy Caribs of Hispaniola?[100] In part its roots lay in the historical formation of the broad *hidalgo* class with its distinctive ideological self-definition:

> the very character of the *Reconquista* as a southwards migration in the wake of conquering armies encouraged a popular contempt for sedentary life and fixed wealth, and thus imbued the populace with ideals similar to those of the aristocracy.[101]

But more particularly, gold itself had been a regular and sought-after prize in the looting of the Moorish kingdoms. For the latter controlled the land routes via Morocco to its African source, and thus, alone among the societies of early medieval Europe, were able to use a gold coinage.[102] Even during the two hundred year pause after 1250, the Castilian monarchy was able to secure a steady supply in the form of tribute from the kingdom of Granada.[103] This flow was interrupted after 1415, first by the Portuguese capture of Ceuta, then by their direct contacts with Guinea.

None of this, however, would have carried the Castilians across the Atlantic had it not affected wider interests. The fourteenth and fifteenth centuries witnessed a partial but significant redeployment of Italian mercantile activity to the western Mediterranean. This was conditioned partly by the deteriorating geopolitical and commercial situation in the Levant (the final collapse of the Byzantine Empire under Ottoman pressure came in 1453), and partly by the expanding luxury market of Castile. In addition, the production of sugar-cane on slave plantations managed by Italian merchants had itself migrated westward – from the Levant to Cyprus, to Sicily, to the Algarve and beyond – as military pressure from the East and the shifting supplies of slave labour dictated. (By 1450, Portugal was importing 2,500 African slaves annually.) But equally important was the Italian (and in particular, Genoan) commercial involvement with both Castile and the coastal ports of Morocco as a means of drawing off gold specie to drive the eastern trade in spices. The importance of this direct penetration was already considerable in the fourteenth century due to a marked fall in European silver production on the one hand,[104] and rising prices in the spice trade following the collapse of the Mongol Khanates on the other. From 1471, Portuguese direct contacts with Guinea diverted the Moroccan supply of bullion. And by the time central European silver production revived in the latter half of the fifteenth century, this 'bullion hunger' was further compounded by the sharply rising demand for specie which accompanied the early economic recovery after the Black Death. Between 1460 and 1620, the European population nearly doubled and the volume of money transactions may have increased ten- or twentyfold.[105] It now seems to be agreed that this burst of growth was already generating the inflationary pressures of the sixteenth century *before* the discovery of American silver – which in any case did not come 'on stream' until halfway through the century.[106] And while it remains true that Mexican and Peruvian imports later superimposed a monetary inflation onto this 'real cost inflation', it follows that their *first* effect was to relax those restraints on growth which were due to the objective scarcity of the means of exchange. As Davis observes, on the eve of the Discoveries, '[t]he European economy urgently needed a large increase in the supply of silver, and to a lesser extent of gold.'[107]

It might be asked: How can we reckon this urgency as a factor in our historical explanation of European expansion – without posing the issue in unacceptably functionalist or teleological terms? As we noted axiomatically in chapter 2 above, systems do not have 'needs', and we cannot therefore assume an automatic causal link between a dispersed systemic 'pressure' and subsequent outcomes. The challenge is not dissimilar to our earlier task of making sense of the idea of a 'momentum of reconquest', and it must be answered in the same way: that is by spelling out how the social structures under view (in this case those which organized late medieval trade and finance) comprised sets of social relationships reproduced by knowledgeable, concretely located human agents, what the broader conditions (and dynamic tendencies) of this reproduction were, and how they were met – or not. In this case we find that some groups, notably mercantile interests, would have experienced this scarcity not simply as a diminished stock of wealth available for individual engrossment (as did the Spanish *hidalgo* class), but additionally, and more particularly, as a brake on circulation itself. And since for these groups access to the means of exchange is vital to their basic social reproduction, it is hardly surprising that the scarcity of the money-form was expressed as a fixation with and determination to accumulate the finite supply, and discover new sources:

> With metallic coinage shrinking, trade rising, and a lag in the spread of Italian methods of credit ... bullionism was not a simple fallacy, like that of misplaced concreteness.[108]

Thus it may well be that, as the aged Bernal Diaz reflected, 'all men alike covet gold, and the more we have the more we want';[109] but it is also clear that the lethal obsession of the *conquistadores* was historically overdetermined: behind the personal greed shaped by the collective memory of Moorish booty were gathering the dispersed pressures of a social system beginning to strain against the objective limits of the conjuncture.

It would be a simplification to conclude that the southwards momentum of the crusading *Reconquista*[110] met a westwards thrust of Italian mercantile speculation racing the Portuguese to the eastern sites of spice production – a thrust which, while it failed in its own purpose, unwittingly catapulted the Castilian engine of plunder to within reach of the hapless Amerindian civilizations. But there have been worse simplifications. For Columbus, it will be remembered, was not a Castilian, but an Italian, who had been in the employ of a Genoese bank. (The New World itself came to be named after the Florentine businessman Amerigo Vespucci.) Moreover, Ferdinand and Isabella agreed to support his venture only after a guaranteed loan was secured from private sources by the Royal Treasurer – quite possibly from a group of Genoese financiers with whom the latter was linked.[111] And certainly, there is no doubt that the aim of the voyage was to discover a westward route to the Spice Islands. Included within this brief was the search for new sources of gold, 'a metal that he mentioned at least sixty-five times in his diary during the passage'.[112] Columbus apparently never gave up the belief that the Caribbean islands he discovered lay off the eastern coast of China. And even after this was proved false, the search for a passage through to the riches of the Pacific remained the most powerful inspiration of seaborne exploration of the Americas.[113] Magellan's heroic voyage of 1519–22 was supported by Charles V on the (spurious) grounds that 'if the line of Tordesillas were extended to the other side of the globe, it would leave the Spice Islands on the eastern, or Spanish, side.'[114] And over a century later, the Anglo-French competition in the American fur trade which was to become of such geopolitical moment *began* largely as a by-product of the search for a North-West Passage.[115]

Such were the motives of the Italian vanguard, motives which underlay the so-called 'Mediterranean approach' associated with Columbus.[116] Although on his return from the first voyage, Columbus promised the monarchs gold and 'slaves, as many as they shall order',[117] the second trip to the West Indies (1493) was not planned as a campaign of conquest. The 1,500 passengers included soldiers, but composed 'a microcosm of male Spanish society'.[118] The purpose was rather 'to establish trading factories on the pattern of Genoese establishments in the Levant'.[119] This, however, required that contacts be made with the Far East as rapidly as possible. Failure to achieve this exacerbated strains between the Italian leadership (Columbus was attended by his brother Bartholemew) and the Castilian settlers who were more interested in extorting gold from the Caribs of Hispaniola. In an attempt to contain this rift, Columbus was compelled to distribute land and natives among the settlers in the form of *encomiendas*. And when, in 1499, he was replaced by the Catholic kings and sent back to Spain in irons, the social organization of European expansion in the Americas reverted decisively to 'the Iberian tradition of conquest and settlement'.[120] Banned from returning to Hispaniola, Columbus was allowed one final chance by his patrons to discover the sea-route to Cathay. As the westward Italian reconnaissance petered out along the shoreline of the Gulf of Mexico, the fate of the Carib populations (collapsing under the combined pressure of intensive slave-raiding, overwork in the forced search for gold and disastrous vulnerability to alien pathogens), prefigured the impact of the reviving *conquista* about to burst onto the American mainland.

Conquest and Settlement

As J.H. Parry puts it, the age of the professional explorer gave way swiftly to the age of the *conquistador*; and the latter was itself to prove 'quarrelsome and brief'.[121] The conquest of Cuba (1511) was followed by two exploratory voyages to the Yucatan peninsula (1517–18) which returned with intelligence of a large empire inland. A third voyage (1519) carried 600 men under the leadership of a former treasurer's clerk, Hernando Cortés. The events which followed, culminating in the rapid and complete destruction of the Aztec Empire, compose a narrative of reckless and breathtaking courage, astonishing historical coincidence, a fatal, dreamlike cognitive dissonance enabling spectacular plunder – all of these in a conjunction that must have seemed unrepeatable, until it recurred a dozen years later in the high Andean heartland of Inca power.

Cortés seems to have been mistaken for the reincarnation of an Aztec god, Quetzlcoatl, 'whose return to earth was expected by Mexican augurers about the time that the Spaniards landed'.[122] This would perhaps explain the contradictory behaviour of the Aztec ruler, Montezuma, and the fact that the Spaniards were initially welcomed into Tenochtitlan (the capital city comprising 60,000 dwellings built on an island in lake Texcoco), and lodged in a palace adjacent to that of the Emperor. Within weeks, Montezuma, by a mixture of psychological manipulation and physical force, had been reduced to a puppet of Cortés; and the formal political structures of the Empire were being mobilized to raise tribute in gold from subject populations. Montezuma handed over the contents of the royal treasury, and Aztec warrior-guides escorted Spaniards to the mines and rivers where the gold was extracted.[123] Inevitably, Montezuma's increasing subservience generated rising tensions within the Aztec political elite, tensions which exploded into open rebellion following Spanish interference with the routine ceremonies of mass human sacrifice. Expelled from Tenochtitlan, the *conquistadores* fell back on native allies. In the final assault, several hundred Spaniards led a native army of over 100,000 in ninety-three days of continuous fighting, 'systematically looting and destroying [the capital] building by building'.[124]

Pizarro's conquest of the Incas was no less spectacular. The first European to find the Indian coastal city of Tumbes in northern Peru in 1527, he returned first to Spain, securing from Charles V a *capitulacion* ceding the governership of any territories captured. By another fatal historical coincidence, the Inca Empire, whose engineers had constructed a military communications infrastructure surpassing even that of the Romans,[125] was at the time of Pizarro's arrival approaching the climax of a five-year war of succession. As the 180 or so Spaniards set out from Tumbes, the 80,000 strong victorious army of Atahualpa, 640 kilometres away on the high Andean plateau, was preparing for its triumphant descent to the capital Cuzco, having finally defeated the reigning Inca, Huascar. Why Atahualpa allowed the Spaniards to approach unhindered – indeed, even evacuating the small town of Cajamarca for their use – remains unclear.[126] Even stranger was his acceptance of Pizarro's invitation to a parley in the town's main square – a natural setting for the ambush which followed. Completely unprepared for the Spanish onslaught, the 5,000 unarmed royal escorts died (or escaped) without offering any resistance.[127] And the remainder of the army melted away. Once again, the captive ruler retained his divine status and was used to command the labour of the empire in its new task of delivering gold to the conquerors: 'Atahualpa's Ransom' (which failed to save him from execution by his captors) was assembled by a two-month, officially promulgated mass stripping of the artefacts of Inca civilization,[128] and amounted to no less than 1,326,539 pesos of gold and 51,610 marks of silver.[129] And here, too, early attempts to rule through Inca puppets led to open rebellion (1537) requiring a more substantial military conquest. In two major respects, however, the Peruvian theatre of expansion differed from the Mexican. First, for reasons of logistical supply, Pizarro did not retain the Inca mountain city of Cuzco as the capital of Spanish rule, preferring instead to operate from the new coastal city of Lima. As a result, the topographical disjuncture between coast and mountain (together with its associated contrast of forms of social organization) came to underlie – as it has done ever since – the weakest seams in any project of unified political rule. But second, this geography informed not only Spanish–Indian relations, but also the intra-Spanish civil wars in which rival *conquistadores* fought out first their claims for territorial dominium and then their resistance to the consolidation of the bureaucratic authority of Charles V.[130]

As mentioned above, the *conquistadores* organized their settling of the new territories using institutions carried over and modified from the *Reconquista*.[131] In particular, the distinctive articulation of urban and rural social relations was reproduced. Cortés's immediate followers lived in the new Mexico City, relations among them being organized through the rotation of municipal offices. Their material reproduction, however, was secured outside the city by the conferment of *encomiendas* – grants of territory with an assigned number of Indian households from whom tribute in kind and in labour could be levied, and towards whom the *encomenderos* assumed a general responsibility of religious conversion and military security. (Cortés himself aquired an enormous *encomienda*, numbering no less than 23,000 households.) Strictly, the *encomienda* involved no cession by the Crown either of land ownership or of jurisdiction over persons. However, the evident desire of the *conquistadores* to make their positions heritable, coupled with the despotic power enabled by the right of forced labour, confirmed the Crown in its determination to abolish the institution.

The displacement of the *conquistadores* was undertaken in two stages. First, the Crown established structures of legal and administrative authority staffed by peninsular Spaniards and answerable directly to the Council of the Indies in Castile (set up in 1524). The *audiencia* (court) of Mexico was not resisted on its inauguration in 1528; and the first governor of New Spain, appointed over the head of Cortés, arrived in 1535. At the same time, the Crown gradually aquired the power of appointment to the main city councils (*cabildos*) and curtailed their political independence. Local fiscal and legislative control passed into the hands of another royal appointee, the *corregidor*, whose responsiblity for supervising the collection of taxes (including among the Indians) and acting as a local court of appeal further blocked the development of the *encomendero* class into a feudal aristocracy.[132] Thus at every level the settlers were to be hedged about by the royal bureaucracy unfurled from Seville. And this in turn was not simply government for the sake of government. The same organized structure of social relations which carried royal authority from the Council of the Indies down to the local adminstration of Mexico also comprised a structure of public finance which relayed resources upward, level by level, until all the costs of government had been met, whereupon the balances could be remitted to Spain.[133] (The other major source of New World income lay in the royal supervision of colonial trade.)

Second, this progressive displacement of the *encomenderos* within the government of the New World was followed in 1542 by a direct assault on the *encomienda* itself. The New Laws of that year, fruit of a temporary but powerful confluence of interest between a centralizing monarchy and a proselytizing Church, provided for the abolition of

Indian slavery, the close restriction of personal labour services, and the permanent reversion to the Crown of every *encomienda* as it fell vacant on the death of its tenant.

The New Laws provoked such a storm of opposition – including, in Peru, outright rebellion and the killing of the viceroy – that they were never implemented, and were formally revoked in 1547. The *encomienda*, however, did not survive. Slotted in at the apex of pre-existing Aztec and Inca tributary structures, it was undone by the physical and institutional collapse of the Indian societies on which it bore so heavily. Between 1520 and 1650, the native population of Mexico may have fallen from 25 million to 1.5 million, while that of Peru dwindled from 5 million to less than 300,000.[134] As the free fall continued, control of Indian labour passed increasingly to the Crown's *corregidores de indios*, who allocated coerced labour recruited through a rotating native levy system to a new class of Spanish farmers. This *repartimiento* gave way in turn to the *haciendas*, large estates occupying the lands of extinct Indian communities, now held in full ownership by private individuals and repopulated under the rule of wage-labour and debt peonage. The falling numbers of Indians meant a proportionate rise in the burden of the *repartimiento* on the survivors. Since the latter was levied on Indian communities rather than on individuals, and since Indians could escape communal obligations by dispersing to *haciendas* (or to the mines), the *repartimiento* acted historically as a bridge between the natural modes of production taken over by the *conquistadores* and the reconstituted tributary colony of New Spain.[135]

The Spanish Theory of Empire

The Spanish conquest of the Americas is a minor *locus classicus* for those students of the modern international system who chart its historical emergence in terms of a normative evolution from a culturally monolithic Christendom to a self-conscious 'international society' accommodating an extensive cultural diversity.[136] Now, it is indeed the case that first the conquest and then the governance of the Indies provoked vigorous legal and theological controversies in sixteenth-century Spain concerning the political rights of non-Christian subject peoples. It is also true that these debates turned on more than humanitarian appeals, or the cosmopolitan rights of individuals already developed in the Roman tradition of *jus gentium*: if they were not yet a discussion of the rights of states in the modern sense (though it can be claimed that Vitoria 'assumed, though without stating, the now familiar doctrine of the equality of States'[137]), their core was none the less the jurisprudence of an extension of specifically political rule. This much is evident from the 'conspiracy of silence'[138] which they maintained on the contemporaneous expansion of African slavery, which raised no equivalent legal dilemmas: the Amerindians, for all their subordination, remained political subjects in a way that slaves, entering the New World as privately traded commodities, did not. Finally, it is also true that these legal questions agitated the Spanish monarchy itself, which not only permitted the controversies but actively solicited contributions and provided an official forum – as in the set-piece debate between Las Casas and Sepulveda at Valladolid in 1550 or the earlier *Junta* of theologians and jurists convened by order of the Emperor at Barcelona' in 1529.[139]

What is much less certain, however, is any attempt to picture the cause and significance of these debates as the emergence of a new conception of international society called forth by the expansion of European political rule beyond Christendom. While this may indeed have been their formal content, it is arguable that their centre of gravity and their political momentum are to be found elsewhere, in the aforementioned partial and temporary congruence of interests between the proselytizing orders and an absolutizing monarchy.

The Franciscan and Dominican Orders charged with the conversion of the indigenous population had set about creating new urban centres where Indian communities would be both segregated from their Spanish conquerors and concentrated for the purposes of conversion and Church regulation. This 'necessarily interfered with the control of Indian labour upon which Spanish economic activity depended';[140] in particular it competed directly with the semi-feudal system of *encomiendas* by which the *conquistadores* had institutionalized their booty. Dominican campaigns (from 1510) for the reform of colonial property and government found a willing audience in the Habsburg court, which had its own reasons for hostility towards the *encomienda*: 'A growing royal absolutism could not tolerate the emergence of a new feudal aristocracy overseas.'[141] It is perhaps significant therefore that the formal arguments of the leading campaigner for Indian rights, Las Casas, are organized around *a theory of kingship*, which insists on the inalienability of royal jurisdiction.[142] Las Casas's proposals fed, in some cases directly, into the unsuccessful attempt to abolish the *encomienda* in the New Laws of 1542. By contrast, Sepulveda's arguments defending the rights of the *conquistadores* draw on the notion of a natural aristocracy.

Thus the wide-ranging debate on the political rights of the Europeans over the Indians reveals a subtext about the rights of absolutist monarchy over the emergent colonial aristocracy. And the importance of this subtext may be seen from the fact that when, in the reign of Philip II, demand for Indian labour in the silver mines switched royal interests out of the legal and organizational tracks laid by the missionary project, the issue of Indian rights simply dropped out of view:

> after the middle of the sixteenth century the political theory of imperialism has to be deduced from imperial practice and from the opinions of imperial administrators ... [for it] disappeared from serious academic debate in Spain.[143]

Now, we may remember this episode for its novel philosophical significance. We might, however, remember it also for a slightly different reason. For what Parry calls 'the Spanish theory of empire' was indeed the IR theory of its day, the language with which privileged groups within an imperial formation figured to themselves the superior right of their ascendancy, and fought out the fate of subject peoples. Because we know that great human interests were at stake in this debate, we do not underestimate its importance. Yet equally (perhaps partly because, as twentieth-century observers, we no longer believe in either kingship or aristocracy), we do not read it literally or take its categories for granted. We look for clues about how these categories resonated with the structures of social power specific to that society. If it comes much less naturally to us to adopt the same approach to our own contemporary intellectual frameworks in IR, this is surely not because the clues are any less compelling. This discipline is almost entirely Anglo-Saxon, the preserve of those national centres which have played a directive role in the modern states-system. It would therefore be surprising if its core discourses were not managerial ones, articulating and legitimating the exercise of particular forms of international power.

Conclusions

This review of Iberian expansion has two implications for our wider argument. First it illustrates the contention that the dynamics and forms of geopolitical expansion are structurally specific – specific, on the one hand, to the historical identity of the social order which is expanding its reach, and, on the other, to the particular social relations which it seeks to encompass and direct. It would therefore be pointless to construct an exclusively geopolitical account of these episodes or to attempt to explain them by reference to some property of geopolitics *sui generis*, as in the following:

> It is the nature of powers to expand ... the expansion of powers is the product of two causes: internal pressure and the weakness of surrounding powers. When an equilibrium is reached between the outward pressure and the external resistance, expansion stops.[144]

The second implication points forward to what must be our task in the remainder of this book. It is not difficult to see that the early modern empires were reproduced as composite social orders: structured sets of social relations which resist attempts to distinguish between 'power and plenty'. Although the Portuguese moved for the most part in the interstices of the Asian world, their commercial operation comprised relations of exchange commanded by the political authority of the Crown. The Spanish Empire, for its part, was literally an extension of Castilian society. Because in both cases political relations travelled with the commodities, the lines of social power effecting the relaying of surpluses are clearly visible: they take the form of an extension of the political jurisdiction of the metropole. Thus the Iberian empires, like nearly all precapitalist structures of geopolitical power, can be visualized as geographical entities.

This unseparateness of politics and economics (the perception of 'economies' as social orders) is harder to visualize today. Indeed, the contemporary international system could hardly look more different. Lines of political jurisdiction halt at fixed national borders, while those of economic activity speed on through a myriad of international exchanges without undermining the ramparts of formal sovereignty above. This appearance might seem to suggest that our structural method of analysis will not find the same purchase in the modern international system as it did when applied to the past. For, it could be argued, as long as traditional societies and states prevented the emergence of a self-regulating market, politics and economics were indeed intertwined and a sociological analysis was therefore needed to specify the particular structures of interference and corruption which resulted in each case. But once the wealth-creating properties of a free market were understood, the state conceived an interest in allowing the latter to regulate itself, and increasingly restricted its own activity to the more properly political functions of government.

As a result, the business of wealth-creation now takes place in the market, whose workings are analysed by the science of economics.

Meanwhile, the struggle for power takes place within the state, a domain scrutinized by political science. The empirical interaction between the two spheres is studied by political economy. And sociology forms a residuary discipline, combining under the general rubric of 'society' the remaining accoutrements of social reproduction: the family, social class, deviance, education and so on.[145] An equivalent separating out at the international level gives us a world market studied by international economics and a states-system studied by IR.

If this view of history is correct – if what distinguishes the modern international system is simply freer markets and better behaved states – then no amount of demonstrating the interconnection between social structure and geopolitical system in past historical epochs need have any critical implication for the division of labour among the contemporary social sciences. After all, we are now living in a different world, one whose institutional differentiation does in fact correspond to this intellectual division of labour. If this were so, then our conclusions up to this point, and the historical materialist method we have deployed, would indeed be of historiographical interest only. 'Thus', wrote Marx, drawing out the extraordinary assumptions which such a view would entail, 'there has been history, but there no longer is any.'[146] On the other hand, if it is not true, if the division of labour is, on the contrary, a naturalizing of the social forms of modernity which also mystifies them, then Marx's method may be the key to a world of insight which the orthodox social sciences could never unlock. This is the issue to which we turn in the next chapter.

5

The Empire of Civil Society

As we have seen in the chapters above, Marx's method (tracing the correspondence between the strategic relationship and the wider forms of social power) can be used as a general method in historical sociology. But the principal deployment of it by Marx himself was of course in the analysis of capitalism. For it was by elaborating the structural uniqueness of capitalism as a mode of production that Marx sought to explain the distinctive institutional forms of modernity. Our purpose in this chapter is to extend this explanation to the dominant forms of modern geopolitical power.

The argument will be set out in six parts. First, we must identify the strategic relationship in modern Western societies and examine its connection with the political form of the state. This leads, second, to the suggestion that sovereignty needs to be understood historically as a form of political rule peculiar to capitalism. Third, it is suggested that these structural connections (between capitalist relations of production and the sovereign form of the state) underpin the distinctive form of modern international power – and indeed explain how it is that we can have a global states-system at all. This observation is then developed, on the one hand, into a challenge to the widespread notion that the modern states-system dates from the era of absolutism, and, on the other, into a reinterpretation of another category of realist theory, namely the balance of power. In turn, reinterpreting the balance of power makes it apparent that Marx himself provides a theory of anarchy – not as the timeless condition of geopolitics, but as the characteristic social form of capitalist modernity. The argument therefore includes the theoretical redefinition promised earlier of the two core categories of realist IR. In a nutshell, the structural specificity of state sovereignty lies in its 'abstraction' from civil society – an abstraction which is constitutive of the private sphere of the market, and hence inseparable from capitalist relations of production. Meanwhile, anarchy – which, for realism comprises a presocial state of nature – is rediscovered as a historically specific condition defined by Marx as 'personal independence based on dependence mediated by things'.

The Structural Basis of Civil Society

Let us begin, as Marx recommended, with the relationship between the direct producer and the owner of the conditions of production. In capitalist societies the direct producers are no longer in possession of their own means of subsistence, and what binds them to the processes of surplus extraction is no longer political command, but rather the requirement to sell their labour in order to gain this subsistence. This necessity supports the distinctive capitalist relations of surplus extraction themselves: a legally sanctioned contract of exchange between formal equals in which the labourer accepts authoritative subordination in the private realm of production and forgoes any rights over the product in exchange for an agreed wage payment.

There is a very striking contrast here. In precapitalist societies the apparatus of public rule was implicated directly in the process of surplus extraction and the producers were therefore, as we would regard it, politically unfree. This does not mean that all precapitalist societies were prison camps. The non-economic means used to extract the surplus varied, as Marx observed, 'from serfdom with enforced labour to a mere tributary relationship',[1] and an apparatus of domination might bear down more or less heavily on the peasant majority. It does mean, however, that formal political inequality was basic to social reproduction. Not so with capitalism. Under capitalism the formal subordination in production which accomplishes the extraction of the surplus is not exercised through the state. Formal political inequality is therefore not inscribed in the relations of production. This does not mean that all capitalist societies are havens of human rights. Once again, the historical variation is considerable, and only a tiny number of capitalist societies have been able to sustain durable political democracies.[2] But if any have been able to do so, and to institutionalize a formal political equality among the citizenry, this reflects the fact that under capitalist relations of production the direct extraction of a surplus is accomplished through 'non-political' relations associated with new forms of social power.

What, then, are these new forms of social power? This is the riddle
that Marx sets himself to answer in Volume I of *Capital*. We call them
'market forces' and the rule of law. But what, after all, is the market?
In the first place it is, as Sayer puts it, not just a thing we inhabit
as individuals, but simultaneously a way we collectively are as a society.[3]
It is a historically specific set of social relations between persons which
effects the reproduction of the social order in a determinate form.
And what makes the capitalist market different from all other markets
in history is the generalized commodification of labour-power. Where
this occurs, the market ceases to be simply a set of voluntary exchange
relations which circulate only a small fraction of the social surplus.
It becomes a compulsory association, which subordinates all its
members to the impersonal rule of value. To uncover exactly what
this new form of rule comprises, and how it operates, is the central
object of Marx's substantive theory of capitalist modernity, the social
theory of value elaborated in *Capital*.[4] However, the crucial point here
is simply this: because incorporation into this association through the
labour contract takes the form of a relation of exchange between legal
equals, the process of surplus extraction is reconstituted as a private
activity of civil society.

This is called economics. But what *is* economics? We are so used
to assuming the presence of this distinct branch of social life that it
is always surprising to recall how little the word itself discloses about
the novelty and character of what it describes. A combination of the
Greek terms for house and law, 'economics' originally referred to the
management of the household. And as late as the 1740s, Adam Smith's
teacher, Francis Hutcheson, still included marital, parental and master–
servant relations under the heading of 'Principles of Economics'. In
short, there is nothing in the earlier use of the word (unless it be the
hint of a private sphere) which accounts for why it should have come
to refer exclusively to market relations. And nothing is explained
therefore by using the term 'economic' in its modern sense unless one
already assumes (consciously or otherwise) the capitalist relations of
production which create its object.[5] Similarly, if one looks up any of
the words we habitually use to describe the process of surplus extraction under capitalism – market, business, industry, commerce – one
finds that each of them is an etymological dead-end in the same way
that 'economics' is.[6] The tracks of modernity are well covered.

At the same time, while the state no longer carries out the process
of surplus extraction itself, it has on the other hand assumed a new
centralized monopoly of jurisdiction which it asserts through an

impersonal rule of law.[7] Thus we see a redefinition of political power in public, communal terms: it guarantees contracts between private individuals, it keeps the peace both internally and externally, it imparts a degree of collective management to the overall social development of the society. But there are also things that it no longer does, social roles which are by the same token removed from the domain of political power and redefined as private. Among these, the most striking is the process of surplus extraction.

The emergence of distinct institutional spheres called the state and the economy is the signature of capitalist society. But no adequate social theory can take it at face value. For, as Ellen Wood put it, in a passage we have already cited in chapter 3 above:

> the differentiation of the economic and the political in capitalism is, more precisely, a differentiation of political functions themselves and their separate allocation to the private economic sphere and the public sphere of the state. This allocation reflects the separation of political functions immediately concerned with the extraction and appropriation of surplus labour from those with a more general communal purpose. ... the differentiation of the economic is in fact a differentiation within the political sphere.[8]

If this is true, then the very least that can be said is that under such an arrangement the activities denoted by the term 'politics' – or, indeed, 'the state' – are going to be radically different from what these terms would refer to in other kinds of society. There is a kind of emptying out of certain powers and functions from the formal political realm of the state. The inverse applies, as already suggested, to the term 'market'. Here we see a kind of filling up with new social powers and functions, centred on the processes of surplus extraction, which exchange relations never previously encompassed. Historically speaking, it is a very strange form of social organization.[9]

Sovereignty as a Capitalist Political Form

These observations may turn out to be of considerable relevance to IR. For what is the political form under discussion here if not the conceptual building-block of the discipline, namely the sovereign state? This is a category in need of some clarification. Most commentators accept that the primacy denoted by the term 'sovereignty' cannot be defined straightforwardly as the ability of the state to control activities within its borders or resist external constraint on its freedom of action. Apart from anything else, there are just too many small, weak states in the world for this to be empirically plausible. For this reason, we all learn that its absolute properties refer to its juridical status. A sovereign state does not share jurisdiction with Church and nobility as under feudalism, or suffer systematic subordination to a party organization as under Soviet communism. Yet sovereignty is not just the legal paramountcy of the state – and even if it were, it is not easy to see how this could be sustained without exercising a preponderance of power. Much IR theorizing on the subject seems to waver uncertainly between these two definitions, substantive and formal, switching back and forth depending on the particular issues being discussed. Excited claims that the latest wave of military or communications technology, or the latest round of 'globalization' in the world economy, are rendering the concept of sovereignty obsolete alternate with firm denials of any diminution in the political, legal and military monopolies commanded by the state. As a result, students often find the whole issue of sovereignty deeply enigmatical: an absolute form of rule which seems never to be absolute in practice even though, for some reason, the formal constitution of the international system rests on the assumption that it is so.[10]

What are we to do with what Waltz has called this 'bothersome concept'?[11] Perhaps a first step might be to cease thinking about sovereignty as a self-evident starting point – which is what we do if we accept its own legal or political self-definition. Perhaps instead we should think of it as a form of political rule historically specific to the distinctive configuration of social relations which define capitalism as a kind of society. For sovereignty also, crucially, involves the idea of the state being outside, over against civil society, autonomous, 'purely political'. What do these phrases mean?

In part, they mean that 'the primacy of geopolitics' gives the state executive a warrant to override internal interest groups in the conduct of foreign policy. However, something like this could apply in any hierarchical society incorporated into a geopolitical system, and it is therefore not specific to sovereignty, the form of rule held to distinguish the modern state. Nor do they mean that the state is not involved in regulating civil society. It is, after all, the state which frames laws, upholds contracts, raises taxes and implements policies designed to promote the development of the sphere of production.

None of these, however, need involve the state moving into that other realm of political command, namely the privatized sphere of production, by taking over the process of surplus extraction itself. Where it does do this, for example by extending its direct ownership through nationalization,[12] it can find that the *sovereign* character of its

rule diminishes. It no longer stands over against civil society. Industrial disputes are immediately political disputes. The appropriation
of the surplus becomes an object of public 'political' struggle within
the state rather than private political struggle within the productive
corporations of civil society. The private despotism of the workplace
becomes the public despotism of the state.[13] A process such as this
seemed to be a factor in the British 'Winter of Discontent' of 1978–
79: the sovereignty of the state was eroded because the day-to-day
separation between politics and economics was blurred, and the
government therefore found itself dragged into one industrial dispute
after another.

Conversely, however, the restoration of the sovereignty of the state
in such circumstances is also the restoration of the private political
sphere and of the class power of capital in this sphere of production.
In fact, is this not what happened next in the British case? The Labour
government fell, and was replaced by Margaret Thatcher's Conservative administration, which came into office with a commitment to
'roll back the frontiers of the state'. On the face of it, this commitment
seemed to be contradicted by the evidence, namely the failure to
reduce public spending levels, the reinforcement of the coercive arm
of the state, and the transparent use of state legislative authority to
intervene in industry by reducing the legal power of organized labour.
But if we understand the capitalist separation of politics and economics in the manner suggested by Ellen Wood, then a real underlying
consistency emerges which concerns the *sovereignty* of the state.

For the sovereignty of the state does depend on both a kind of
abstraction from production and the reconstitution of the state-
political sphere as external to civil society. But this is not an abstraction which means that the sovereignty of the state is neutral. On the
contrary, its very form is a dimension of class power because it entails
the parallel consolidation of private political power in production. An
illustration of what this can mean in practice was the British miners'
strike of 1984–85. Since it is known that the government gave the
Coal Board every possible assistance behind the scenes,[14] its insistence
that the strike was an industrial dispute and not the business of the
state can be made sense of only in terms of a determination to redefine
'the political' as outside and separate from surplus extraction, a redefinition whose other half was necessarily the restoration of private
political power in production. Perhaps the two most oft-repeated goals
of the government during the dispute were that an impersonal rule
of law should be upheld, and that 'management should be allowed

to manage'. In other words, the state was neither withdrawing from civil society nor necessarily encroaching further upon it. It was reimposing the separation of political functions between public and private spheres which is the *form* of both class power and state power under capitalism.

All this suggests that we should define sovereignty primarily not in terms of the practical ability of the state to command the behaviour of its citizens, nor yet as a kind of residual legal paramountcy. To be sure, without these there would be no sovereign states. But these descriptive attributes, enormous though their practical significance is, do not comprise an explanation of why the modern state assumes its distinctive 'purely political' form. By contrast, if we define sovereignty as the social form of the state in a society where political power is divided between public and private spheres, it becomes apparent that at least some of the confusion over whether modern state power is strong or weak, autonomous or determined, sovereign or constrained has been unnecessary. For under capitalism, these are not necessarily dichotomies.

The Sovereign States-System

The Structural Implications of Sovereignty

The historical rise of the sovereign state is thus one aspect of a comprehensive reorganization of the forms of social power. The change that it works in the form and content of the international system is no less startling. For under this new arrangement, while relations of citizenship and jurisdiction define state borders, any aspects of social life which are mediated by relations of exchange in principle no longer receive a political definition (though they are still overseen by the state in various ways) and hence may extend across these borders. And if political functions which used to be in state hands are now assigned to a private political sphere fronted by a set of exchange relations, then these political functions will travel.[15]

This is indeed what has occurred. It is now possible, in a way that would have been unthinkable under feudalism, to command and exploit productive labour (and natural resources) located under the jurisdiction of another state. This is because capitalist relations of surplus extraction are organized through a contract of exchange which is defined as 'non-political'. It must be reiterated that it simply will not do to call this 'economics' and think we have explained anything unless we *either* say that this is the first time there has been such a phenomenon as 'economics' *or* define it more closely as capitalist economics. And either way, we have to include in our definition the peculiar state-form which is its other half, because these functions can be regarded as non-political only on the assumption that politics has been redefined to restrict it to general communal functions.

Historically, this transformation seems to have been accomplished in Europe in two broad, overlapping phases. The first phase comprised the processes of state-building, that is, the centralizing of political authority by absolutist monarchs, the suppression of rival centres of power and the construction of a bureaucratic machinery of government. This made it possible for monarchs to exercise a much more absolute and exclusive jurisdiction, so that states became much more sharply defined territorially. The modern political map of the world is a perfectly fitting jigsaw in which all the separate, interlocking pieces are clearly marked in different colours.[16] For much of orthodox IR, the modern world begins here, where the impossible patchwork of medieval Christendom is replaced by territorially unified jurisdictions. However, lagging some way behind this process of state-building there followed the liberal transformation of the state discussed above – which eventually overthrew absolutism. And as a result of *this* process, it actually becomes less and less realistic to try to theorize the international system in terms of relations between states alone. Moreover, if we take the two processes together over the whole period, we must say that what looks to the naked eye like an unprecedented concentrating of power in the hands of the state apparatus (as certain functions are centralized as never before) is simultaneously a dramatic *disaggregation* of social functions and social power, between public and private spheres.[17]

Clearly, the trick here, as this overall shift takes place, is to keep our eye on *both* political spheres which emerge (that is, public and private), otherwise we will assume that what we are seeing is simply a shift from empire to states-system, which could safely be treated purely in its external aspect. In the public political sphere this is indeed the form of the shift. And if we watch only that external, public sphere, it would then seem that we could theorize the international system by listing the *differentia specifica* of a states-system as compared with an empire, and understand its properties *sui generis* as those of anarchy. This is the path of realism. But it ignores the changing structural definition and content of 'the political'. And its effect is precisely to occlude the distinctive character of modern international power.

For it is this formal disjuncture (between public and private political realms) which explains part of the paradox of sovereignty: why
it is both more absolute in its 'purely political' prerogatives than other
historical forms of rule, and yet highly ambiguous as a measure of
actual power. It explains how we can see simultaneously an enhanced
territorial differentiation between states together with an unprecedented porousness and interdependence.[18]

Viewed in this way, it becomes increasingly apparent that in realism reality is standing on its head. Realists tell us that the modern
international political system is different because it is a states-system
organized by anarchy rather than an empire organized by centralized
command. However, if the above discussion is sound, then, to be true,
this statement needs to be turned right way up. It is not so much that
modern international politics is different because it is a states-system;
rather, we can have a global states-system only because modern
'politics' is different. And the surest way to misunderstanding here
is precisely the attempt to theorize this difference in abstraction from
the historically specific kind of society which produces this form of
politics. For the form itself is not inert or neutral, but rather suffused
with determinations deriving from its capitalist character.

Once this point is seen, we can (and will) go on to explore the
distinctive properties of this social form of geopolitics – including the
character of anarchy. But if empire is taken to mean the expansion
of political command beyond the territory of the originating community in order to accumulate resources from outside, then the last thing
this portends is the end of empire. Rather it means that the exercise
of imperial power, like domestic social power, will have two linked
aspects: a public political aspect which concerns the management of
the states-system, and a private political aspect which effects the
extraction and relaying of surpluses.[19] It means the rise of a new kind
of empire: the empire of civil society.[20]

Political Implications of Sovereignty

It has just been suggested that what we witness in the emergence of
the modern states-system is actually the development of a new form
of imperial power characteristic of a fundamentally new kind of (capitalist) social structure. It was also implied that a theoretical understanding of contemporary international relations would therefore have
to encompass both the public political and the private political aspects of international power which emerge in the modern period.

This may seem to invite the charge that we have done no more than reinvent the wheel. For each of these aspects, public political and private political, has its own specificities: military, legal and territorial for the one; and civil, profit-seeking and transnational for the other. Moreover, they are largely carried out by identifiably distinct actors: states and private corporations. And therefore has not the work of international political economy already produced the necessary re-formulation by posing the discipline in terms of the interaction of states and markets?

The answer must be negative. For assuming the separation of politics and economics as a starting point in this way is not a theoretically innocent assumption. It is to assume the automatic reproduction of the particular human social relations which bring about and sustain this institutional separation. And we cannot assume this, partly be-cause these relations have not obtained for most of history, perhaps more importantly because there are still large areas of humanity where they do not obtain; but mainly because even where they do obtain, they are continually being contested. Much of the content of inter-national relations, past and present, is the outcome of continuous struggle over the reproduction of these capitalist social relations. If we assume their reproduction, then we exclude from our account the very human agency and historical *process* we are trying to recover as the basis of the social world. We see that world not as the daily outcome of definite social relations between real living individuals, but as the timeless clash of disembodied social forms: the remorseless grinding of the balance of power, the ghostly motions of the invisible hand.

But this is to imply that, in some way parallel to the earlier ex-ample of the miners' strike, the sovereign form of the states-*system* is itself the object and outcome of struggle and contestation. What could this mean?

Consider the fate of the New International Economic Order (NIEO).[21] From the mid 1970s, emboldened by the example of OPEC, a large group of Third World governments (organized as the Group of 77) used their numerical majority in the General Assembly of the United Nations to press through demands for a reform of the inter-national economy. In 1974 the General Assembly adopted a 'Charter of Economic Rights and Duties of States' which included provisions for linking commodity prices to prices of manufacture, the expropria-tion of foreign investments, increased controls on the activities of multinationals, and so on. Here, then, was an attempt to challenge the separation of politics and economics, the separation which enabled the private dimension of the relationship between Western and Third World societies to count as non-political. Of course, majority votes in the General Assembly have no binding force, and the campaign for the NIEO failed for a number of reasons, including disunity among the southern states pressing for it. The point, however, is the form that this failure took.

By the mid 1980s, the UN was in financial difficulties due to the reduction or delay of funding by disenchanted Western governments. Moreover, a number of the Group of 77 were now submitting themselves to International Monetary Fund (IMF) restructuring packages in exchange for debt-rescheduling agreements. Now, the negotiation of economic terms by indebted countries with the IMF does not count as a political process; none the less, it did embody a dramatic reversal of the very programme which these countries had been attempting to advance by political means. For a prominent feature of these packages was a withdrawal of the state from direct control of prices through subsidy and tariff – a withdrawal which effected, in principle at least, a new separation of politics and economics, and thereby opened these societies further to the world market. The geographical progress of this outcome among the countries involved could be followed throughout the 1980s in the spread of what became known as 'IMF riots' – mass demonstrations against price increases implemented by governments as part of IMF restructuring packages. By January 1989, these had occurred in twenty-three countries.[22]

It would be hazardous to draw any substantive conclusions from these events. But the overall pattern of this episode is surely too suggestive to pass without comment. The Group of 77 pressed for further public political regulation through the UN; their defeat was registered in a fuller than ever subordination to private economic mechanisms through the IMF. By reimposing the separation of the world economy from the formal political institutions of the states-system, the West was able to restore simultaneously the private freedom of capital and the purely political sovereignty of the states-system, both of which were challenged by the NIEO.

Significantly, this denouement of the 1980s coincided historically with a vigorous revival of both neo-liberal economic theory (and deregulation) and neorealist state theory (and flexing of the coercive military arm of the state). These supplanted the 1970s vogue for 'complex interdependence' and fears of international ungovernability, replacing them with a revived definition of the sovereign individuality of the state.[23]

The NIEO, however, was a comparatively minor episode. What *was* the entire Soviet experience and the Cold War which dominated world politics for the last four decades, if not an enormous geopolitical challenge to the social form of the modern states-system? The Soviet Union was precisely not a sovereign state, in the sense that we have been discussing sovereignty. It did not stand outside a distinct private sphere of surplus extraction. It moved in and took it over. And it supported other governments who did the same – who, by overthrowing the separation of politics and economics, withdrew their societies from the world market, and hence from the reach of private Western power. This was ultimately the political content of the Cold War. With the best will in the world, it would be impossible to understand the Soviet presence in the international system in terms of states and markets. It was precisely an attempt to abolish both of them.

Marx would have us go even further. For him, the increasingly global, continuously fought-over separation of politics and economics – meaning the actual construction of the world market and the linked emergence of a sovereign states-system – was the central unfinished theme of modern world history. In fact, for Marx it is what has 'produced world history for the first time'.[24]

Let us pause for a moment to take stock of where our argument has led us. We began, in accordance with the overall method of this work, by specifying the 'strategic relationship' of modern Western society. The contrast with earlier kinds of society seemed to confirm that it was the distinctive character of this relationship which underlay or constituted the institutional differentiation of spheres we call economics and politics, civil society and the state. We also saw that this differentiation was not a substantive separation or 'autonomy', and we illustrated the structural interdependence involved, using the examples of the 'Winter of Discontent' and the miners' strike of 1984–85. By this stage we had already noted the descriptive affinities between the political institutions of the society in question and the theoretical ambiguities of the treatment of sovereignty in IR. These affinities led us to merge the two in a redefinition of sovereignty as the abstracted social form of the state specific to (and partly constitutive of) capitalist social relations. Once this connection was made, we sought to develop its implications for theorizing the sovereign states-system. These implications were of two kinds. First, the differentiation of spheres provided the structural precondition for a simultaneous enhancement of territorial definition of polities and yet deepening of material integration of social reproduction across borders. This was seen to give rise to a wholly new idiom of geopolitical power which we named 'the empire of civil society'. But second, our attention to the under-lying structural interdependence of the public and private spheres led us to identify sovereignty itself as a contested social form because of its profound imbrication in the reproduction of these new forms of (private) power. Searching for manifestations of this within contemporary international history, we found first the NIEO, then the Cold War, and finally, pursuing a hint from Marx, the emergence of the modern international system itself.

Now, if sovereignty is redefined as a social form, and hence is specific to a very distinctive kind of society, then the consolidation of sover-eignty and its generalization into a global states-system must imply a concrete *historical process* of social upheaval and transformation. And since this process is what produces the states-system in its modern form, then arguably it is here – rather than strictly in the diplomatic interchange between preconstituted states – that we shall find the real and continuing history of the international system. With this move, we have finally broken out of the realist framework for thinking about the origins of the sovereign states-system, and have instead linked up our account with the broader historical processes of social transfor-mation involved in the making of the modern world. The agenda for historical research to which this points will be spelled out in a little more detail in the last chapter.

The Question of Absolutist Sovereignty

We now have a historical puzzle to solve. The emergence of the modern idea of sovereignty is conventionally traced to the absolutist monarchies of early modern Europe. This seems at first sight to constitute a straightforward empirical refutation of our argument. For it was central to the definition of absolutism as a political form that the monarchy was a direct and major appropriator of the surplus. It could not constitute itself as sovereign in the sense in which we have redefined that term because it was based not on taxing surpluses already extracted in a separate private sphere – the European aris-tocracies did not pay tax – but rather on consolidating the grip of the state as a gigantic landlord, a centralized apparatus of surplus extraction (on behalf of an emasculated noble class). This was a very distinctive political form, very different from the classic model of European feudalism. Bringing it about involved many of the rigours we associate with state-building: breaking the independent power of the nobility and the Church, maintaining standing armies, creating a bureaucratic apparatus, enforcing the King's law evenly across the territory, elaborating new diplomatic forms, and so on. In many ways it looks quite modern. Furthermore, it was indeed the absolutist monarchies who elaborated the concept of sovereignty to legitimate their suppression of rival centres of power within the state. No doubt for this reason, there remains within IR a broad consensus that the modern states-system dates from the absolutist epoch – in particular, from the Peace of Westphalia of 1648. What are we to make of this? Did the sovereign states-system emerge with absolutism or not?

If one defines sovereignty very broadly, then the significance of Westphalia is indeed considerable. Let us take Hedley Bull's definition:

> On the one hand, states assert, in relation to this territory and population, what may be called internal sovereignty, which means supremacy over all other authorities within that territory and population. On the other hand, they assert what may be called external sovereignty, by which is meant not supremacy but independence of outside authorities.[25]

Now, the terms of Westphalia were not wholly unprecedented; the Treaty of Augsberg in 1555 had already established a principle of *cujus regio, ejus religio*. Nor is it claimed that the treaties themselves accomplished the overall development which they recognized – that is, the emergence of a secular states-system. But they did mark an end to the religious wars of Europe; they did (much to the fury of Pope Innocent X[26]) abolish the competing political rights of the papacy in the territories of the states concerned; and they did undermine the hierarchical geopolitical structure centred on the Holy Roman Empire by proclaiming the freedom of the German princelings to make alliances.[27] In Bull's broad sense, both internal and external sovereignty were recognized. However, the matter cannot rest there, for an intriguing inconsistency creeps into the orthodox account at this point.

It is generally recognized that 'the first systematic statement of the theme' of sovereignty is that of Jean Bodin.[28] Given this, it is perhaps surprising that in the Anglo-American discipline of IR we find so little discussion of the *Six Livres de la république*. Indeed, for the most part Bodin is only ever mentioned as a prelude to invoking a far more familiar icon of realist accounts of sovereignty – Thomas Hobbes. The inconsistency involved here cannot be seen unless we take some measure of the societal distance between the two formulations of sovereignty involved.

An illuminating account of this distance has recently been advanced by Ellen Wood.[29] Bodin's formulation was a defence of an absolutizing monarchy confronting a parcellization of the state due to the persistance of feudal corporate forms. This reflected the structural basis of French absolutism: between 85 and 90 per cent of cultivated land was in the direct possession of the peasantry, with the consequence that the mechanisms of surplus extraction were heavily concentrated in the local jurisdictional prerogatives of the nobility, forming an immediate barrier to juridical centralization.[30] Bodin's argument therefore takes the form of a plea for a superordinate power to join together

> the corporate constituents of the polity, and especially the three Estates, into an organic unity, a balanced hierarchical order based on 'harmonic justice', the justice of 'proportional' equality among unequal corporate entities.[31]

This is in strong contrast to Hobbes's method, which seeks to derive the need for a sovereign power from the self-destructive effects of the liberty of individuals in a state of nature – the famous 'warre of every man against every man'. As Wood points out, although this response to the turmoil of the Civil War wears French clothing (sixteenth- and seventeenth-century English thought is notable for its *lack* of an indigenous tradition of theorizing about 'sovereignty'[32]), the body of the argument reflects the strongly divergent path of English social development. For the English state did not face the same obstacles of feudal parcellization confronted by its French counterpart. Not only had it achieved effective juridical and legislative centralization at an early stage,[33] but also the much wider direct ownership of land by the aristocracy facilitated a lesser dependence on jurisdictional mechanisms of surplus extraction. Under these conditions, the way was more open for a unitary state to become not a competing form of politically constituted property, but rather – through the formula of the 'Crown in Parliament' – the public 'political' corollary of an incipient private 'economic' mode of surplus extraction.[34]

While Wood's argument can be given only the briefest and most partial of summaries here, the conclusion to which it points for the place of Hobbes (and Westphalia) in IR theory is remarkable. For it suggests that insofar as the English Civil War was fought over control of the centralized state apparatus (rather than being a contest of particularism and centralization) the issue was precisely *not* sovereignty in the continental sense. Rather, Hobbes uses the language of sovereignty to elaborate what is becoming a very different problematic,

namely that of order in a 'purely political' state made up of legally
equal individuals:

> In transplanting the idea of absolute and indivisible sovereignty to English
> conditions, Hobbes was obliged to impose it not on Jean Bodin's collection
> of 'families, colleges, or corporate bodies' but on Sir Thomas Smith's
> 'multitude of free men collected together' in a unitary state. This did not
> mean that Hobbes's conception of sovereignty was any less absolute than
> Bodin's. If anything, it seems even more unlimited and uncompromising,
> perhaps because no corporate mediations stand between the individual
> and the sovereign state.[35]

More absolute precisely because it was not absolutist? Here, surely,
we begin to pick up echoes of the modern form of sovereignty discussed earlier in this chapter.

But what has all this to do with Westphalia? Quite simply this: one
major state was not represented at that Europe-wide convocation of
powers – England. And yet it was Hobbes's England, not Bodin's
France, which was to go on to play the leading role in extending the
sovereign form of rule beyond Europe and defining the institutional
form of the global states-system of today – England, followed by the
United States, an even more thoroughgoing liberal polity, even further removed from the spirit of Westphalia. As Sayer puts it:

> a political form that was, much later, to become general throughout Europe
> (and the world), was sucessfully pioneered [here] rather earlier than else-
> where.[36]

Could it be, then, that when we talk about sovereignty in IR we are
really, without being fully aware of it, assuming this new and very
special form of state – even if we hold formally, with Bull, to the
absolutist definition? Certainly this would help explain the ambiguity
of the term in IR. For the concept of sovereignty, which under
absolutism really did add up to a kind of despotism, now means
something else which the absolutist (and hence by extension realist)
doctrine of sovereignty could never grasp.[37] It might also explain why
we do not read Bodin.

But in that case, we should also be somewhat sceptical of the
orthodox claim that the modern states-system came into being in
1648 – or 1713, 1515, 1494, much less the maverick 1414. An absolutist
states-system was initialled at Westphalia. But this is not modern
politics. To define the state in absolutist terms is to miss the specificity
of 'purely political' institutions under capitalism. Modern sovereignty
is only allowed to be so absolute because it involves restricting much

more closely what is to count as the legitimate domain of politics. To miss this is, in Augustine Thierry's words, to 'lack the comprehension and sentiment of great social transformations' – which for Thierry at any rate was such a powerful lever of sociological insight.

Historicizing the Balance of Power

As we round this bend of our argument, something else comes into view, something which perhaps ought to have been visible all along. It was hinted earlier that a comparison might be drawn between the 'invisible hand' of the market and the balance of power. At that point the suggestion was that both of these phenomena appeared as impersonal, 'automatic' mechanisms needing to be translated back into the historically specific social relations which give rise to them, in order to rediscover the human agency which must lie at the heart of the social world. It was not noted at the time that this suggestion flies in the face of conventional wisdom about the balance of power, which understands the latter precisely as an automatic function of a plurality of competing decision-making centres in the absence of superordinate coercive power – a necessary function, that is, of anarchy. On this view, the emergence of a balance of power under such circumstances derives from a timeless logic, of which history provides merely illustrations. This, the *fons et origo*, if ever there was one, of realist theory, has always seemed unsatisfying and suspicious to its critics – not so much in its internal logic (the mathematics is flawless, even if the exponents of game theory have pressed it to absurd lengths) but rather with respect to how much it *does not* tell us, or illuminate, about the balance of power as a historical institution. Yet the problem always was: what else *is* there to say about it? We now have the beginnings of an answer to this problem.

If the line of argument developed in this chapter is valid, then the balance of power is not just *like* the invisible hand. It is its other half, the equivalent in the public political realm of the alienated social form of the invisible hand in the private political realm of 'the economy'. This can be seen more clearly once we recognize that what is distinctive about the modern balance of power is actually *not* the plurality of armed actors. It cannot be that, for history is awash with geopolitical systems which fit this criterion. The twenty-odd *taifa* kingdoms which emerged from the eleventh-century break-up of the Caliphate of Cordoba spent over three hundred years wheeling and dealing their way into oblivion – weaving, no doubt, a moving tapestry of alliance, calculation and counter-alliance which would gladden the heart of any game theorist. During the Hundred Years' War, Edward III played his hand of coalitions with a cynicism and manipulative skill that might have made Machiavelli blush.[38] Yet these cases – and the many hundred others like them – are rarely, if ever, discussed in IR. Why?

Perhaps the answer is that the modern balance of power is indeed different from either the grasping of empire or the contending of princes. And what is so distinctive about it is not the number of players. It is its impersonality, its emptiness, its abstraction, its anonymity, its almost scientific technicism. Indeed, this mechanical quality was an object of fascination for Enlightenment observers; it encouraged discussion of a political arithmetic of equipoise, and suggested the spread of Newtonian reason to the affairs of states.

By contrast, feudal geopolitics was anything but impersonal: it revolved around personal (dynastic) claims to property in land, and wars were fought by armies levied through ties of personal allegiance. While everyone, no doubt, calculated his own advantage, there was no sense in stabilizing the system territorially through a military balance, for war and political expansion were a major mechanism of surplus appropriation. This reflected feudal relations of production in which economic ownership and political jurisdiction were fused in the heritable fief. Just as there was no sense of the state standing outside, over against civil society, so too there was no abstraction of the geopolitical system. In feudalism we find not an impersonal balance of power compelling its members to adjust levels of military preparedness internally, but rather a militarily defined struggle over surpluses expressed in the form of territorial competition between political units. In feudalism, the last thing anyone wanted was a balance: that would have stopped the game.

For contemporary capitalist societies, however, war plays a different role because imperial processes of expansion (or, rather, those connected directly with surplus extraction) are now accomplished principally in the private sphere. Under these circumstances, war and military competition in general become instruments for managing the international public political realm – which is itself now empty of the material sources of wealth that used to be the object of war, namely property in tied labour, trading monopolies, and so on.

As a result of this emptying out, when modern Western states contend it is not because one has what another wants – like Louis XIV enviously eying the Dutch monopoly in Baltic shipping; they contend over *public policy*, that is, over the collective, linked organization of public international and private transnational spheres. Advanced capitalist states do resort to military means in order to prosecute policy, where this is judged necessary. But because the use of military force is no longer itself the means of surplus appropriation, it, too, takes on a 'pure', 'technical' character, in line with the abstracted, sovereign form of the state as a whole.

The balance of power is a pressure system which shows an unmixed, 'purely political' aspect to the world. By this is meant that the immediate goals pursued through it are not plunder of wealth or territorial expansion, but rather the bending of other states to one's own will. The pursuit of power does not come any purer than this. As Morgenthau famously put it, 'statesmen think and act in terms of interest defined as power.'[39] But this purity is not a function of some timeless essence of statehood. The 'pure' power of the political scientists, the medium of the balance of power, is in fact the power of the 'purely political' state, the sovereign state, the state which stands outside production and is therefore abstracted from the particularities of civil society – in short, the capitalist state.

But for what purposes should one state wish to bend others to its will if it is not going to invade and plunder them? What is all the power-mongering *for?* There is simply no answer to this question unless one can point to those political functions which have been shuffled off into the private sphere, where the business of surplus extraction now takes place. But realist IR has twice forbidden itself to look in this direction; once, because the private sphere is formally non-political, and a second time because it subsists in the domestic realm. This is why, whenever realism tries to theorize the international system, it can see only an empty, purely political struggle for domination. The fruits of power lie elsewhere. All that breaks surface in the public political sphere is the mechanics of domination; and no amount of mapping the patterns and rehearsing the internal logic of these mechanics will ever tell us either what the balance of power is about at any given point, or why modern geopolitics assumes this distinctive, impersonal form. In this sense, strange as it may sound, and precisely because it takes it for granted, *realism has no theory of the balance of power*. Since realism has been known to rest its entire claim to authority on the assertion that the balance of power is the only international theory possible, this is a remarkable failure.[40]

Yet a theory of the balance of power must be able to do more than identify the historically specific character of the states making up a

geopolitical system. To say simply that the goals of geopolitical competition lie outside the formally demarcated sphere of geopolitics is
to give a hostage to fortune. For such a claim might reinforce further
the notion of a discrete logic operating within that realm, irrespective
of the ends to which policy is turned. Thus if we truly wish to lay
the ghost of realism, we have not only to insist that a full understanding of the international system requires us to look beyond the realm
of the purely political; we have also to show that the abstracted
competitive logic which haunts the purely political sphere, a logic
which seems to derive precisely from the absence of society, is itself
a social form whose surface appearance belies the reality of what it
accomplishes. We need, in short, a social theory of anarchy.

Karl Marx's Theory of Anarchy

An Unexpected Discovery

It is often remarked that the same absolute character of the sovereignty of the modern state which is the foundation of order *within*
national borders simultaneously dictates the persistence of an *external*
condition of anarchy among states. Where no higher authority is
recognized, an underlying 'war of all against all', whether violent or
not, must endure. Against those who condemn this arrangement as
a chaos which must be mastered, two points in particular are usually
urged. First, it is suggested that the condition of anarchy does not
actually promote the random behaviour of states. Rather, it gives rise
spontaneously to a distinctive, decentralized form of regulation –
namely the balance of power – which tightly constrains the multilateral relations of states like an objective law of their existence. Despite
having no centralized agency of enforcement, this regulation continuously 'socializes' states into the common norms and practices of the
states-system. Second, the defenders of anarchy point out that the
only conceivable alternative to this dispersed form of authority would
be its centralization in a world state (or empire); and since this global
Leviathan could exist only by overriding the sovereign independence
of individual states (and with it the self-determination of nations) it
would perforce consititute a kind of global despotism. In this respect,
the balance of power, by automatically producing coalitions against
hegemonial pretenders, preserves the states-system and with it the
liberty of the individual states. Such are the *differentia specifica* of 'the
international', properties which distinguish this environment from the
society which exists in the domestic realm.[41]

It might therefore come as something of a surprise to a student of IR, innocently leafing his or her way through the pages of Volume I of *Capital*, to encounter the following set of reflections:

> Division of labour *within the workshop* implies the undisputed authority of the capitalist over men. ... The division of labour *within society* brings into contact independent producers of commodities, who acknowledge no authority other than that of competition, of the coercion exerted by the pressure of their reciprocal interests, just as in the animal kingdom the 'war of all against all' more or less preserves the conditions of existence of every species. The same bourgeois consciousness which celebrates the division of labour in the workshop ... denounces with equal vigour every conscious attempt to control and regulate the process of production socially as an inroad upon such sacred things as the rights of property, freedom and the self-determining 'genius' of the individual capitalist. It is very characteristic that the enthusiastic apologists of the factory system have nothing more damning to urge against a general organization of labour in society than that it would turn the whole of society into a factory ... in the society where the capitalist mode of production prevails, anarchy in the social division of labour and despotism in the manufacturing division of labour mutually condition each other.[42]

What would make this passage doubly arresting is perhaps not just the uncanny detail of the parallels between the condition of states and the condition of firms – internal authority coupled with external anarchy, the Hobbesian state of nature, the nexus of competition, equilibrium and freedom, even the nightmare vision of a world state/ factory. Rather, diligent readers of *Capital* would have another, more compelling reason to linger over the passage quoted above. For they would recall that the anarchy in production to which Marx refers is not only central to his whole conception of capitalism as a kind of society – 'The point of bourgeois society', he says in a famous letter to Kugelmann, 'consists precisely in this, that *a priori* there is no conscious, social regulation of production'[43] – it is also, albeit under a different heading, the subject of detailed theoretical exposition in the earlier chapters of the work. The remarkable parallels between the condition of states and the condition of firms have not gone unnoticed in orthodox IR. For the most part, however, they have been used to legitimate either a conception of anarchical systems *sui generis*, or the importing of theoretical frameworks from neoclassical economics into IR theory.[44] Since there exists such a powerful methodological as well as substantive contrast between these idioms and that of Marx's social theory, the question naturally arises whether an elaboration of Marx's theory of anarchy in production might suggest an alternative way of understanding the interaction of states which we call anarchical.

The case may be stated more broadly than this, however. For if there is an overall historical schema in Marx's oeuvre, then it is arguably not that of the succession of five modes of production so often inferred from *The Communist Manifesto* and the '1859 Preface', with its suggestion of the transhistorical continuity of class struggle.[45] Rather, in *Capital* Volume I (and in the *Grundrisse*, which includes Marx's longest discussion of precapitalist societies[46]), the emphasis is much more on the *dis*continuity of modern world history, the fundamental rupture with *all* previous forms of human society which capitalism is held to comprise. Nor is this discontinuity registered in terms of a new pitch of social oppression contrasting with the more humane modes of society which went before.[47] Its characteristic formulation strikes a quite different note:

> Relationships of personal dependence ... are the first forms of society, in which human productivity develops only to a limited extent and at isolated points. Personal independence based upon dependence *mediated by things* is the second great form, and only in it is a system of general social exchange of matter, a system of universal relations, universal requirements and universal capacities, formed.[48]

'Dependence mediated by things' constrasts here with all earlier forms of social organization, which rested 'on blood ties, or on primeval, natural or master–servant slave relations'.[49] In place of 'direct relations of domination and servitude',[50] we now see an unending 'collision of unfettered individuals who are determined only by their own interests ... the mutual repulsion and attraction of free individuals'.[51] However, as Marx almost immediately goes on to warn, this new condition does not mark the abolition of relations of dependence. It constitutes rather 'the dissolution of these relations into a general form', a structural dispersal as a result of which they now 'confront the individual ... as external necessity'.[52] With this shift from personalized domination to impersonal necessity as the organizing 'form of social connectedness' we enter the paradoxical world of anarchy in which, to borrow Wight's characterization of the international anarchy, social 'action is most regularly necessitous'[53] – despite (or precisely because of) the fact that it remains formally uncoordinated by any overarching authority.

Whether or not this contrast suppresses the historical diversity of human societies (as Sayer suggests[54]), its relevance to IR theory should be apparent. For *Capital*, as is well-known, contains no theory of the state, no explicit account of 'the relation of the different forms of the state to the different economic structures of society'.[55] This is generally taken to rule out the possibility of a Marxian theory of international relations, where the requirement is to explain not the exploitative relations between persons and classes, but rather the anarchical relations between states. Yet in the passages cited above we seem to have a contrast which installs anarchy – conceived not as a technical feature of the economy but as a constitutive social form – as central to Marx's overall conception of capitalist modernity. And while realism argues that an anarchical order will always be something less than a 'real' society in the traditional sense (meaning one raised out of the state of nature by the operation of superordinate government), the implication of Marx's account seems to be that *this* anarchical order is already much more than a society in the traditional sense.

It might be argued that such a contrast does not entail the possibility of a Marxian theory of anarchy, because the single term 'anarchy' is being used to describe distinct phenomena in the two cases: the bare fact of independent, competing units in the realist case, as against some much more specific condition in that of Marx. This involves us in a methodological question which Marx addresses directly in the 'General Introduction' of 1857, and it may therefore be worth recalling his discussion here.[56]

In Marx's discussion, the category in question was 'labour in general', a deceptively simple abstraction which provided one of the conceptual foundations for the tradition of classical political economy. This abstraction was derived as a straightforward generalization: all acts of production must involve labour (though in practice its form differs in each case); therefore labour is a general precondition of all production. For Marx, the objection to such a method lay partly in the fact that it was doomed to barren circularity:

> There are characteristics which all stages of production have in common, and which are established as general ones by the mind; but the so-called *general conditions* of all production are nothing more than these abstract moments with which no real historical stage of production can be grasped.[57]

Beyond this, however, the abstraction 'labour' as a descriptive generalization across history not only ignored differences between modes of production, it also persistently obscured the way in which the abstraction of labour *as an actual social process* (which in turn forms the historical condition of being able to think the category 'labour in general') is unique to capitalism. In this society the abstraction of useful labour, its reduction to a homogenous 'abstract labour', is a key mechanism of social reproduction, and one which differentiates this society from all others:

> The simplest abstraction, then, which modern economics places at the head of its discussions, and which expresses an immeasurably ancient relation valid in all forms of society, nevertheless achieves practical truth as an abstraction only as a category of the most modern society.[38]

There are likewise two senses in which the term anarchy may be applied to the modern international system. First, that system lacks superordinate government. But this has almost always been true. There has never actually been a world government, so there has always been an element of 'Thucydidean realism'. However, this very general point (like 'labour in general') is routinely conflated with a second sense of the term anarchy: when it is used to denote the dynamics of power characterizing the *modern* states-system. For what distinguishes the modern form of geopolitical power is not that it is exercised by a plurality of independent units (anarchy in general), but that it no longer embodies personalized relations of domination (which cancel the formal independence of the dominated), being impersonal, mediated by things. It is this structural shift which explains why the units are no longer empires but bordered, sovereign states. This anarchy, anarchy as a structurally specific social form, is persistently obscured by being conflated with the transhistorical generalization 'anarchy in general'. So mystifying was the concept of 'labour in general' (obscuring even, or perhaps especially, the historicity of its own formulation) that Marx's eventual discovery of 'abstract labour' as a real historical form appeared, in Engels's words, 'like a thunderbolt out of a clear blue sky'. But Marx's method here, the deciphering of the historicity of concepts, is fit for wider use. And we must turn it now on the realist concept of anarchy.

The Clear Blue Sky

Where, then, do we find 'the anarchical society' in the work of Marx? It is to be found principally in part one of Volume I of *Capital*, where the analysis of the commodity as a social form is initiated.[39] There we encounter a community made up of isolated individuals who secure their diverse material needs and desires by exchanging the products of their own private labour with those of others. This recourse is dictated by the conjunction of a significant division of labour with the private character of their production (which renders each individual the proprietor of all he produces). Individuals therefore are constrained to produce social use-values for the purpose of exchange: that is, they secure their own subsistence by producing commodities.

This immediately distinguishes this community from most societies known to history. For as a rule the process of production is directly social: the total labour carried on by the society is organized through personal relations of dependence which authorize command over labour and its product.[60] Here, however, such relations are not to be found, and seem to be ruled out by the formal equality and independence of individual proprietors. Yet all collectivities with any degree of division of labour must have some means of co-ordinating their divided labours in order to accomplish the overall task of social reproduction. As Marx put it, 'this necessity of distributing social labour in definite proportions cannot be done away with by the *particular form* of social production, but can only change the *form it assumes*.'[61] How, then, do the private labours of these individuals become social? How are they assimilated into (and in turn organized by) the overall labour of collective reproduction? Or, to recall the formulation current within the problematic of IR: in what way do they constitute a society?[62] The answer is that in this case the private labours of individuals become social only through the exchange of products as commodities. And this in turn gives a unique role to exchange-value as a central mechanism of overall social co-ordination:

> the form in which this proportional division of labour operates, in a state of society where the interconnection of social labour is manifested in the *private exchange* of the individual products of labour, is precisely the *exchange value* of these products.[63]

Thus, where other collectivities constitute themselves as societies through direct (personalized) relations of authority, this one is reproduced through exchange relations between things.

This mediation of human social relations by exchange relations between things has three principal effects. First, it depersonalizes the processes of social reproduction such that the individual confronts his material incorporation into society in the form of external, quantifiable relations between the prices of things.

Second, because the exchange-value of a commodity is not inherent in it but is rather a function of the totality of relations among the whole world of commodities, the actual mechanism which determines price and hence organizes the distribution of social wealth is not under the control of any individual. It is alienated onto a dispersed or anarchical property of the society as a whole – the market. How this mechanism operates 'behind the backs of the producers'[64] to bring order to their collective labours is truly a thing of wonder. For it can have no substance apart from their active relations with each other, and yet it reflects that collective agency back to them in the form of an automatic, impersonal movement:

> It has been said and may be said that this is precisely the beauty and the greatness of it: this spontaneous, this material and mental metabolism which is independent of the knowing and willing of individuals, and which presupposes their reciprocal independence and indifference.[65]

Finally, the perceptual corollary of this linked objectification and alienation is a recurrent mystification of the processes of social life in the minds of their authors, an unavoidable tendency to lose the constitutive social relations between persons beneath the price relations between commodities which mediate them and are their only visible expression – commodity fetishism:[66]

> Their own movement within society has for them the form of a movement made by things, and these things, far from being under their control, in fact control them.[67]

Marx has some striking observations to make about the connection between the role played by the exchange of things in this anarchical order and the bases of individual human freedom. This connection centres on the formal character of the act of exchange itself, which makes no distinction of status or right between the actors involved. On the contrary,

> As far as the formal character is concerned, there is absolutely no distinction between them. ... Each of the subjects is an exchanger, i.e. each has the same social relation towards the other that the other has towards him. As subjects of exchange, their relation is therefore that of *equality*.[68]

The variety of specialized labours in which individuals are engaged, which might be expected to endanger this equality, in fact only reinforces it by compelling all producers to enter continuously into acts of exchange which posit their mutual formal equality.[69] Moreover, because the individuals involved do not simply take what they want by force, but rather implicitly recognize one another each as the sovereign proprietor of the product of his own labour,[70] they also thereby posit each other as *free*, formally not subordinate to the will of another. This line of reasoning is pressed to a startling climax:

> Equality and freedom are thus not only respected in exchange based on exchange values but, also, the exchange of exchange values is the productive, real basis of all *equality* and *freedom*. As pure ideas they are merely the idealized expressions of this basis; as developed in juridical, political, social relations, they are merely this basis to a higher power.[71]

One further dimension of these relations may be noted here. The formal properties of the act of exchange as positing equality and independence may be seen as constitutive of the distinctively modern conception of 'the individual'. For as Marx elsewhere observes, far from being the natural starting point of social evolution, part of the *explanans* of social theory, this individual, apparently existing in 'dot-like isolation'[72] is a historical outcome:

> The more deeply we go back into history, the more does the individual ... appear as dependent, as belonging to a greater whole. ... Only in the eighteenth century, in 'civil society', do the various forms of social connectedness confront the individual as a mere means towards his private purposes, as external necessity.[73]

The above discussion suggests that the organization of social reproduction via exchange relations does not simply accord greater recognition to individual rights. It actually constitutes the individual as a novel social form. Take away the anarchical form of regulation, and the individual as ideal must go with it; for then the members of the society must submit once more to direct relations of domination.[74] The predominance of exchange relations thus actively creates the boundaries around the person which other societies do not recognize. As Marx puts it:

> The less social power the medium of exchange possesses ... the greater must be the power of the community which binds the individuals together, the patriarchical relation, the community of antiquity, feudalism and the guild system. ... Each individual possesses social power in the form of a thing. Rob the thing of this social power and you must give it to persons to exercise over persons.[75]

Personal independence (hence the category of the individual) is based on relations of dependence (individuals depend upon mutual exchange) mediated through things (the exchange relations established between their commodities).

Here, then, we have an anarchical society: the plurality of independent individuals; the lack of superordinate direction; the emergence none the less of an impersonal mechanism of social organization which lies beyond the control of individuals; the paradoxical role of this collective alienation as the basis of individual freedom; and the peculiar objectified form in which individuals confront their relations with each other.

Now let us look again at the parallel conception of anarchy encountered in IR. It clearly belongs to the same genus: the plurality of sovereign independent states lacking superordinate direction; the emergence none the less of impersonal mechanisms of social organization (the balance of power and the invisible hand of the market) which escape the command of individual states; the paradoxical role of this collective alienation as the precondition of sovereign independence; and the novel forms of international power which characterize such an order.

This similarity points to a remarkable implication. For orthodox IR, as we saw in chapter 1, claims to be founded upon the opposition between realism and idealism. And yet it now appears that these two, far from being opposites, are actually variations on this single theme of anarchy, emphasizing respectively its public and private articulation. Cobden predicted that the triumph of free trade would enable the reversion of the international environment to a municipal form of government.[76] Palmerston insisted, against Cobden, upon the efficacy of the balance of power.[77] In this they advanced against each other the claims of rival, differentiated public and private political spheres. But it is striking that the mechanisms they invoked (the invisible hand and the balance of power) bore the same stamp for all that – namely that of personal independence based on dependence mediated by things. And the pragmatic interdependence of these mechanisms was clearly recognized on both sides. Cobden and Bright saw non-intervention as the other side of free trade – 'God's diplomacy', Cobden called it.[78] But, arguably, Palmerston himself saw free trade (and the consolidation of the liberal political institutions which went with it) as a necessary condition of the doctrine of non-intervention, and hence of the organization of the international system through a balance of power.[79] In fact it was the memorable boast of the British state in the age of Palmerston that it gloried in the anarchy of both spheres. Two quotations from that ebullient statesman will perhaps, in their combination, serve to make the point:

> Why is the earth on which we live divided into zones and climates? Why, I ask, do different countries yield different productions to people experiencing similar wants? Why are they intersected with mighty rivers – the natural highways of nations? Why are lands the most distant from each

other, brought almost into contact by the very ocean which seems to divide them? Why, Sir, it is that man may be dependent upon man. It is that the exchange of commodities may be accompanied by the extension and diffusion of knowledge ... multiplying and confirming friendly relations. It is, that commerce may freely go forth, leading civilization with one hand, and peace with the other, to render mankind happier, wiser, better.[80]

Therefore I say that it is a narrow policy to suppose that this country or that is to be marked out as the eternal ally or the perpetual enemy of England. We have no eternal allies, and we have no perpetual enemies. Our interests are eternal and perpetual, and those interests it is our duty to follow.[81]

Here we see adopted, as the very watchword of foreign policy, that presupposition of 'reciprocal independence and indifference' which Marx noted above as fundamental to his anarchical society.

Now, if the invisible hand and the balance of power are not the stark opposites which they are often presented as being, this suggests that their *doctrinal* antagonism, consolidated in the disciplinary opposition of liberal utopianism and political realism, might be equally misleading.[82] Although it coloured the language of British foreign policy debates throughout the nineteenth century, the contrast none the less reflects an oscillation wholly internal to the problematic of an emergent liberal international order. Given this, it is hardly suprising that these anarchical themes have a definite historical anchorage. Far from being timeless, they emerge in the course of the eighteenth century, and their development is anticipated as the geopolitical corollary of the broader social transformation which we associate with the emergence and spread of capitalism as a kind of society.

The Thunderbolt

Thus far, liberalism. Yet Marx's unravelling of these social forms has only just begun.[83] For despite its appearance as a presocial state of nature, this anarchy entails a very *advanced* form of society, in which the direct producer is separated from the means of subsistence and obliged to sell his or her labour-power as a commodity in exchange for money-wages:

Only where wage-labour is its basis does commodity-production impose itself on society as a whole; but it is also true that only there does it unfold all its hidden potentialities.[84]

Thus Marx's anarchical society reviewed above has no historical existence except on the basis of wage-labour. Wage-labour, however, as we know from our previous discussion, is the strategic relationship of capitalist society. Generalized commodity-production, it turns out, is thus not the idyllic precursor of capitalist society: *it is its surface form.*

Let us look a little further into this. In the previous section, we noted that individual freedom consists in not being formally subordinated to the will of another, a condition avoided by relating to others through the exchange of things. In addition, mutual recognition of property (meaning here the ownership of things) was in turn the basis of equality in the relation of exchange. Now we are told that human labour-power (whose expenditure previously established the ownership of the things produced) has itself assumed the social form of a 'thing' (that is, has been commodified). And as we work through the implications of this new fact, we see, before our very eyes, the 'laws based on the production and circulation of commodities become changed into their direct opposite through their own internal and inexorable dialectic.'[85]

First, anyone who relates to another through the alienation of *this* thing in exchange has contracted to make himself subordinate to the will of another, since labour power as a commodity is not physically separable from the living activity of its owner. Thus we have an exchange relation which entails (albeit beneath the realm of circulation where the exchange takes place) precisely what relations mediated by things were supposed to avoid: direct relations of power by one person over another. At the same time, the law of property which was the bulwark of equality at the anarchical surface now sanctifies the right of the new owner of this commodity to consume it as his own. But consuming labour-power means setting it to work in production. And labour power, conjoined with the means of production, can be made to produce a greater sum of values than comprise the cost of its reproduction. (This is indeed the only reason for purchasing it in the first place.) So long as this holds good, the formally equal relation between buyer and seller of this commodity, though they exchange equal values, becomes one of actual appropriation. For the product of labour no longer belongs to the direct producer but rather to the owner of the commodity whose consumption produced it. 'The separation of property from labour thus becomes the necessary consequence of a law that apparently originated in their identity.'[86]

So anarchy is based on 'dependence mediated by things' – hence both its impersonality and the new forms of freedom and subjectivity associated with it. But, in turn, 'dependence mediated by things' is based on the commodification of labour-power, a strategic relationship between the direct producer and the owner of the conditions of production – in short, a relation of surplus extraction – hence the new forms of social power.

When this is first realized, it might seem to imply that the play of anarchy is mere appearance, 'the surface process, beneath which, however, in the depths, entirely different processes go on, in which this apparent individual equality and liberty disappear'.[87] Should we therefore ignore it, and concentrate on the underlying processes? To do so would be to miss the real power of Marx's social theory. For if, instead, we now reverse the direction of our explanation and work our way back up from 'the depths' to 'the surface', we find that in *this* society relations of exchange between things (anarchy) are not the opposite of relations of domination and appropriation between persons (hierarchy): they are the social form through which *this* kind of hierarchy is reproduced.[88] As Isaac Rubin put it:

> Marx did not only show that human relations were veiled by relations between things, but rather that, in the commodity economy, social production relations inevitably took the form of things and could not be expressed except through things.[89]

Thus when Saint-Simon anticipated that 'The government of men would give way to the administration of things',[90] he was at best only half right. What capitalist society has actually given us is more like the government of men *through* the administration of things. When social relations are routed through things in this way, those things themselves become suffused with social determinations. Marx calls this the secret of the commodity. What is then required is a theory which can show us the actual social relations between persons which underlie this form without *either* abbreviating their sociology to the visible relations between things *or* denying the effectivity of the anarchical character of their reproduction. For this reason, vulgar Marxist attempts to play down the importance of anarchy because it seems to dilute the explanatory power of 'class' are as wide of the mark as their inverse: the liberal or realist apprehension of anarchical liberties at face value. In the end, a class analysis of anarchy needs also to embrace the anarchical constitution of class. This is the unique achievement of Marx's theory of value, which is grounded in a distinction between value (as a relation between persons) and exchange-value (as the relation between things which mediates the value relation). And, as the reader of *Capital* soon discovers, in the space opened up between these two emerges a sociology of *bürgerliche Gesellschaft* which is simply beyond the analytical reach of the orthodox disciplines of economics and politics.

In this context, we may recall again Ian Craib's third criterion for assessing rival social theories.[91] For by posing historically specific social relations between persons as the key to understanding anarchical social forms (such as the market and the balance of power), Marx identifies and illuminates a constitutive dimension of the social world whose existence is not even suspected by liberal theories which take those social forms to be natural – the logically determined outcome of unregulated interaction between preconstituted individuals. There is, as it turns out, rather more than this to be explained. And there is therefore, contra Wight, every need for international theory. For this anarchy is no ordinary state of nature: it has 'ontological depth' – and the depths powerfully subvert any understanding drawn straightforwardly from observation of the surface appearance.

Marx's analysis is conducted at the level of 'domestic' social reproduction. Yet it is full of implications for IR. These implications may be grouped into two categories: formal and substantive. An immediate formal implication can be seen if we recall that in IR anarchical social forms and hierarchical structures are emphasized by competing schools of thought (realism and structuralism) which supposedly represent incommensurable paradigms. It follows from our discussion that this is a false dichotomy. And just as the earlier discussion of public and private political spheres resolved the contradiction between realism and idealism, so here Marx's theory of anarchy provides a means of overcoming this so-called 'paradigm debate'. Theoretically, after all, the supposed incommensurability is simply an elaboration of the formal theoretical challenge set up by Marx as *the* central object of his theory of value at the end of chapter 5 of Volume I: namely, to understand how an anarchical interaction of independent individuals resolves into systematic class relations of subordination and appropriation without introducing either unequal exchange or any formal qualification of individual freedom and equality. (It might be added that our broader discussion suggests also that the third, 'pluralist' paradigm is really just a descriptive encounter with the differentiation of state and civil society. And there the redefinition of sovereignty advanced above would hence seem to have greater explanatory power.)

Satisfying though this formal, disciplinary clarification may be, the real excitement must attach to the new possibilities for substantive theoretical explanation of international phenomena which now come into view. For the implication is that with the international anarchy, too, beneath the realm of 'Freedom, Equality, Property and Bentham', the domain of 'the free trader vulgaris',[92] 'entirely different processes go on, in which this apparent individual equality and liberty disappear'. Is it true, then, of the international anarchy of states that there is an 'ontological depth' to the structures of social reproduction which must be plumbed before their apparently self-evident surface appearance can be understood?

In one respect, such a speculation might seem inappropriate: states are not biological individuals who buy and consume each other's labour- power. There can thus be no simple mapping of the condition of states onto that of persons. But this is not the point. What holds for both is the condition of social relations mediated through things, rather than through personalized relations of domination. It is this difference which underlies the historical shift from empire to states-system. But, by the same token, it is this same alienation of social relations onto impersonal mechanisms – the balance of power and the invisible hand of the market – which provides the social forms through which the new kinds of power peculiar to value relations operate in the international system. There is therefore a determinate task of sociological recovery yet to be undertaken, in order to resolve the actual workings of these anarchical mechanisms of the international system back into their constituent social relations. It is a task which needs to be addressed both as theoretical explication and as historical reconstruction. The major obstacle standing in the way of such a project has always been the realist definition of anarchy as a presocial state of nature.[93] For insofar as the international system could not attain the settled properties of a society, it was for the same reason held to be resistant to sociological analysis: the rules of existence in the state of nature are unforgivingly brief. Anarchy has therefore always represented the strongest argument for those resisting the intellectual integration of IR into the broader social sciences. But if anarchy is not presocial, if it can be shown to be the geopolitical form of capitalist modernity, then this last, most basic argument for realism need no longer hold us back.

In fact, there is a much broader warrant for this intuition, which emerges if we contrast our understanding of anarchy point for point with the realist understanding. Realists have argued variously that anarchy is a property of international politics which distinguishes the character of that domain from domestic politics and requires an analysis *sui generis*. They have supposed that as such it is a transhistorical, timeless feature of states-systems. And they have assumed that because it comprises a presocial state of nature, there is no ontological depth to the recurrent patterns of anarchical behaviour: the logic informing these patterns is already manifest in the two-dimensional game-plans of the balance of power.

Against this composite realist understanding, we have argued that the experience of anarchy studied in IR is not transhistorical but peculiarly modern. We have suggested that, far from being a peculiarity of geopolitics, it is *the* constitutive social form of capitalist societies. And we have glimpsed how this apparently simple and natural form of interaction can in fact be understood only by uncovering the ontological depth of its daily reproduction through a very particular kind of social relations between people.

This rediscovery of anarchy as a social form comprises a decisive break with realist theory in much the same way as the earlier redefinition of sovereignty enabled us to break decisively with realist history. There the effect was a release from the tyranny of diplomatic history which finally made it possible to connect the emergence of our international system with the wider processes of social transformation involved in the making of the modern world. Here the result is a sudden collapse of *theoretical* partitions which reveals something equally startling. To see what this is, we need only look out into the surrounding terrain of classical political economy and classical sociology which is no longer barred from view.

Sociology is commonly defined as 'the study of society'. Yet this apparent universality bears its own historical stamp. For 'society' does not present itself as an object of study outside political philosophy before the institutional differentiation of public and private spheres, state and civil society, which characterizes the modern West. As Frisby and Sayer suggest: 'the very possibility of abstractly conceptualizing society at all would seem to have been historically dependent upon the concrete development of *bürgerliche Gesellschaft*: market society, civil society, bourgeois society.'[94] And once this differentiation of spheres has occurred, what most immediately needs to be explained is precisely how social reproduction is organized by means other than direct political co-ordination. (Polanyi argued that the same requirement underlay the emergence of classical political economy. In a chapter entitled 'Political Economy and the Discovery of Society' he suggests that new forms of understanding were needed because 'no human community had yet been conceived of which was not identical with law and government.'[95]) The intellectual novelty of this problematic thus reflects the historical novelty of an actual historical formation.

Much of classical sociology is therefore implicitly a reflection on the theme of anarchical regulation. Is this not the meaning of Durkheim's question: 'How does it come about that the individual, whilst becoming more autonomous, depends ever more closely upon society?'[96] It echoes through Herbert Spencer's notion of an 'evolution from militant to industrial societies, from 'compulsory cooperation' between the elements of the whole society to 'voluntary cooperation, from centralization to decentralization'.[97] Simmel's speculation on 'how is society possible?'[98] has a strangely familiar ring to any student of IR theory reared on the question 'Can there be a society of states?'

It might be suggested that the significance of these parallels has gone unremarked because of the disciplinary remoteness of IR from sociology. In one respect, however, this would not be accurate – and here we come upon one of the most bizarre twists in the whole story. The central, organizing category of the English School of IR is 'international society'. What is the sense of the term 'society' here? One of its sources is undoubtedly the 'great society of states'[99] which Grotius describes as the outcome of the 'impelling desire for society' which even sovereigns conceive on account of their mutual dependence:

> there is no state so powerful, that it may not some time need the help of others outside itself, either for purposes of trade, or even to ward off the forces of many foreign nations united against it.[100]

However, we may also identify a second strand of analysis, deriving from classical sociology, which seeks to fix as a definite quality the comparative looseness of international association which might otherwise be regarded simply as a kind of incompleteness due to the absence of world government. Notable in this regard is the work of Georg Schwarzenberger, who drew upon Ferdinand Tönnies' distinction between *Gemeinschaft* and *Gesellschaft* – usually translated as 'community' and 'society':

> Whereas the members of a community are united in spite of their individual existence, the members of a society are isolated in spite of their association.[101]

Now although it is true that Tönnies formulated *Gemeinschaft* and *Gesellschaft* as ideal-types, it is also the case that he had a definite historical application in mind. As he put it: 'Gemeinschaft (community) is old; Gesellschaft (society) is new as a name as well as a phenomenon.'[102] Schwarzenberger – unlike, for example, Charles Manning[103] – retains this historical dimension, arguing that 'the inter-Christian State system [i.e. medieval Christendom] had many features which make us inclined to classify it as a community', and that the emergence of modern geopolitics therefore comprised 'its transformation from a community into a society'.[104]

But once the anarchical character of the modern international system has thus been identified as a definite historical form – its *Gesellschaft*-type relations distinguishing it descriptively from the *Gemeinschaft*-type geopolitical relations of feudal Europe – it is clearly of some relevance to ask: *why* does it now assume this different form? Schwarzenberger does not press this question – perhaps because he is content to have found an ideal-type which captures his sense of the quality of modern relations between states – 'isolated in spite of their association'. Tönnies himself, however, did not hesitate to make this final link:

> Gesellschaft ... is to be understood as a multitude of natural and artificial individuals, the wills and spheres of whom are in many relations with and to one another, and remain nevertheless independent of one another and devoid of mutual familiar relationships. This gives us the general description of 'bourgeois society'.[105]

Whatever conclusions we may draw from this, the main point may perhaps be allowed to stand: the problematic of anarchy, so long regarded as the *differentia specifica* of IR theory, turns out instead to be perhaps *the* central preoccupation of modern social thought.

At a certain point in the *Grundrisse*, Marx asserts that 'The analysis of what free competition really is, is the only rational reply to the middle-class prophets who laud it to the skies or to the socialists who damn it to hell.'[106] Something very similar may be suggested concerning our subject here: namely, that the analysis of what anarchy really is is the only rational reply to the realists who laud it to the skies or to the idealists who damn it to hell. It would be difficult to imagine a more decisive affirmation of the structural unity of social forms and geopolitical systems – unless it be the writing of that alternative history of the emergence of the international system to which the considerations developed in this chapter now point.

6

Tantae Molis Erat: Prospectus for an Alternative History of the International System

Tantae molis erat to unleash the 'eternal natural laws' of the capitalist mode of production.

MARX[1]

The Method

Towards the end of *Capital*, Volume I, Marx breaks off from the detailed analysis of the dynamics of capitalist production and devotes the last eight chapters to the subject of 'so-called primitive accumulation'. Classical political economy had recognized that the preconditions of a capitalist 'economy' – in particular, the conjunction of some individuals possessing money and means of production with a much larger group who possess no means of subsistence and are hence compelled to sell their labour-power in order to survive – were not naturally occurring. In order to explain this conjunction which makes capitalism possible, some authors therefore posited a preceding phase of social development in which the diligence and frugality of a few enabled them to accumulate sufficient wealth to employ others, while a much larger number failed to husband their resources so well and, having squandered their property, came to maintain themselves by hiring out their labour. The deepest inadequacy of this account of 'primitive accumulation' is not so much its 'nursery tale' naïvety.[2] It is rather that by representing the emergence of capitalism as a quantitative accumulation of money rather than a qualitative transformation of social forms it reads back into what is supposed to be a 'state of nature' the very differentiation of politics and economics which constitutes capitalist society. It offers an explanation of the emergence of capitalism which unwittingly presupposes the existence of capitalist social relations as part of the explanation.[3] In such a 'state of nature', the labour of modernity is already accomplished, and it remains only for the multitude of naturally occurring 'unencumbered selves' to sign the requisite contracts – that is, the social contract and the labour contract.

It is not difficult to see the parallels with the supposed 'state of nature' of IR theory, and its nearest equivalent to the 'civil state', namely 'international society'. There, too, the sovereign individuality of the state is read back into the state of nature, hence suppressing the labour of its historical emergence, and leaving only the signing of treaties to make the difference between a state of nature and international society. This is very clear in Bull's work, which, as we saw in chapter 2, draws a contrast betweeen international system and international society, the latter obtaining by virtue of formal mutual recognition and shared rules and practices among the states involved.[4] The injunction *pacta sunt servanda* ('treaties are to be obeyed') may not be as law-inspiring as the gaze of the Leviathan, but they have this much in common: each is a contractual solution to a problematic of anarchy which is assumed to be natural but which actually requires historical explanation. How then do we get at this hidden history?

Marx did not reject outright the 'nursery tale' of primitive accumulation. Instead, he reworked it into an empirically open category for charting the entire series of actual historical processes and transformations which comprise the emergence of capitalist society. Exactly what these processes are cannot be specified in advance: this is a matter for empirical research. Indeed, Marx later objected vigorously to any attempt 'to metamorphose my historical sketch of the genesis of capitalism in Western Europe into a historico-philosophical theory of the *marche générale* imposed by fate upon every people, whatever the historic circumstances in which it finds itself'.[5] What *can* be said, however, is that since for most of history most humans have been peasants in possession of the means of subsistence, the emergence and spread of capitalist society must be brought about by a historical process of expropriation which reconstitutes them as propertyless individuals compelled to sell their labour. This historical process he calls 'the secret of primitive accumulation'.

> So-called primitive accumulation, therefore, is nothing else than the historical process of divorcing the producer from the means of production. It appears as 'primitive' because it forms the pre-history of capital, and of the mode of production corresponding to capital.[6]

We should add that since over the same period most appropriating groups have been politically constituted elites extracting a surplus by extra-economic coercion at the end of the production process, the consolidation of the capitalist property form must also involve a historical process of internal pacification or state-building, by which their personalized political and military power is broken and reconstituted in the impersonal form of the sovereign state, leaving them with predominantly 'economic' forms of power. In other words, state-building is an integral part of primitive accumulation.[7] These things do not come about spontaneously or without violence. They form an uneven history which, as Marx put it, 'is written in the annals of mankind in letters of blood and fire'.[8] They are the object of fierce struggle which 'assumes different aspects in different countries, and runs through its various phases in different orders of succession, and at different historical epochs'.[9]

The question then arises: can we extend the scope of this reworked category of primitive accumulation beyond individual societies in order to recover the emergence of the capitalist *international* system as a determinate set of historical processes of structural change? (Can we, in other words, uncover a historical 'secret of primitive accumulation' buried within the international 'state of nature'?) The core assertion of this book has been that there is a connection between the strategic relation of production and the social form of the geopolitical system. And this, of course, does entail that the generalizing of a new strategic relation would be associated with a transformation of the geopolitical system.

As we noted in chapter 4, Marx himself was by no means insensible to the international components of primitive accumulation, nor to their association with a sequence of leading 'national' centres:

> The different moments of primitive accumulation can be assigned in particular to Spain, Portugal, Holland, France and England, in more or less chronological order.[10]

Nor did he assume that these were merely developments within 'civil society', having nothing to do with the state. Of the same processes he writes:

> These methods ... all employ the power of the state, the concentrated and organized force of society, to hasten, as in a hothouse, the process of transformation of the feudal mode of production into the capitalist mode. ... Force ... is itself an economic power.[11]

The *Grundrisse* shows Marx projecting a huge multi-volume critique

of political economy which, from the evidence of his correspondence,[12] was to have included a volume on the state, and which singles
out the themes of war and the 'influence ... of international relations'
on internal social development.[13]

These observations are scattered and incomplete in Marx's work.
They certainly do not comprise an explicit theory of the international
system. But taken together with the discussions of the British in India
and some *eight hundred* pages of journalism on the Eastern Question,[14]
they might make one think twice before endorsing a claim that 'international relations did not particularly interest the two founders of
marxism.'[15]

But how can Marx's insistence that 'the expropriation of the
agricultural producer, of the peasant, from the soil is the basis of the
whole process'[16] be applied to the emergence of the modern international system?

The Data

It is a curious feature of IR theory that the nineteenth century seems
largely to have dropped out of view. Wight's academy of 'international thought'[17] is fully staffed by the end of the eighteenth century,
while the *locus classicus* of the political realism imported by Morgenthau
into the US after World War II is Max Weber's 1918 lecture 'Politics
as a Vocation'.[18] In the first case, the implication must be that the
experience of the nineteenth century did not add anything significant
which was not available at the end of the eighteenth.[19] As for the
second, by 1918 the international world of the previous century was
already a distant, shattered memory. If Churchill looked fondly back
on it – 'The old world in its sunset was fair to see'[20] – Weber's eyes
were fixed sternly on the world ahead. And all he saw was 'a Polar
night of icy darkness and severity'.[21] Moreover, such extended treat-
ments of the nineteenth century as we do possess in IR tend to focus
on the eruption of European nationalism, the evolution of international institutions among pre-existent states, or the alternation of
concerts and balances within Europe.[22] To be sure, these are all
important themes. Yet it was the nineteenth century which saw the
incorporation of nearly the whole of the earth into a single geopolitical system, thus inaugurating the era of *world* history. And this did
not come about through the progressive entry of more and more pre-
existing political entities into balances and concerts.[23] On the contrary, its main dynamic was visibly the expansion – not to say explosion

– of European societies outwards, which eventually brought the larger part of humanity under the formal or informal rule of European states and the white settler states of the Americas. In other words, the actual historical path to the modern global states-system – the world of anarchical freedoms – lies not through the widening interaction among pre-existent sovereignties, but rather through the construction of the greatest colonial *empires* the world had ever seen. Thus the state of nature of IR theory, for all its elemental appearance, is in fact the historical outcome of determinate processes of change. These processes are not far to seek.

For the nineteenth century was also, as Hobsbawm described it, 'a great machine for uprooting countrymen'.[24] If we could visualize the European social formation and its connections with the wider world early in the second half of that century, the most striking feature would undoubtedly be the gigantic movement – local, regional and intercontinental – of populations. This 'greatest migration of peoples in history'[25] in fact comprised three distinct but crucially related movements: from the European countryside to the towns, from Europe to the Americas and other regions of white settlement, and (by non-Europeans) between Asian and African regions under European political control. These three movements, each made up mostly of dispossessed direct producers (peasants), were dynamically and structurally related. To understand how this is so is to begin to appreciate something of the vast labour of social transformation which the emergence of the capitalist world market entailed at its birth.[26]

When we referred a moment ago to the nineteenth century in terms of the explosion of European societies, this may have seemed like a colourful exaggeration. But in fact the metaphor is apt in at least three ways, each one of which relates to one of the vectors of migration listed above.

First, an alternative phraseology such as the 'expansion' of Europe would miss the extent to which European societies themselves were in a turmoil of transformation, visible above all in the 'flight from the land' and the periodic revolutionary crises which formed the aftershocks of the great earthquake of 1789–1815. Between 1600 and 1800 the urbanized population of Europe had undergone no significant increase as a proportion of the (expanding) total.[27] After 1800, however, it showed a continuous heady ascent: newly unified Germany crowded its people into towns at such a rate that the proportion doubled from one-third to two-thirds in four and a half decades.[28] In mid-nineteenth-century Manchester, more than two-thirds of the population over twenty years of age had been born elsewhere.[29] As Colin Murray suggested, 'the study of migration is the study of processes of structural transformation'.[30] And certainly, this migration to the towns involved far more than a simple physical relocation of population.

The dynamo here at the heart of all three movements was the capitalist industrialization of Europe. Having said that, the actual process was uneven in the extreme. And it would be misleading to say simply that all over Europe the introduction of liberal property laws on the land was rapidly expropriating the peasantry, raising agrarian productivity to feed the towns and creating a supply of landless labourers to work in the expanding industrial sector. The French peasantry remained more or less intact.[31] The Russian 'Great Reform' of 1861 did not generalize private property in land.[32] The peasants of southern Italy, 'privatized' in the early part of the century, were not actually dislodged till after the 1860s, when the conjunction of agrarian recession with new cheap imports of grain from the US began suddenly to turf them out almost by the million. In fact it is arguable that the only country which followed the 'classical' road to capitalist industrialization was Britain – and that Britain itself could do this only by dint of being the first to industrialize. Britain's priority was more fundamental than this, however. For when the early cotton-mill owners of Lancashire looked out into the countryside they beheld an advanced agrarian order unlike anything in any other major country: no peasantry clinging tenaciously to the land or bolted to it by legal subordination to semi-feudal landed elites. On the contrary, the processes of expropriation of the direct peasant producer and the parallel consolidation of private property in land had already been largely accomplished, leaving behind a capitalist agrarian economy dominated by the triad of private land-owner, tenant farmer and landless labourer. By contrast, every other state that wished to compete with the world's first industrial power confronted an 'agrarian problem' which often reached into the heart of the state itself. The imperative to industrialization entailed the transformation of property relations on the land in order to raise productivity and liberate labour for redeployment into the urban industrial sector. But these property relations were the foundation of the political power of landed classes who were strongly represented within the state. Thus industrialization spelled not only population movement and social transformation but also political contradiction and crisis. Partly for this reason, much of the geopolitics of nineteenth-century Europe was preoccupied with managing the tensions between old and new classes, the constitutional struggles of liberalism and absolutism, and the territorial and political consequences of the divergent strategies pursued by different states to produce industrial economies.

Thus the Europe which plunged into the catastrophic general crisis of 1914–45 was no longer the same kind of social formation which the legitimists had vainly attempted to restore a century earlier.[33]

Europe's societies were also exploding in a second sense. The period saw a massive outflow of population from the continent. Most crossed the Atlantic, forming an 'enormous and continuous flood of humanity driven year in, year out, onto the shores of America'.[34] But others travelled to areas of white settlement elsewhere. Over the century up to 1914 some fifty *million* people left Europe. These people were almost all peasants shed by the revolution on the land gathering pace across Europe. As Wolf notes:

> The main factors pushing these people out of Europe were the spread of industrial capitalism and the commercialization of agriculture.[35]

Indeed it is possible to observe successive national waves of transatlantic migration corresponding to 'the timing of the industrializing process in the various countries ... a process which initially liberated labour power on a massive scale in the agricultural and handicraft sectors everywhere.'[36] Thus Britain provided three-quarters of European emigrants between 1821 and 1850, something over half between 1851 and 1880 (when numbers were swelled by other north European states) and just over a quarter between 1881 and 1915 – by which time the outflow from south-eastern Europe comprised over half the total.[37] There are partial exceptions to this pattern, such as the exodus in the middle decades of the century from Ireland and Germany, spurred not by industrialization but by famine. Moreover, as the century wore on, cyclical downturns in international trade displaced cohorts of workers from European industry itself.[38] However, as Kenwood and Lougheed aver, 'most European migrants during the nineteenth century were rural workers'.[39] And although it was land-hunger which drove them out, they too were mostly reconstituted as (unskilled) industrial wage labour.[40]

In 1800 the United States was 'a small agricultural nation settled along the Atlantic seaboard',[41] numbering some five million people. By 1914 it was a leading industrial power of over one hundred million.[42] In the intervening years it had absorbed some two-thirds of the fifty million people who left Europe for the areas of white settlement overseas.

Now, it is a commonplace that European emigration underwrote American industrialization. But this formulation drastically understates the extent to which Europe and America were caught in a single explosion. For Europe's role in shaping the new society was not only demographic. Woodruff suggests that the westward movement of the US frontier was itself paced in part by the expanding European demand for American products,[43] a demand which multiplied as European industrial production expanded. This was certainly the case in the South. It was the mechanical tempo of the Lancashire mills which (absorbing a 1,500-fold increase in US cotton production between 1790 and 1860) beat out the westward march of the planters, leading to the Indian wars and political expansion of the period.[44] (Indeed at this time, cotton comprised some two-thirds of US exports[45] and was, overall, 'the most important proximate cause of expansion' in the US economy.[46]) But in the North, too, later on in the century, European demand for wheat played its part in bringing areas newly accessible by rail under the plough. This latter development, in turn, had further important consequences. For, as Wolf notes, the 'massive inflows of American and Russian wheat' which came on stream during the Great Depression 'shook the foundations of European agriculture and intensified the outward flow of migrants to the Americas'. Indeed in some cases it seems that the very ships which brought the American grain to Europe carried on the return run Italian peasants dislodged by the trade.[47]

The stimulus of external trade should not be exaggerated. The expanding internal market of the North soon became the principal dynamo of expansion. But the deeper relevance of these observations lies elsewhere: they remind us of what the United States actually is, historically. Far from being just another great power,[48] this great, defining fixture of postwar international relations is the child of the industrial-capitalist transformation of Europe.[49] Indeed, having no formal ethnic definition, its national (constitutional) identity is practically indistinguishable from the purest ideological expression of capitalist relations of production. The truths declared to be self-evident in the Declaration of Independence are, as Marx might have put it, 'the idealized expression of this basis; as developed in juridical, political, social relations, they are merely this basis to a higher power.'[50]

Thus when Max Weber sought to characterize 'the spirit of capitalism', he quoted (citing its 'almost classical purity') not a tract of German Protestantism but a pamphlet by a signatory of the American Declaration of Independence, Benjamin Franklin.[51] Similarly, when,

in 1845, Marx singled out what he called 'the most perfect example
of the modern state', he chose not France – the birthplace of the
absolutist idea of sovereignty and site of the revolution regarded as
the very fount of modernity – not even Britain – pioneer of agrarian
and industrial capitalism – but rather 'North America'.[52] For here was

> a country where bourgeois society did not develop on the foundation of
> the feudal system, but developed rather from itself; where this society appears
> not as the surviving result of a centuries-old movement, but rather as the
> starting-point of a new movement; where the state, in contrast to all earlier
> national formations, was from the beginning subordinate to bourgeois
> society, to its production, and never could make the pretence of being an
> end-in-itself; where, finally, bourgeois society itself, linking up the produc-
> tive forces of an old world with the enormous natural terrain of a new one,
> has developed to hitherto unheard-of dimensions and with unheard-of
> freedom of movement.[53]

This is the power which (with the assistance of its liberal forebear,
England) was to remake the institutional framework of the international system in the 1940s and after. Should it really be a matter
for controversy to suggest that, whatever the enormous diversity and
uneven development of human societies in the world today, the
dominant institutions of the international system reflect the distinctive social forms of capitalism?

The third and final way in which the metaphor of 'explosion' is
apt concerns the direct co-ordination of Europe's internal transformation with its external reorganization of the non-European world
outside the areas of white settlement. For the non-European societies
which, as it were, caught the force of the blast and came under
European rule were not only shattered militarily. Nineteenth-century
imperialism was not simply what is referred to generically as 'the
imperialism of great powers'. Almost everywhere they went, the
Europeans sought either to transform the social order directly (sometimes by abolishing traditional forms of land-ownership and replacing them with private property) or at least to reorientate production
in order to integrate it directly or indirectly with the needs of European industry. Again, practices varied considerably between the
different imperial powers. But what holds for all of them is that
European external expansion was not just an external geopolitical
process. It always also involved a forcible reorganization of social life
in order to facilitate commercial extraction of resources. And whatever the amnesia of later generations, the sheer immensity of what
this involved was not lost on those involved at the time. As Lord

Lytton, Viceroy of India, expressed it in 1878, in a justly famous passage:

> It is a fact which there is no disguising ... and also one that cannot be too constantly or too anxiously recognized that ... we have placed, and must permanently maintain, ourselves at the head of a gradual but gigantic revolution – the greatest and most momentous social, moral, and religious, as well as political revolution which, perhaps, the world has ever witnessed.[34]

The colonial echo of Cobden's irenic hymn to free trade was thus a crash programme of compulsory social transformation.[35] This rolling upheaval contributed in turn to large-scale migrations within and between these non-European societies as labour was redeployed out of traditional forms of life onto plantations and European-owned farms or mobilized for the infrastructural projects that would facilitate the material integration of the regions into the expanding world market centred on Europe. In the hundred years after the British abolition of slavery in 1833, this new system of bonded labour, or 'coolieism', organized the international movement of between twelve and thirty-seven million people.[36] And when the colonial empires withdrew – the last step in the *formal* emergence of a global states-system – they left behind not only political apparatuses commanding demarcated territories, but also a pattern of economic linkages by which the societies were partly integrated into the transnational structures of the world market.

One must be careful not to overstate the immediate impact of European colonialism, in particular the speed and scale of the social transformations wrought by it. The latter were highly uneven, and, as Kiernan has observed, Marx's own journalism on India tended 'to pull out the thread of history faster than the Three Sisters were weaving it'.[37] That said, we need to retain a sense of the overall sociological content of imperialism. And if we take Marx's formulation as an empirically open tool for thinking about this, then it surely remains the best way of sidestepping empty debates about whether nineteenth-century imperialism was primarily 'economic' or 'strategic':

> England has to fulfil a double mission in India: one destructive, the other regenerating – the annihilation of old Asiatic society, and the laying of the material foundations of Western society in Asia.[38]

Outflow of population, internal transformation, external conquest and upheaval: the intellectual challenge of IR is surely to grasp these several dynamics as a whole. For what we witness in these linked processes of geographical expansion and structural transformation is nothing less than the dawn of the modern international system – the object of study of IR.

The Result

If we now step back from the turmoil, we can see this emergence more clearly by observing the basic historical shift in the form of imperial power which has been associated with this world-wide 'uprooting of countrymen'. In the sixteenth-century Spanish Empire, accumulation of resources could not have been accomplished without territorial expansion. This was clearly not a 'purely political' state. Whether in the Habsburg domains of Europe[59] or in the lands of the Aztecs and the Incas, the scale of Spain's imperial structure could be measured by the extent of its formal jurisdiction. Not so with the British some three hundred years later. Taking British material expansion as a whole, the bulk of it was concentrated in Europe and the Americas, where it did not involve formal political command. So much so, that it may even be that the vast formal empire ran at a loss.[60] The postwar Pax Americana was different again: no territorial expansion this time, but pressure on the colonial powers to grant sovereign independence, and considerable military intervention to stabilize the emerging system internally and preserve it from the Soviet threat from without. No map of sovereign jurisdictions could show us the extent of US international power. For its rise went hand in hand with the globalizing of the sovereign states-system.[61]

When do the interests of a rising imperial power promote not political subjection but political independence? They do so when the political independence in question is not substantive political possession of resources by an autarchic state (in either communist or radical nationalist forms) but rather the consolidation of sovereignty. This breaks the political link with the former imperial power, while opening the newly demarcated sphere of 'the economy' to the private power of foreign capital,[62] that is, to the social form of dependence mediated by things. Historically, the US fought communism and anti-Western radical nationalism and supported the emergence of sovereign independence, irrespective of whether it took a democratic political form. In other words, it promoted the separating out of private and public spheres at the international level.

Like Lord Lytton before them, US foreign policy planners during World War II, many of them associated with the think-tanks of the

Council on Foreign Relations, showed themselves quite aware (albeit in a more pragmatic sense) of the historical specificity, and hence the necessary institutional form, of their coming ascendancy. As recorded in chapter 1 above, by May 1942 it was recognized that 'the British Empire as it existed in the past will never reappear and that the United States may have to take its place.'[63] Since at the same time it would have to 'avoid conventional forms of imperialism',[64] America could step into Britain's shoes only if it innovated (and dominated) institutions which internationalized the exercise of formal political power. Such were the reflections of Isaiah Bowman which fed directly into the drafting of the US proposal for the establishment of the United Nations. In this strategy, implying a determination to universalize the exercise of geopolitical power through the control of things, we see the attempted global extension of the anarchical social form of capitalist geopolitics – for all that it was hedged about by the Soviet system on the one hand and the actual recalcitrance of non-captialist social formations on the other.

But why then was British empire part formal and part informal? Gallagher and Robinson long ago pressed this question with great insistence. They argued that where, as in the 'import–export sectors' of the regions of white settlement, the movement of commodities and investment could proceed without either meeting political resistance or generating new social instability, there was no need for direct rule. The institutionally demarcated sphere of the economy, presided over by local 'satisfactory political frameworks',[65] facilitated the expansion of private political power. The British foreign secretary, Canning, referred to the new form of international power which would be deployed in this expansion when he commented in 1824: 'Spanish America is free, and if we do not mismanage our affairs sadly she is *English*.'[66] In the decades which followed, British capital built the railroads and the cattle ranches of Latin America, and 'by 1913 over a quarter of [all British] investment abroad was invested in that region.'[67] Of course this was not a socially harmonious process and the public political power of the British state was repeatedly required to intervene on behalf of the private stockholders against expropriating nationalist regimes.[68] But so long as the separation of public and private was maintained (partly accomplished here, as elsewhere, by 'purely political' pressures), imperial expansion (the widening command over productive resources) could assume a 'non-political' form.

The main factor which prevented non-European societies from being treated in the same way was the very different social structure of those societies, in which labour was not a 'thing' able to be commanded by money, production was oriented towards subsistence, and financial investment was therefore unable to lay hold of the means of wealth-creation. Thus, as already mentioned, although much of imperialism was devoted to straightforward plunder, a great deal of effort was also made, in particular by the British, to bring about social changes which would integrate these populations into the expanding realm of the world market – whether by compelling a shift to export crops or by forcibly changing the institutional forms of authority and ownership in order to open the society to commercial penetration. As Ronald Robinson summarized it elsewhere:

> Afro-Asian economies, being largely undifferentiated from their socio-political institutions, were more or less invulnerable to the play of the international market. The institutional barriers to economic invasion proved intractable; economic reform was subject to the political veto of social conservatism. ...
>
> In white colonies the international economy worked through neo-European attitudes and institutions which enabled their export–import sectors to convert British economic power into colonial political collaboration with empire. In most Afro-Asian examples, institutional gaps kept industrial imputs too small to empower such a mechanism. Small as they were, they had to be driven in by the hammer of European intervention. External political pressure had to supply the lack of economic leverage on the indigenous political economy before a measure of economic collaboration could be obtained.[69]

These contrasts may be viewed in one further aspect. For the changing political form of the imperialist states was paralleled over the same period by an equivalent shift in the form in which surplus labour was extracted by the agencies of imperialism from the foreign direct producer. The Iberians used slave and forced draft Amerindian labour, followed by African slaves. The British were the principal overseers of the peripheral coolie migrations of bonded, or semi-free, labour. The internationalization of American production has depended for the most part on the availability of free labour forces and private property rights upheld by alien state authorities.[70]

In the course of his discussion of primitive accumulation, Marx observes that

> the historical movement which changes the producers into wage-labourers appears ... as their emancipation from serfdom and from the fetters of the guilds.[71]

Similarly, the historical movement of 'geopolitical' expropriation (imperialism) which brought about the partial integration of non-European peoples into the world market (in some cases effected by a forced 'liberation' of labour) appears in its outcome, the world of independent 'nation-states', as the sovereign emancipation of the peoples. What we actually see emerging here is the geopolitical corollary of capitalism: sovereign independence based on dependence mediated by things. Behind the contemporary world of independent, equal states stands the expropriation of the direct producer.

It is in this respect, then, that the spread of the world market, the emergence of a global sovereign states-system, the internal explosion of Europe, and its tumultuous impact upon peripheral societies – in short, the linked processes of geopolitical expansion and social transformation which created our modern international system – must all be seen as parts of a single enormous upheaval: the ongoing world-historic upheaval of capitalism.

Conclusion

Every historical episode of imperial expansion elaborates its own distinctive ideological legitimation according to the specific forms of domination and surplus appropriation involved in its reproduction. For sixteenth-century Castile this meant theories of kingship and theological disputes about the rights of non-Christian Amerindians. For the twentieth-century United States it means the liberal idea of freedom, and a discipline of IR which concentrates on the purely political world of sovereign equality and anarchical competition in which the imperial character of American world power is least visible.

If we want to understand the modern international system we cannot take this purely political world at face value. For the formal shift from territorial empire to sovereign states-system does not mean that direct political command over persons no longer extends across borders. Rather it means that this extension of command assumes a different *form* as a result of the disaggregation of political functions between public and private spheres, coupled with the organization of material relations between persons through social relations between things. Any theory of international relations therefore needs to begin by grasping the historical uniqueness of both sovereignty and anarchy as *social forms* arising out of the distinctive configuration of social relations which Marx called the capitalist mode of production and reproduction of social life. Only then will it be able to see its object for what it is: a set of social relations between people.

Arguably, it is in this determined rediscovery of our own collective human agency in the anonymous social forces and processes around us that social theory finds both its surest methodological and its deepest political premiss. For, as Marx himself put it:

> It is nothing but the definite social relation between men themselves which assumes here, for them, the fantastic form of a relation between things.[72]

IR has not been without its mavericks and principled oppositionists. (Morgenthau himself opposed the Vietnam War.) Nor has it lacked for writers and teachers possessed of a sincere revulsion against war and injustice. But it has failed to reappropriate the fantastic forms of states and markets, and thereby to explain what the great modern drama of our international system has actually been about. Surveying the systematic character of this failure, one is driven to conclude that the US has found in the modern clerisy of this 'American social science' a rather more serviceable ideologue than Charles V was able to command in the Dominican Order of his day.

Afterword to the Second Edition[1]

The Empire of Civil Society (hereafter *Empire*) was written as a PhD thesis under the mentorship of Fred Halliday at the London School of Economics during the years 1988 to 1992. It therefore coincided with the most dramatic changes to the international order in almost half a century – the end of the Cold War and the collapse of the Soviet Union. The implications of these changes for Marxism in the academic discipline of international relations (IR) were contradictory. On the one hand, with the end of the Soviet system, Marxism was finally relieved of its association with a repressive political regime; and the way was suddenly open, for anyone who so wished, to shake off that deadening incubus and to think afresh the relevance of Marx's original ideas for international theory. On the other hand, the Soviet collapse also removed overnight a major reason why orthodox Marxism had achieved what standing it had alongside realism and liberalism in IR: namely, its connection to, and assumed influence upon, a great power. Once it was deprived of this support, 'the broad consensus in the study of international relations was that Marxism had little if anything to offer the serious analyst'; and it was quite rapidly replaced as the third major approach by the much more insipid and easily assimilated 'constructivist' paradigm.[2] Any future return to relevance would now depend upon two things: the ability to demonstrate in

---

1 I would like to express my thanks to Verso for proposing a second edition, and especially to Grey Anderson for very helpful editorial guidance and feedback while preparing this Afterword.
2 A. Linklater, 'Marxism', in *Theories of International Relations*, third edition, S. Burchill et al., Basingstoke 2005, p. 125.

new ways the profound significance of Marx's ideas, and the tendency of capitalism to generate fresh contradictions and crises which only those ideas could fully explain. Despite the sudden demotion of Marxism in IR (and despite its own internal limitations), this seemed to me (and still seems) a safe double bet. And *Empire* was devised as an attempt to underwrite the first half of the wager: to uncover the fundamental, and even astonishing, relevance of Marx to international theory.

Timing was also important to this work in a second sense. Throughout the postwar period, political realism had, despite various challenges, remained 'the primary or alternative theory in virtually every major book and article addressing general theories of world politics'.[3] Indeed, its core thesis – that states inhabit a timeless, anarchical, power-political realm which governs their interactions irrespective of their internal social composition – had received a dramatic new formulation in Kenneth Waltz's 1979 *Theory of International Politics*. So influential was this 'neorealist' reformulation that one later survey suggested of international theory that 'all theoretical development since 1979 has been a series of footnotes on Waltz'.[4] For Waltz had stripped realism down to its bare essentials; and in doing so he also reasserted both the separation of domestic and international realms and the transhistorical continuity of power politics, or, as he described it, 'the striking sameness in the quality of international life through the millennia'.[5] These moves contradicted two of the most essential premises of Marxism as a social theory: that the social world in all its aspects is an internally related totality rooted in the collectively organized human metabolism with nature (the mode of production); and that the emergence of capitalist society had comprised a fundamental *dis*continuity in human history. After surviving a liberal critique by the 'interdependence' literature of the 1970s, political realism had already, from the mid-1980s, been subjected to a renewed assault by neo-Gramscian, feminist and poststructuralist approaches (the so-called fourth great debate of disciplinary IR). But the sudden ending of the Cold War added considerable weight to this attack. For here, surely, was a major

3 J. Legro and A. Moravcsik, 'Is anybody still a realist?', *International Security* 24: 2, 1999, p. 5.
4 T. Dunne, L. Hansen and C. Wight, 'The end of international relations theory?', *European Journal of International Relations* 19(3), 2013, p. 413.
5 K. Waltz, *Theory of International Politics*, Reading, MA, 1979, p. 66.

historical discontinuity: the collapse of the bipolar structure of the postwar international order. Moreover, the *geopolitical* shift was visibly connected to internal *social* change: the rise of neoliberal capitalism in the West and the exhaustion of 'state socialism' in the USSR. It was a denouement which realism, along with most other approaches, had failed to predict.

These interlinked political and intellectual contexts of *Empire* account for the work's three most insistent refrains: that geopolitical systems cannot be understood so long as their analysis is separated from a study of the *forms of society* involved in them; that these forms of society (and hence the geopolitical systems too) are always *historically specific* to a given time and place, a specificity which has to be uncovered by empirical research; and finally that one such specificity – industrial capitalism – is so significant that it introduced a *fundamental discontinuity* into human history, and irreversibly transformed both the nature and the subsequent empirical contents of international relations on a global scale. Modern international relations were henceforth capitalist international relations. And it followed that this historical specificity must somehow be inscribed even within the two features most regularly invoked by realism as emblematic of the supposedly separate, self-contained realm of geopolitical existence: namely sovereignty and anarchy. *Empire* was an attempt to show how.

It was of course by no means the first Marxist or Marxisant critique of orthodox international theory. Leninist, *dependencia* and neo-Gramscian authors had already set out their understandings of modern world affairs. Fred Halliday had argued for 'a necessary encounter' between historical materialism and international relations.[6] And numerous others had criticised orthodox IR from a Marxist point of view. But *Empire* was the first (and to my knowledge remains the only) book-length attempt to apply *Marx's original* intellectual method and his social theory of value to the field of international theory in general, and to the realist concepts of sovereignty and anarchy in particular. As we shall see further below, there is a reason why Marxists in IR have often bypassed the thought of Marx himself in order to concentrate on apparently secondary sources – Lenin's theory of imperialism, for example, or Gramsci's concept of

6 F. Halliday, 'A Necessary Encounter: Historical Materialism and International Relations', in *Rethinking International Relations*, Basingstoke 1994, pp. 47–73.

hegemony. But while these latter resources may (or may not) be necessary completions of Marx's thought in IR, it would be a mistake to treat them as substitutes for it. Hopefully, therefore, there is still room for a work like *Empire* which, before supplementing the ideas of Marx, pauses to investigate the remarkable implications of those ideas – in their own right – for international theory.

Beyond *Empire*: Uneven and Combined Development

In the years since *Empire* was written, the relevance of its core argument – that we live in an international world fundamentally shaped by capitalism's differentiation of the 'economic' and the 'political' – seems only to have strengthened. In the early 1990s, the major geopolitical constraint on the reach of this differentiation – the USSR and its allies in Eastern Europe and the Third World – dissolved almost overnight, with its differing parts subjecting themselves to varying degrees of 'shock therapy' in a bid to shorten the transition to market societies. Western neoliberal doctrines of 'rolling back the frontiers of the state' received a canonical policy formulation in the Washington Consensus, a universal neoliberal prescription which now replaced Western tolerance of the high levels of protectionism that many 'developing countries' had maintained since decolonization. Meanwhile, the cover-all term 'globalization' came to signify three interlinked processes: the widening abstraction of the state from civil society in one country after another; the institutionalization of this separation in new international bodies such as the World Trade Organization; and of course, enabled by these socio-political changes, the outpouring of Western capital to take advantage of cheaper labour power in the less developed 'Global South', fundamentally altering the world economy via the transfer of manufacturing production and the proliferation of globally networked supply chains. In a world-historic shift, even Maoist China, by far the largest demographic obstacle to the global expansion of capital, finally opened itself to the foreign exploitation of its workers, simultaneously initiating the process of 'uprooting countrymen' which would liberate what seemed like an unending flow of fresh labour power to service its 'imported industrial revolution'.[7] Marx's prediction that capitalism

7 Eric Hobsbawm's phrase cited above, p. 163; E. Vogel, *Deng Xiaoping and the Transformation of China*, Cambridge, MA, 2011.

would universalize itself through its inbuilt tendencies of endless accumulation, geo-social expansion and technological momentum had come true with a vengeance. Little wonder then that Perry Anderson, reviewing the scene in 2000, could comment that 'neo-liberalism as a set of principles rules undivided across the globe: the most successful ideology in world history'.[8]

In the 1990s too, the United States reached the pinnacle of its international power, the 'unipolar moment' which it exploited not through territorial expansion but through the construction of international organizations based on sovereign participation, facilitating the extension of the private power of its capital across national borders. If empire means the outward expansion of political power coupled with the deployment of transnational structures of surplus extraction, then the 1990s were witness to the intensification of a peculiarly modern form of empire. Based on the organizational principle of abstract sovereignty and multilateral anarchy, it was the empire of *bürgerliche Gesellschaft*, of *société bourgeoise*, of 'civil society'.

When *Empire* was published, I imagined that it would be the first of two volumes. The second would provide the fuller international history of capitalist world development for which Chapter 6 provides only the 'prospectus'. I also fondly envisaged using an intuitively attractive idea of 'combined and uneven development' to guide this narrative. From a Marxist perspective, it seemed obvious that, over time, the expansion of capitalist social relations had not only 'combined' (or interconnected) all societies into a single world market, but had also globally reproduced the fundamental inequality ('unevenness') inscribed in their inner structure. The phrase 'combined and uneven development' seemed to capture this double effect perfectly.

Before I could begin work, however, this plan was overtaken by events. In 1994, *Empire* was awarded the Isaac and Tamara Deutscher Memorial Prize. In order to prepare for the delivery of the memorial lecture the following year, I decided to read Deutscher's most famous work – his three-volume biography of Leon Trotsky.[9] The effect was transformative. Not only was the

8 P. Anderson, 'Renewals', NLR 1, January–February 2000, p. 10.
9 The lecture was published in *New Left Review* 215, January–February 1996, pp. 3–15, under the title of 'Isaac Deutscher and the Lost History of International Relations'.

literary genius of the work breathtaking; that genius was also used to recover and expound a theoretical framework of whose existence I had not even been aware: Trotsky's theory of 'uneven and combined development' (UCD). The much more widely referenced idea of 'combined and uneven development' would certainly have filled out the argument of *Empire*; but it would have done so by superimposing Marx's *societal* model of capitalist expansion onto the *inter-societal* plane without making any fundamental theoretical addition to that model. By contrast, it seemed that Trotsky's lesser-known idea, though sounding very similar, contained truly radical implications.

That it was in fact a quite different theory can be seen from Trotsky's patient correction of a follower who had confused the two ideas. 'I would', he wrote, pinpointing what would be lost by the apparently harmless inversion of terms, 'put uneven before combined, because the second grows out of the first and completes it.'[10] The difference then should be clear: 'combined and uneven development' sees inequality ('unevenness') growing out of capitalist interconnection ('combination'). By contrast, UCD posits a *pre-existing* unevenness of some kind which gives rise to a phenomenon called 'combined development', which then overdetermines ('completes') the original condition of unevenness. What looks like a simple inversion of terms in fact alters the very referents of the terms themselves. And it produces a quite different theory. At any rate, and perhaps due to later sectarian conflicts within Cold War Marxism, the implications of UCD were never fully drawn out.[11] Indeed, by the 1990s the original theory had all but been forgotten, even among Trotskyist writers. And yet its implications for Marxism, for IR and even for social theory in general are enormous.

10 L. Trotsky, 'A serious work on Russian revolutionary history', in G. Breitman (ed.), *Writings of Leon Trotsky*, supplement (1934–40), New York, p. 857.
11 An important exception is M. Löwy's *Combined and Uneven Development*, London 1987. However, even Löwy's excellent study is focussed much more on the politics of 'permanent revolution' than on UCD as a social and international theory. And, of course, its title misnames Trotsky's theory. For a brief history of the forgetting of Trotsky's theory, and of its revival in the field of international relations, see J. Rosenberg, 'Results and Prospects: An introduction to the CRIA special issue on UCD', *Cambridge Review of International Affairs* 34: 2, 2021, pp. 146–63.

Some ideas are so counter-intuitive that they seem almost destined to circulate in mainstream thought as bowdlerized versions of themselves, reproducing precisely the vulgar appearances that they were originally designed to overturn. Marx's social theory of value, reduced by so many of his followers to a shallow economism, is clearly in this category. But so too is Max Weber's concept of 'rationalization' and Carl von Clausewitz's famous dictum on war and politics.[12] The fact that UCD itself almost disappeared, or was even jettisoned,[13] while its apparent synonym continued to enjoy an easy currency, suggests a similar logic at work.[14] Where then lies the counter-intuitive kernel of UCD? And what does it reveal? The answer carries the question of Marxism's relation to international theory to a new level.

Empire emphasizes the significance of social structures for international relations; but it is largely silent on the obverse connection: the significance of 'the international' for societal development. In

[12] J. Rosenberg, *The Follies of Globalisation Theory*, London 2000, pp. 113–14.

[13] Even Neil Smith's major work on *Uneven Development*, which no one could accuse of lacking rigour, has contributed to the background noise blurring the meaning of UCD. For him (in line with the general notion of 'combined and uneven'), it was the logic of capital which produced the unevenness of development, confirming the normal directionality of a Marxist analysis. *Uneven Development* was an expansion of the theory of capital, but not a counter-intuitive one requiring fundamental adjustment of the theory itself. Perhaps for this reason, it was paired with a direct attack on Trotsky's idea, which Smith rightly sensed was very different from his own. Alas, his referencing of UCD as 'a theoretical and conceptual embarrassment' was an unfortunate misunderstanding which only added to the general confusion. See N. Smith, 'The geography of uneven development', in B. Dunn and H. Radice (eds), *100 Years of Permanent Revolution: Results and Prospects*, London 2006, p. 182. See also N. Smith, *Uneven Development: Nature, Capital, and the Production of Space*, third edition, London 2010, pp. 3–6, 132–5.

[14] The analogy is not perfect. The counter-intuitiveness of the theory of value lies in its claim that the social world is not what it appears. By contrast, UCD works by showing that apparent anomalies – 'peculiarities' – are in fact the historical rule, and that they appear anomalous only in the eye of (unwittingly) unilinear theory. What holds in both cases, however, is the substituting for the original theory of a more accessible representation which in fact obscures the theory's most important insight.

this it mirrors Marx's thought. For despite the prominence of international affairs in Marx's writings as a whole, he never formulated the co-existence of multiple societies as a *theoretical* premise of the materialist conception of history. With this omission came also a unilinear liability in which it could be tacitly assumed that all countries were on the same developmental path from pre-capitalist, through capitalist to socialist forms and would have to pass through the same stages in order to arrive there. Marx himself explicitly renounced any such unilinear, stageist view, rejecting all attempts 'to metamorphose my historical sketch of the genesis of capitalism in Western Europe into a historico-philosophical theory of the *marche générale* imposed by fate upon every people, whatever the historic circumstances in which it finds itself'.[15] What he did not do, however, was to formulate in positive theoretical terms the consequences of multilinearity for the materialist method of social and political analysis. This is why the Russian Marxist Vera Zasulich could write to Marx in 1881, asking whether it was really the case that in her country 'all that remains for the socialist, as such, is more or less ill-founded calculations as to how many . . . centuries it will take for capitalism in Russia to reach something like the level of development already attained in Western Europe', at which point socialist revolution could finally be attempted.[16] The five drafts of Marx's reply to Zasulich show him wrestling intensely with the problem of developmental stages, only to draw back in the brief final draft – the one that was actually sent – leaving the problem unsolved. And thus Marxism (along with liberalism) would later become a byword for 'reductionist' approaches in international theory. After all, a tendentially unilinear social theory must by definition exclude any *systematic* role for interactive multiplicity – that is, for the international per se – in its method of analysis.

All this, however, was not a necessary outcome. Two decades later, Trotsky confronted the same paradoxical situation in Russia: Marxist activists pursuing socialist revolution in a largely pre-capitalist setting. But in his case, this led to an intellectual and political solution in which the co-existence of multiple, differentially developed societies – 'the international' – played a central role.

Trotsky was of course – and remained to the end – a revolutionary Marxist. And yet, without fully realising it, he introduced a

15 Cited above, p. 160.
16 T. Shanin (ed.), *Late Marx and the Russian Road*, London 1983, p. 98.

fundamental modification into the materialist conception of history. Marx's explanatory method began with a given mode of production, and then explored its consequences for all dimensions of social existence. This, once again, Trotsky never questioned. But he wrote from the semi-periphery of capitalist world development. There was no point in applying Marx's theory of capital directly to early twentieth-century Czarist Russia because it was not (yet) an industrial capitalist society. And yet nor could the Russian situation be explained *without* locating it in the wider process of capitalist world development. Trotsky's solution was to recognize – as a *theoretical* premise – that that process of world development was necessarily a spatio-temporally 'uneven' one. It occurred in different countries at different times and under different conditions. Marx had, as we earlier saw, recognised this empirically. But Trotsky sensed instinctively that this unevenness had profound *theoretical* implications too. For it meant that at any given historical moment, capitalist development involved a multiplicity of *co-existing* societies of different kinds, at different levels of development and so on. And because their real-time conjunction meant that they could affect each other in various ways, the overall process was not only 'uneven' but also 'combined'. What would be the effect of this combination? That depended, Trotsky argued, on the particular conjunctions of different social formations, with their differing forms and temporalities, which the international unevenness of the historical process would unavoidably produce. 'It is all', he wrote, 'a question of concrete correlations.'[17] And the effects of these correlations would quite drastically – and counter-intuitively – inflect the historical and geographical trajectory of world capitalism by comparison with the expectations of orthodox Marxism.

In the case of his own country, Trotsky argued that, for a variety of historical and geographical reasons, Russian society had always developed more slowly than its European neighbours. Thus, at the moment when capitalist industrialization was taking off in the Western countries, radically increasing their wealth and power, Russia remained a semi-feudal absolutist state based on agrarian serfdom. The primary effect of this conjunction (or 'concrete correlation') was what Trotsky called a 'whip of external necessity': if Russia did not now industrialize, it would be unable to survive

17 L. Trotsky, *The History of the Russian Revolution*, translated by Max Eastman, New York 1980 [1932], p. 379.

military competition with its neighbours and would lose its independence. And yet paradoxically, the same historical unevenness which placed Russia in this vulnerable situation also generated a 'privilege of historic backwardness': precisely because it would industrialize later than the others, Russia would not have to reinvent the process for itself and go through the same steps that they had followed.[18] More developed technologies (and weapons) could be imported; organizational structures could be copied; and even the funding of the overall operation could be assisted (through international loans) by the accumulated capital already produced by the more advanced instances of development elsewhere.

However, this would not – *could* not – turn Russia into a copy of the Western societies it was imitating. First, there did not exist in Russia any equivalent to the politically strong capitalist class which, in the West, was carrying out the process of industrialization (and which had already replaced the absolutist state there with a modernizing liberal national order via the so-called 'bourgeois revolution'). It would therefore fall to the Czarist state to take the initiative and introduce modern factory production into the Russian economy. This state-led industrialization would already mark off the Russian experience from that of its Western forebears. But second, the state in question was an absolutist state whose social power still rested upon a servile agricultural population. Hence it would seek to carry out only a partial transformation: one that preserved its foundations in the countryside and blocked any urban-based political modernization. Modern social forms would be selectively 'grafted onto' an archaic economic and political structure. The result was a 'combined' social formation that fused together modern and archaic, capitalist and non-capitalist, foreign and indigenous societal forms. Here we can see once again just how different are the referents of 'unevenness' and 'combined development' in UCD, as compared with 'combined and uneven development'. And it was UCD – and not CUD – which produced the particular bundle of impossibilities that confronted and so paralyzed the Russian Marxists at the time: a pre-modern state armed with the latest modern weaponry; a tiny, politically ineffective capitalist class entirely dependent on the semi-feudal state that had spawned it; modern factories springing up in the midst of a rural peasant economy; and a new militant class of proletarians

18 Ibid., p. 5.

calling for socialism long before capitalism itself had been consolidated. This proletariat was radicalized in part by the sheer speed of change which had produced it, in part by the repressive nature of the state which had called it into being, and in part too by its exposure to the more advanced Marxist ideas already reaching it from the West (even in the *earliest* years of its own historical formation). All three of these conditioning factors, along with the peculiar characteristics of the other classes, of the economy and of the state, were effects of Russia's 'lateness' which expressed the spatio-temporal unevenness of capitalist world development as a whole. Russia's 'belatedness . . . was thus not only a matter of chronology, but also of the social structure of the nation'.[19]

It might be thought that this inchoate social structure would turn Russian development into an historical cul-de-sac. After all, even Trotsky did not believe that it brought Russia within reach of socialism. But this was where the significance of 'the international', captured in the idea of UCD, rose to its full height. Czarism had initiated Russia's belated industrialization through the import of foreign technologies and ideas. This was financed by enormous international loans which were serviced in turn by the proceeds from ever-growing exports of serf-produced wheat. Thus, while the internal effect was to twist the social structure into an unstable 'amalgam' of capitalist and pre-capitalist elements, there was an external effect too: by the same process, Russia was being integrated materially and politically into the expanding international structure of capitalist world development. That structure too exhibited an uneven and combined form. And this made it pregnant with new revolutionary possibilities.

According to Trotsky, the advanced capitalist countries were now 'over-ripe' for socialism. There, uniquely, the social conditions for capitalism's self-overcoming as itemized in Marx's *Capital* were already present. But political opportunities had been missed by the workers' movement, and its leading cadres had become a 'labour aristocracy', bought off by concessions financed in part by the proceeds of imperialism. However, Russia was now integrating into the capitalist world order. A Marxist-led revolution *there* would throw the political, military, financial and trading bases of that order into turmoil and trigger the long-awaited proletarian revolutions in the West. And these in turn would rescue the Russian

19 Ibid., p. 12.

revolution from the inevitable degeneration that awaited it if it were left without external support.

If we now step back and view Trotsky's argument as a whole, we can see something remarkable: at every step, the logic of capital as expounded by Marx has incorporated the international effects of capital's operation in a context of multiple co-existing societies. First, capital's transnational expansion is driven not only by an inner logic of 'reproduction on an expanded scale' but also by the 'whip of external necessity' and the 'privilege of historic back-wardness'. Second, capitalist development within societies that are incorporated under these conditions is necessarily diversified by its fusion of external with internal social forms. As Trotsky put it, 'the peculiarity of a national social type is the crystallization of the unevenness of its formation.'[20] And finally, the causal chain of social revolution itself is now distributed across multiple, differen-tially developed societies and their interactions, rather than being confined within a single society or even a single mode of produc-tion. Thus, while the idea of 'combined and uneven development' would visualise the international system as the societal logic of capital writ large, Trotsky's theory argued that in real history that logic was necessarily overdetermined by its operation in an *inter*-societal context. It was from this difference that the counter-intui-tive implications of UCD flowed. And they transformed both the sociological method and the political implications of a Marxist analysis.

Still, to view the full significance of all this, we must relate it back, beyond Marxism, to the problem of political realism. And we must do this in two steps, taking in successively the implications for inter-national theory and for social theory in general. First, the theory of uneven and combined development proves in a new way that real-ism's separation of the logic of anarchy from theories of society and social development is unnecessary and counterproductive. Not only does capitalism (as *Empire* argues) shape the modern form of the geopolitical 'anarchy'; but that geopolitical anarchy also inflects the overall course of capitalist world development – and in ways that the idea of UCD enables us to comprehend theoretically. In fact, in Trotsky's perspective the international looms even larger than in realism because (via mechanisms such as the 'whip' and the

20 L. Trotsky, *The Permanent Revolution* and *Results and Prospects*, trans-lated by Brian Pearce, London 1962, p. 24.

'privilege') it reaches into the internal historical constitution of societies themselves. And anarchy is rediscovered too as the interactive co-existence of entire *societies*, not only geopolitical actors. Not just politics then, but also social structures, belief systems, cultures, languages, artistic production and so on – all are now opened by UCD to an international analysis because all of them exist and evolve in the 'concrete correlations' among multiple, differential, interacting societies.

But there is a second, even larger, implication. 'Unevenness', wrote Trotsky, is 'the most general law of the historic process'.[21] This means not only that it applies to all empirical phenomena – nothing in reality is completely pure or absolutely regular – but also that it extends back beyond the capitalist epoch across world history. Due to the unevenness of social development, human society has never been singular and hence there has always existed an inter-societal dimension to social existence. This installs the interactive multiplicity of societies as a foundational premise of any social theory – including the materialist conception of history. In fact, 'unevenness' even 'goes behind' political realism to explain sociologically why the fact of geopolitical anarchy exists in the first place.[22] But how?

In a much-discussed passage in the 1857 'General Introduction' to the *Grundrisse*, Marx distinguishes between the transhistorical idea of 'labour in general' and the historically specific, commodified form of labour found uniquely in capitalist societies.[23] Chapter 5 of *Empire* compared this to the difference between 'anarchy in general' (the transhistorical claim espoused by realism) and the peculiar capitalist form of anarchy (which could, using Marx's method, explain the replacement of territorial empires by the modern state system).[24] Most commentaries on Marx's 'General Introduction' treat the passage in question as a simple rejection of transhistorical categories. In line with this, *Empire* discarded the idea of 'anarchy in general' as an empty truism. In fact, however, a

21 Trotsky, *History of the Russian Revolution*, p. 5.
22 J. Rosenberg, 'Basic Problems in the Theory of Uneven and Combined Development. Part II: Unevenness and Political Multiplicity', *Cambridge Review of International Affairs* 23: 10, 2010, pp. 165–89.
23 K. Marx, *Grundrisse*, translated by Martin Nicolaus, Harmondsworth 1973, pp. 103ff.
24 See above, pp. 145ff.

closer reading of Marx's discussion reveals a more complex picture, in which transhistorical and historically specific categories are interdependent.[25] It follows that the dismissal of 'anarchy in general' (given the undeniable fact of political multiplicity across human history) incurs a major liability: it leaves open a way for realism to restore its credentials through an appeal to pre-capitalist world history. Such an appeal would end by suggesting that even the historically specific anarchy of capitalist geopolitics was merely a variation on a perennial theme, rather than the exclusive product of a new, capitalist form of society. This was indeed a dangerous gap, but *Empire* did not have the theoretical tools to close it. Only by working through the ontological foundations of UCD did that become possible.[26] For UCD provides a means by which the particular form of modern society and the transhistorical fact of a plurality of social formations ('anarchy in general') can be thought together, with all the implications they have for each other. It provides, in effect, that great *desideratum* not only of international theory but also of the wider field of social theory, beset as it is by the problem of 'methodological nationalism': it provides a socio-logical template for integrating 'the international' into our general understanding of the social world.[27]

Integrating *Empire* and UCD

The question then arises: what are the implications of UCD for the argument of *Empire?* The answer, hopefully, is that it completes and strengthens the latter, but in a very particular way. Chapter 6 of *Empire* invoked Marx's identification of the social preconditions of capitalist accumulation, namely the privatization of property and the generalization of wage labour; like Marx, it used 'so-called

25 For the detailed argumentation, see Rosenberg, *Follies of Globalisation Theory*, pp. 69ff.
26 For this working through, see, in particular, Rosenberg, 'Basic Problems in the theory of uneven and combined development', pp. 165–89; 'The "philosophical premises" of uneven and combined development', *Review of International Studies* 39: 3, 2013, pp. 569–97; 'Kenneth Waltz and Leon Trotsky: anarchy in the mirror of uneven and combined development', *International Politics* 50: 2, 2013, pp. 183–230.
27 J. Rosenberg, 'Why is there no international historical sociology?', *European Journal of International Relations* 12: 3, 2006, pp. 307–40.

primitive accumulation' as an empirically open category for assembling all the different historical events and processes that fed into the widening production of those social preconditions; and it then correlated that widening to the changing forms of social power which eventually resulted in the modern international system. In doing so, however, the argument was forced to draw a line between theory and history. What could be theorized, with almost ideal-typical clarity, was the relationship between changing modes of production and the forms of geopolitical power. But the ways in which these changes had come about remained the stuff of history – contingent, messy, taking different forms in different places. Beyond asserting a general tendency of capital to universalize itself in a relentless process of geo-social expansion, *Empire* did not seek to extend its ideal-typical theorization of 'so-called primitive accumulation' into this contingent, messy, multiform stuff of historical process. The book's theoretical resources did not extend to that – largely because it had neglected the ontological signifi-cance of what it called 'anarchy in general'.

As we have seen, however, UCD repairs this neglect. It does so by adding 'unevenness' to the theoretical premises of historical mate-rialism itself. And it is this addition that enables it to integrate 'the international' into social theory. To wit: from the unevenness of human social development as a global whole arises the perennial multiplicity of societies; within that multiplicity arises the (histori-cally and ecologically rooted) differentiation of forms, scales and levels of development; from the co-existence (the 'concrete correla-tions') of these multiple, differentially developed societies flow both the pressure to interact (the 'whip of external necessity') and the unchaining of development from any unilinear frame (the 'privilege of historic backwardness'); and from these interactions arise not just the contents of international relations (geopolitics, war, trade and so on) but also the particular hybrid characteristics of individual socie-ties, their peculiarities and the necessarily dialectical shape of the historical process as a whole. Modern world history has comprised the emergence, within this dialectical process, of capitalist society with its unique forms of social and geopolitical power. Capitalism in turn has supercharged the historical process and accelerated its developmental tempo, creating for the first time a universal 'social structure of humanity'.[28] But in doing so, it has also proceeded via

28 Trotsky, *Permanent Revolution* and *Results and Prospects*, p. 9.

the inter-societal mechanisms of uneven and combined development, generating paradoxical, counter-intuitive outcomes that
cannot be understood within any unilinear theory.

Thus, *Empire* did not – *could* not – explain why and how the USSR
had come into existence, simply noting instead that its resistance to
the empire of civil society was the sociological content of the Cold
War, the central geopolitical and ideological conflict of postwar
international relations. By contrast UCD showed how the spatio-
temporal unevenness of capitalist world development – and its
resultant international dimension – had produced inside Russia that
social structure of 'belatedness' which generated the supposedly
impossible: a proletarian-led revolution in a largely pre-capitalist
society. In a similar way, *Empire* would have regarded the French
Revolution as simply the particular (and incomplete) manner in
which capitalist society was established in France. As E. P. Thompson
once put it: 'It happened one way in France, and another way here.'[29]
But UCD can be used to explain *why* it took that form in France –
and perhaps even why the very idea of social revolution as a leap
forward into a new form of society is a peculiarly modern (and internationally generated) phenomenon.[30] Finally, *Empire* could certainly
have integrated the rise of China as the delayed expansion of capitalist society into a demographically huge country. But it could not
on its own have explained either why this expansion was being
managed by a *communist* party or how, due to the privilege of historic
backwardness, it was proceeding even faster than other processes of
late industrialization had done, altering the shape of the world economy and generating unexpected political shockwaves.[31]

In short, UCD does not contradict Marx, but it does narrow the
gap between theory and history, enabling his explanatory method
to reach much deeper into the texture of the historical process.
And it does so specifically by reintegrating an inter-societal dimension which *Empire*, in its rush to reject the ahistoricism of political
realism, had too hastily set aside.

29 E. Thompson, *The Poverty of Theory and Other Essays*, London 1978, p. 269.
30 J. Rosenberg, 'Trotsky's Error: Multiplicity and the Secret Origins of Revolutionary Marxism', *Globalizations* 17, 2020, pp. 477–97.
31 J. Rosenberg and C. Boyle, 'Understanding 2016: Brexit and Trump in the History of Uneven and Combined Development', *Journal of Historical Sociology* 32: 1, March 2019, e32–e58.

As noted near the start of this Afterword, *Empire* was written with the aim of showing that Marxism deserves a place at the core of international theory. It later transpired, ironically, that 'the international' also deserves a place in the core of Marxist theorising. Arguably, neither place can be secured without deploying the multilinear perspective of UCD. But they cannot even be invoked without first applying to international relations Marx's principles of historical specificity and social totality. That was the foundational task that *The Empire of Civil Society* sought to undertake.

Notes

Introduction

1. E. Heller, *The Artist's Journey into the Interior*, London 1966, p. 3.
2. Cited in G. Therborn, *Science, Class and Society*, London 1976, pp. 172–3.
3. *The Twenty Years' Crisis*, 2nd edn, London 1946, reprinted Basingstoke 1981, p. 116.
4. The work of Susan Strange provides a leading and impressive example of the elaboration of the task of international political economy in these terms. See her discussion in *States and Markets: An Introduction to International Political Economy*, London 1988, pp. 13–14.
5. 'However natural it may appear to us to make that assumption, it is unjustified: market economy is an institutional structure which, as we all too easily forget, has been present at no time except our own ...' (K. Polanyi, *The Great Transformation*, Boston 1957, p. 37).
6. *The German Ideology* (Parts I and II), ed. R. Pascal, New York 1947, p. 15. This vocation should not be confused with the practical transcending of these social relations, which are sustained by material relations of power. However much one may wish to affirm the emancipatory potential of human self-understanding, it clearly does not follow that structures of power can be dissolved simply through a cognitive reappropriation of alienated social forms. This fallacy is something of an occupational hazard for political intellectuals, but seems most seriously to afflict sociologists of a phenomenological disposition and Hegelian Marxists. The latter case – which perhaps includes the epistemological concerns of some contemporary 'critical theory' – is especially puzzling given the merciless satire deployed against the 'innocent and child-like fancies' of the 'critical critics' in the opening pages of *The German Ideology*. Marx caricatures the Young Hegelians as follows: 'The phantoms of [men's] brains have gained the mastery over them. ... Let us revolt against the rule of thoughts. Let us teach men, says one, to exchange these imaginations for thoughts which correspond to the essence of man; says the second, to take up a critical attitude to them; says the third, to knock them out of their heads; and – existing reality will collapse.' (Ibid., p. 1.) For Marx, by contrast, 'commodity fetishism' is the perceptual component of a real process of alienation of human agency arising out of a specific configuration of social relations. Consciousness can apprehend this; it cannot, by itself, undo it. As Sayer puts it: 'Reification is a social process, not a mere category error.' (*Capitalism and Modernity*, London 1991, p. 65.)

7. For example, Waltz: 'Domestic systems are centralized and hierarchic. ... International systems are decentralized and anarchic. The ordering principles of the two structures are distinctly different, indeed, contrary to each other.' (Keohane, ed., *Neorealism and Its Critics*, New York 1986, p. 81.)

8. Ibid, p. 340.

9. Ibid, p. 53.

10. *War and Change in World Politics*, Cambridge 1981, p. 211. And Martin Wight held this to be the answer to the question 'Why is there no international theory?': 'If Sir Thomas More or Henry IV ... were to [contemplate] ... the international scene [of 1960] it is more likely that they would be struck by resemblances to what they remembered. ... The stage would have become much wider, the actors fewer, their weapons more alarming, but the play would be the same old melodrama. International politics is the realm of recurrence and repetition; it is the field in which political action is most regularly necessitous.' ('Why is There No International Theory?', in H. Butterfield and M. Wight, eds, *Diplomatic Investigations*, London 1966, p. 26.)

1. The Trouble with Realism

1. See Introduction, n. 10, above.

2. Each of these texts enjoys the status of a classic within the discipline. Carr's *The Twenty Years' Crisis*, first published on the eve of World War II, remains the most celebrated and powerful indictment of the 'peace through law' school of thought (also known to its realist critics as 'idealist' and 'utopian') which had pinned its hopes on the League of Nations and vainly imagined that the role of war in relations between states could be superseded by international law and arbitration. Hans Morgenthau's *Politics among Nations* (first published 1948) was the work of a German émigré to the US who sought to counter 'the depreciation of political power' and the excessive idealism of US foreign policy which, in his view, threatened to interfere with a responsible pursuit of the national interest. Writing in 1977, Stanley Hoffmann declared that 'If our discipline has any founding father, it is Morgenthau' ('An American Social Science: International Relations', *Daedalus*, Summer 1977, p. 44). This work, in its many editions, remained the the leading textbook on IR in US colleges for several decades. Finally, Kenneth Waltz's *Man, the State and War* (1959) is perhaps the best-known attempt to distil the essence of realist thought (anarchy/the balance of power) and to reconstitute it in the idiom of a deductive proof. For a fine historical survey of the realist school, see M.J. Smith, *Realist Thought from Weber to Kissinger*, Baton Rouge and London 1986.

3. In what follows I shall use 'realism' to indicate the critical mode of thought discussed by Carr, and realism to indicate the specific assumptions of Realist International Relations listed above. Numbers in parentheses indicate page references to *The Twenty Years' Crisis*, 2nd edn, London 1946, reprinted Basingstoke 1981.

4. *The Twenty Years' Crisis* was conceived in the months following Carr's resignation from a diplomatic career at the Foreign Office in 1936.

5. Carr, *The Twenty Years' Crisis*, 2nd edn, p. 108: 'power ... is organized nationally. ... In its essence, power is an indivisible whole. "The laws of social dynamics", a recent critic has said, "are laws which can only be stated in terms of power, not in terms of this or that form of power."'

6. '[T]he exercise of power always appears to beget the appetite for more power. There is, as Dr Niebuhr says, "no possibility of drawing a sharp line between the will-to-live and the will-to-power." (Ibid., p. 112.)

7. 'In 1914, Austria sent an ultimatum to Servia [*sic*] because she believed that Servians were planning the downfall of the Dual Monarchy; Russia feared that Austria-Hungary, if she defeated Servia, would be strong enough to menace her; Germany feared ... etc.' (Ibid., p. 111.)

8. In fact, Carr was perfectly aware of these themes and their significance. See, for example, his penetrating discussion of the linkage between the nineteenth-century world market and the possibility of a world of nation-states in *Nationalism and After*, London 1945, pp. 6–17. Our concern here, however, is with *The Twenty Years' Crisis* because of its status as a realist classic.

9. A term which Cobden had no scruples in using to describe his involvement in the free trade movement: 'most of us entered upon this struggle with the belief that we had some distinct class interest in the question.' (P. Adelman, *Victorian Radicalism*, London 1984, p. 3.)

10. Hoffman, 'An American Social Science: International Relations'.

11. In the discussion which follows numbers in parentheses indicate page references to Hans Morgenthau, *Politics among Nations*, 6th edn, New York 1985.

12. Cited by T. Taylor, 'Power Politics', in T. Taylor, ed., *Approaches and Theory in International Relations*, Harlow 1978, p. 125.

13. Morgenthau did not live to see the collapse of this order at the end of the 1980s.

14. K. Thompson, 'Toward a Theory of International Politics', in S. Hoffman, ed., *Contemporary Theory in International Relations*, Englewood Cliffs, New Jersey 1960, p. 35.

15. See 'Another "Great Debate": The National Interest of the US', reprinted in M. Smith et al., eds, *Perspectives on World Politics*, Beckenham 1981, p. 52.

16. P. Kennedy, *The Realities behind Diplomacy*, London 1981, p. 257.

17. Carr, *The Twenty Years' Crisis*, 1st Edn, London 1939, p. 14n.

18. It is surely conceding too much to accept, as Trevor Taylor appears to do, that idealism actually held sway over public policy in this period. Taylor writes of 'Utopian theory, whose application would (and did) lead to policy disaster.' (*Approaches and Theory in International Relations*, p. 124.) Even the claim for a purely intellectual ascendancy has been questioned. William Olsen noted of the interwar realist–idealist debate: 'In retrospect, one sometimes wonders ... just how much of a debate it ever really was and how many of the academic analysts of international relations, in contrast to vocal advocates of pacifism in its many versions, were actually "utopian". How many of them really allowed their desire for peace to override their scholarship?' (in B. Porter, ed., *The Aberystwyth Papers: International Politics, 1919–1969*, London 1972, p. 23.) Indeed, it is actually very difficult to pin down Carr himself on the question of how far 'utopian' views were in fact responsible for the failure of interwar policy. In chapter 2 of *The Twenty Years' Crisis* utopian thought is ascribed to ingenuous liberal governments vainly seeking with the support of public opinion to build the League of Nations as an implementation of Lockean principles. Later, however, these same governments are accused of *dis*ingenuously attempting 'to build up a new international morality on the foundation ... of the right of those in possession'. In the meantime, however, Carr has also identified as utopian the 'armchair students of international affairs' whose

fate, however, was to be completely ignored by both governments and public opinion. See *The Twenty Years' Crisis*, 2nd edn, pp. 27–8, 225 and 38 respectively.

19. M.J. Smith (p. 160) records that 'Whenever he faced strong disagreement with his approach and recommendations, Morgenthau called his opponents prisoners of sentiment or moralistic illusion.'

20. 'Political realism wants the photographic picture of the political world to resemble as much as possible its painted portrait' (10).

21. Thus Noam Chomsky cites Morgenthau complaining that revisionist critics of US policy 'confound the abuse of reality with reality itself'. Chomsky unravels this conundrum after his usual fashion: 'It is the unachieved "national purpose", revealed by "the evidence of history as our minds reflect it", which is the reality; the actual historical record is merely the abuse of reality.' 'Intellectuals and the State', reprinted in his *Towards a New Cold War*, New York 1982, p. 74.

22. For an account of the centrality of *Politics among Nations* in the postwar evolution of the American discipline, see J. Vasquez, *The Power of Power Politics: A Critique*, London 1983, p. 17.

23. This applies not only to Waltz's work, considered below, but also to the so-called 'behavioural revolt' of the 1960s which introduced the methodologies of systems theory into IR. As Vasquez suggested: 'The behavioural revolt challenged not the picture of the world that the realists had provided but the realist conception of what constitutes an adequate scientific theory and the procedures used to 'verify' that theory'. (Ibid., p. 23.)

24. In the treatment of Waltz here, explicit consideration is not given to his later *Theory of International Politics* (Reading, Mass. 1979). However, insofar as Waltz in 1979 was still exercising the same problematic as in 1959, albeit at a slightly higher level of abstraction, the same fundamental criticisms apply. In this respect, it could certainly be argued that *Theory of International Politics* is not a theoretical advance on *Man, the State and War*. The latter, however, has achieved the status of a classic text within IR, and is widely used in the teaching of the discipline.

25. The 'level of analysis' problem in IR concerns the 'level' at which theories claiming to explain international outcomes should be constructed. Briefly, should we focus on the psychological dispositions of the individuals or masses concerned, the political character of individual states, or the structural properties of the states-system as a whole? Waltz calls these options the First Image, the Second Image and the Third Image. He uses this classification as the framework for a critical review of a range of answers to the question: What is the cause of war? The range includes religious and psychological theories of human nature (First Image), the liberal and socialist identification of militarism and war with particular – feudal and capitalist – kinds of state (Second Image), and scenarios of the state of nature (anarchy) and unregulated competition from political philosophy and game theory respectively (Third Image). The discussion of Waltz which follows is confined to this Third Image.

26. In this section, numbers in parentheses indicate references to *Man, the State and War*, New York 1959.

27. For a survey of the extensive application of game theory in IR, see J.E. Dougherty and R.L. Pfaltzgraff, *Contending Theories of International Relations*, New York 1981.

28. As Waltz himself was later to put it: 'Students of international politics make distinctions between international-political systems only according to the number of their great powers.' (Keohane, ed., p. 92.)

29. Fred Halliday has provided a stimulating critique of this realist conception of the state, terming it 'the national territorial totality'. See 'State and Society in International Relations: A Second Agenda', *Millennium*, Summer 1987.

30. M. Howard, 'The Concept of Peace', *Encounter*, 61 (4), December 1983, p. 24.

31. A. Giddens, *The Nation-State and Violence*, Cambridge 1985, p. 26.

32. As Stanley Hoffman put it (p. 41): 'Modern sociology and political science emancipated themselves from political and social history, political philosophy, and public law in the nineteenth century. International relations did not.'

33. B. Jenkins and G. Minnerup, *Citizens and Comrades*, London 1984, pp. 146–7.

34. For a systematic elaboration of the significance of revolutions for the study of international relations, see F. Halliday, '"The Sixth Great Power": On the Study of Revolution and International Relations', *Review of International Studies*, 16 (3), July 1990.

35. M. Wight, *Power Politics*, Harmondsworth 1986, p. 92n.

36. A phrase coined by Halliday: 'State and Society in International Relations: A Second Agenda'.

37. Morgenthau, *Politics among Nations*, p. 335.

38. Quotations are from members of the Council on Foreign Relations, cited by L. Shoup and W. Minter, 'Shaping a New World Order: The Council on Foreign Relations' Blueprint for World Hegemony', in H. Sklar ed., *Trilateralism*, Boston 1980, pp. 146 and 149.

2. Social Structures and Geopolitical Systems

1. The term 'geopolitics' is often associated with the geographical determinism of such writers as Friedrich Ratzel, Halford Mackinder and N.J. Spykman. This is not the sense intended here, where it will be used to indicate simply the external relations by which one social order forms part of a larger social formation – irrespective of the form or dynamic which these relations might assume. It is this latter caveat which rules out the use of the more familiar 'international', which designates the specifically modern form of geopolitics.

2. D.J. Hill, *A History of Diplomacy in the International Development of Europe*, Vol. 3, London 1914, p. 339. See also Morgenthau, *Politics among Nations*, p. 199, and Wight, *Power Politics*, p. 174. There are writers who remember Utrecht in rather different terms: 'at the Peace of Utrecht, England extorted from the Spaniards ... the privilege of being allowed to ply the slave trade. ... Liverpool grew fat on the basis of the slave trade.' (K. Marx, *Capital*, Vol. I, introduced by E. Mandel, Harmondsworth 1976, p. 924.)

3. M. Wight, *Systems of States*, Leicester 1977, p. 111. For a discussion of the circumstances, see G. Mattingly, *Renaissance Diplomacy*, Harmondsworth 1965, chapter 8.

4. For detailed discussion of Westphalia, see K. Holsti, *Peace and War: Armed Conflicts and International Order 1648–1989*, Cambridge 1991, chapter 2.

5. Wight *Systems of States*, p. 129.

6. See Hill, vol. 3, pp. 332–4.

7. For the following, see E. Wolf, *Europe and the People without History*, Berkeley 1982, pp. 151–3.

8. J. Viner, 'Power versus Plenty as Objectives of Foreign Policy in the Seventeenth and Eighteenth Centuries', *World Politics*, 1 (1), 1948, p. 10. It must be said that Viner's account provides a striking instance of how 'the pre-bourgeois forms of the social organization of production are treated by political economy in much the same way as the Fathers of the Church treated pre-Christian religions.' (Marx, *Capital*, Vol. I, p. 175.)

9. These points will be considered in more detail in chapter 4 below.

10. See W. E. Minchinton, *The Growth of English Overseas Trade in the 17th and 18th Centuries*, London 1969, pp. 10–11.

11. Wolf, pp. 138–9.

12. The Dutch method was to occupy an island territory, concentrate production in a single spice, and systematically destroy any other cultivation of it within the regions under their control. 'Thus Amboyna became the clove island, the Bandas the mace and nutmeg islands and Ceylon the cinnamon island.' (F. Braudel, *The Perspective of the World*, London 1984, p. 218.)

13. For the following, see ibid., pp. 216–19.

14. Wolf, p. 153.

15. H.G. Koenigsberger, *Early Modern Europe, 1500–1789*, Harlow 1987, p. 172.

16. E. Hobsbawm, *The Age of Revolution*, p. 184.

17. To those who demanded a direct military intervention in Spain in 1823 on the grounds that France's counterrevolutionary invasion had upset the balance of power, the British Foreign Secretary declared: 'If France occupied Spain, was it necessary ... that we should blockade Cadiz? No. I looked another way – I sought materials of compensation in another hemisphere. Contemplating Spain, such as our ancestors had known her, I resolved that if France had Spain, it should not be Spain "with the Indies". I called the New World into existence to redress the balance of the Old.' (Cited in K. Bourne, ed., *The Foreign Policy of Victorian England*, Oxford 1970, p. 210.)

18. Wolf, pp. 172–3.

19. I. Kant, *Perpetual Peace and Other Essays*, ed. T. Humphrey, Indianapolis 1983, p. 108.

20. This insistence on the premodernity of Utrecht could, if due care were not taken, be as misleading as the realist vision which it seeks to displace. For the great beneficiary of Utrecht – namely England – was already an agrarian capitalist society, developing within a non-capitalist social world which it would later revolutionize. This observation underlines the need to move ultimately to a more complex historical understanding than the one deployed polemically here – that is, from monolithic structural contrasts of geopolitical systems to a more empirically open and dynamic account of their combined and uneven development. That said, this injunction only reinforces further the overall argument of this section, namely the need for a *historical* understanding. I owe these points to Ellen Wood.

21. The need for such a periodization has been reiterated recently by A. Linklater in *Beyond Realism and Marxism: Critical Theory and International Relations*, London 1990 (p. 142). It seems, however, that Linklater may not undertake its construction, being more immediately concerned with advancing the Habermasian project of Critical Theory in IR. For his definition of this latter task, see ibid., p. 143.

22. 'The Origins of Our States-System: Geographical Limits', in *Systems of States*, p. 114.

23.   F.H. Hinsley insisted that '...a new European states' system emerged in the eighteenth century and not at an earlier date.' (*Power and the Pursuit of Peace*, Cambridge 1963, p. 153.) David Jayne Hill represents the widest consensus in his affirmation that in the international development of Europe 'the Peace of Westphalia was the most important ... public act of modern history, for from it dates the present political system of Europe as a group of independent sovereign states.' (Vol. 2, London 1906, p. 599.) However, the French invasion of Italy is another commonly cited turning point: for example, Dehio: 'the new structure came into existence at a quite definite moment, the beginning of the struggle among the great powers over Italy in 1494.' (*The Precarious Balance*, London 1963, p. 23.) Further complications are introduced by the precocious behaviour of the major Italian city-states, which not only pioneered the use of standing diplomacy but also concluded what can be regarded as the first collective security treaty, the Peace of Lodi, 1454. (For a discussion of the latter, see Mattingly, chapter 8.)

24.   Wight, *Systems of States*, p. 129.

25.   Ibid., p. 151.

26.   Ibid., p. 131.

27.   Ibid., p. 151–2.

28.   Wight cites these as other examples of 'the kind of states-system we are concerned with' (ibid., p. 22) – though he has doubts about the Indian case. And he is by no means alone in identifying the surface effect of separate sovereignties as the core indicator in any history of the emergence of the modern international system. Dehio's 1963 study, *The Precarious Balance*, declares the same intention in its opening sentence: 'It is possible to imagine a history of the Western world that relates all events to the two principles of unity and diversity' (p. 19). (Was he aware that Ibn Khaldun invoked almost the same oscillatory dynamic as the theme of the Arab civilization of the Maghreb?) F.H. Hinsley's work of the same year is organized almost exclusively around the slow 'shift of emphasis, from concentration on Europe's unity to concentration on the autonomy of its states' (*Power and the Pursuit of Peace*, p. 162). Most recently, Alan Watson's *The Evolution of International Society* (London 1992) offers to organize geopolitical systems from ancient Sumer to the present along a single spectrum from independence to empire.

29.   Anderson's felicitous phrase (*Lineages of the Absolutist State*, London 1974, p. 44n), directed at another work.

30.   The 'transnationalist' school of thought, which sought among other things to make this addition, did not seek to *replace* realism. Rather, Keohane and Nye's model of 'complex interdependence' (*Power and Interdependence*, Boston 1977) was offered as an additional ideal-type, making it possible to register and explain deviations from the realist ideal-type which remained the underlying norm. See ibid., p. 24: 'We do not argue ... that complex interdependence faithfully reflects world political reality. Quite the contrary: both it and the realist portrait are ideal types. Most situations will fall somewhere between these two extremes'. Consistently with this, Keohane himself later embraced a 'neorealist' position as the deterioration of East–West relations gave a renewed centrality in IR theory to the militarily defined balance of power.

31.   A. Giddens, *The Constitution of Society*, Cambridge 1984, pp. 30–1.

32.   This list of questions amalgamates and abbreviates the rival lists advanced by Bull and Kaplan in their philippics of 1966. See H. Bull, 'International Theory: The Case for a Classical Approach', *World Politics*, 18 (3), 1966, pp. 367, and M.

Kaplan, 'The New Great Debate: Traditionalism vs Science in International Relations', *World Politics*, 19 (1), 1966, pp. 10–11.

33. For a summary of 'the injection of history into the social sciences' in the early nineteenth century, see Hobsbawm, *The Age of Revolutions*, pp. 344–7. And for the subsequent *de*historicizing of the same disciplines in the last quarter of the same century, see Hobsbawm, *The Age of Empire*, pp. 269–75.

34. It is a curious feature of the revival of interest in the state within historical sociology that it has tended to adopt a broadly realist perspective, seeking to identify irreducible properties and dynamics of state power. Perry Anderson's reviews (now gathered in *A Zone of Engagement*, London 1992) of Mann's and Runciman's works, albeit not rendered in an IR idiom, contain stimulating theoretical criticisms of the 'power political' perspective implicit in their historical analyses. Paul Cammack, concentrating on the domestic activities of the state, has delivered a strong polemical challenge to the status and coherence of arguments for 'state autonomy' ('Bringing the State Back In?', *British Journal of Science*, April 1989). And within IR, unease has been expressed over what is seen as the uncritical adoption of realist arguments by some historical sociologists – notably Michael Mann. See A. Jarvis, 'Societies, States and Geopolitics: Challenges from Historical Sociology', *Review of International Studies*, 15 (3), 1989. For a discussion of Giddens's work which attempts, perhaps unwisely, to distinguish its provenance from that of the 'bringing the state back in' literature, see J. Rosenberg, 'Giddens' *Nation-State and Violence*: A Non-Realist Theory of Sovereignty?', *Millennium*, Summer 1990.

35. For a clear overview of the postwar evolution of social theory, organized around this question, see I. Craib, *Modern Social Theory*, Brighton 1984.

36. The principal texts relating to this discussion of Giddens's work are *The Constitution of Society*, *The Nation-State and Violence* and *A Contemporary Critique of Historical Materialism* (Basingstoke 1981). Does Giddens recognize the inbuilt limitation mentioned in the text above? 'The concepts of structuration theory, as with any competing theoretical perspective, should for many research purposes be regarded as sensitizing devices, nothing more.' (*The Constitution of Society*, p. 326.) For a powerful challenge to both the originality and the theoretical efficacy of Giddens's work, see D. Sayer, 'Reinventing the Wheel: Anthony Giddens, Karl Marx and Social Change', in J. Clark et al., eds, *Anthony Giddens: Consensus and Controversy*, London 1990.

37. E. Hobsbawm, 'The Crisis of the Seventeenth Century', in T. Aston, ed., *Crisis in Europe, 1560–1660*, London 1965, pp. 18–19. For the debates on the structural location of the early modern market, see R. Hilton, ed., *The Transition from Feudalism to Capitalism*, London 1976; Aston, ed., *Crisis in Europe*; and more generally the work of R. Brenner, especially, 'The Origins of Capitalist Development: A Critique of Neo-Smithian Marxism', *New Left Review*, 104, July/August 1977.

38. J. Merrington, 'Town and Country in the Transition to Capitalism', in R. Hilton, ed., *The Transition from Feudalism to Capitalism*, London 1976, p. 179.

39. 'To be a human being is to be an agent – although not all agents are human beings – and to be an agent is to have power. "Power" in this highly generalized sense means "transformative capacity", the capability to intervene in a given set of events so as in some way to alter them.' (Giddens, *The Nation-State and Violence*, p. 7.

40. The conditions of reproduction may extend far beyond those aspects of social reality which they invoke directly and formally.

41. See, for example, Giddens *The Constitution of Society*, pp. 12–13: 'to say that the existence of a social state A needs a social practice B to help it to survive in recognizably similar form is to pose a question that then has to be answered; it does not itself answer it. The relation between A and B is not analogous to the relation that obtains between wants or needs and intentions in the individual actor. In the individual, wants that are constitutive of the motivational impulses of the actor generate a dynamic relation between motivation and intentionality. This is not the case with social systems, except where actors behave in cognizance of what they take to be social needs.' In other words, 'What "must happen" for certain conditions of system reproduction to occur is posed as a counterfactual question, not as a covert version of functionalism.' (Ibid. p. 191.) See also D. Sayer, *The Violence of Abstraction*, Oxford 1987, chapter 5.

42. *Lineages of the Absolutist State*, p. 216

43. A point reiterated recently by Fred Halliday with reference to Kenneth Waltz's claim that 'The death rate among states is remarkably low'. Cf. 'Theorizing the International', *Economy and Society*, 18 (3), August 1989, p. 355.

44. *The Constitution of Society*, p. 242.

45. This formulation follows, as I understand it, the outline of Roy Bhaskar's position, summarized in Craib, pp. 20–23.

46. Wolf, p. 76.

47. *The Constitution of Society*, p. 164. Incidentally, this formulation does at least avoid the unnecessary embarrassment which some sociologists declare at the sense of closure implied in the word 'society'. For example Mann: 'It may seem an odd position for a sociologist to adopt; but if I could, I would abolish the concept of "society" altogether.' (*The Sources of Social Power*, Vol. 1, Cambridge 1986, p. 2.) It *is* odd. As Giddens suggests (*The Constitution of Society*, p. 163), the ambiguity of the term (totality/association) is actually a fruitful one. John Hall cites the rejection of 'classical sociology's concept of society' as a novel conclusion arising from the work of British historical sociology. (See J. Hall, ' They Do Things Differently There, or, The Contribution of British Historical Sociology', *British Journal of Sociology*, 40 (4), December 1989.) In fact, there is nothing new in the radical rejection of a notion of 'society' as the object of sociological inquiry. The tradition extends back at least as far as Simmel and arguably includes Weber himself. (See D. Frisby and D. Sayer, *Society*, London 1986, pp. 54ff.) That there are ways of introducing the necessary qualifications without abandoning the attempt to theorize social totalities may be seen from Perry Anderson's weighing of the terms 'society' and 'social formation'. (*Passages from Antiquity to Feudalism*, London 1974). And Marx himself inveighed against the use of the term 'society' as an abstraction. See the selections gathered on p. 19 of *Readings from Karl Marx*, ed. D. Sayer, London 1989.

48. For the following, see Wolf, pp. 73–7.

49. Some ethnomethodologists would contest this because of the very use of the notion of structure; but there is no necessary conflict between the insistence that all social action is locally and actively *produced* by the knowledgeable practice of the agents involved and claims for more remote or diffuse forms of social *causality*. Giddens's assimilation of 'practical consciousness' to the recursive definition of structure is one way of allowing for this.

50. Marx, *Capital*, Vol. I, p. 290.

51. Idem, *Capital*, Vol. III, p. 791, italics added.

52. Sayer discusses this point in chapter 6 of *The Violence of Abstraction*, p. 148.

53. For one such treatment, see W. Mommsen, *The Age of Bureaucracy*, Oxford 1974. Beetham also gives some credence to this, albeit nuanced differently: *Max Weber and the Theory of Modern Politics*, 2nd edn, Cambridge 1985.

54. Craib, p. 26.

55. It is a curious feature of Giddens's work that, despite the initially constructive character of its engagement with Marx, it has persistently exhibited this most widespread of caricatures. Indeed, his own generic theory of power, elaborated in the two volumes of *A Contemporary Critique of Historical Materialism*, is premissed upon the claim that historical materialism is incapable of grasping the discrete importance of 'authoritative resources' in the reproduction of social structures, involuntarily reducing them to the class analysis of 'allocative resources' which supposedly defines its optic. But Giddens is actually a great hedger on this issue: he will not say what comprises *his* understanding of the potential of historical materialism. He rarely mentions it without adding a rider such as 'if that term be taken to refer to the interpretation of history that Marx outlines in the "Preface" to *A Contribution to the Critique of Political Economy*' (*The Nation-State and Violence*, p. 8). More than once, the term retreats into scare-quotes. (Compare, for example, the usages on pp. xxix, 34 and 227 of *The Constitution of Society*.) Sayer has described certain aspects of Giddens's account of Marx as 'simply laughable' ('Reinventing the Wheel', p. 242).

56. Marx, *Grundrisse*, foreword by M. Nicolaus, Harmondsworth 1973, p. 472.

57. For a clear account of why the base–superstructure model set out in the 1859 Preface cannot be taken as representative of Marx's historical method, see E. Wood, 'Marxism and the Course of History', *New Left Review*, 147, September/October 1984.

58. A. Gramsci, *Selections from Prison Notebooks*, ed. Q. Hoare and G.N. Smith, London 1971, p. 176.

59. Hedley Bull (*The Anarchical Society*, London 1977, pp. 13–14) sought to distinguish between an international *society* (showing the features just mentioned) and an international *system* (comprising the bare co-existence and interaction of states which however make no formal recognition of common interests and rules of behaviour). In terms of the usage of the term society adopted here, this would be to suggest that we could conceive a system that was not a social system. This is clearly a nonsense, and I recognize that Bull's usage is different; but in that case it must be challenged on historical grounds: did such geopolitical systems ever exist? To reserve the term 'society' for systems which show formal, bureaucratically ordered institutions is misleading – a hangover from a tradition of political theory in which it seems all too easy to mistake the theoretical device of the 'state of nature' for the description of a real historical condition.

60. 'The nation-state, which exists in a complex of other nation-states, is a set of institutional forms of governance maintaining an administrative monopoly over a territory with demarcated boundaries (borders), its rule being sanctioned by law and direct control of the means of internal and external violence.' (Giddens, *The Nation-State and Violence*, p. 121.)

61. This is why it is very difficult to ask a question like 'Why do states compete?' without fortifying proto-realist assumptions about how to explain international politics. Difficult though not impossible: if one were to ask the question 'Why do *people* compete?', two kinds of answer might be returned: a naturalistic answer in terms of human nature; and a sociological answer in terms of historically specific

institutions and practices. It is important to observe, however, that the latter answer, while being more satisfying, does overturn the form of the question. Addressing a similar issue in *The German Ideology* (pp. 34–5), Marx and Engels noted that Feuerbach 'says "man" instead of "real, historical men". "Man" is really "the German".' The paraphrase almost writes itself: realism says 'states' instead of 'real, historical institutions of political rule'. 'The state' is really 'the capitalist state'. These points will be developed in more detail in chapter 5 below.

62. V. Berghahn, *Militarism: History of an International Debate*, Cambridge 1984; M. Mann, 'Capitalism and Militarism', in *War, State and Society*, London 1984; and idem, 'War and Social Theory: Into Battle with Classes, Nations and States', in M. Shaw and C. Creighton, eds, *The Sociology of War and Peace*, London 1987.

63. For a discussion, see Therborn, pp. 168 and 177ff.

64. Polanyi, p. 5.

3. Secret Origins of the State

1. Wight, *Power Politics*, p. 30. This is a fleeting reference. Neither Wight, nor Bull, nor Hinsley gives any systematic consideration to the question of what the conditions of this (by their own account) world-historical development might have been.

2. *The Twenty Years' Crisis*, 2nd edn, p. 63.

3. Petrarch, cited in Anderson, *Lineages of the Absolutist State*, p. 149.

4. Sortition here refers to the drawing of lots as a means of filling public office.

5. Less commonly remarked is the reappearance in strength in Renaissance Italy of another prominent classical institution: slavery. Denys Hay (*Europe in the Fourteenth and Fifteenth Centuries*, London 1966, pp. 374–5) suggests that in fourteenth-century Genoa, slaves may have accounted for 10 per cent of the population. However, as Anderson emphasizes, these tended to be domestic servants, slave labour in production being confined to the overseas sugar plantation and mining colonies (*Lineages of the Absolutist State*, p. 151).

6. 'The Eighteenth Brumaire of Louis Bonaparte', in *Surveys from Exile: Political Writings*, Vol. II, ed. D. Fernbach, Harmondsworth 1973, p. 149.

7. 'State and Society in International Relations: A Second Agenda', p. 217.

8. The Communes were by no means united in their hostility to the Empire. Many of them had, after all, sealed their independence from episcopal rule by winning imperial recognition of their autonomy. (See D. Waley, *The Italian City-Republics*, 3rd edn, Harlow 1988, pp. 32–4.) And the papal–imperial contest would continue to provide the ideological form – though decreasingly the actual content – of both geopolitical and internal factional conflicts for many years to come. On the Guelphs and the Ghibellines, see Waley, pp. 145–56, who also gives instances where this diplomatic partisanship continued to have a very real material basis – e.g. Florentine Guelphism (p. 148).

9. *Lineages of the Absolutist State*, p. 143.

10. Mattingly, p. 65.

11. The ruling groups of the early Communes were the major landholders; the later rise of trade did not produce a landless commercial bourgeoisie (an index perhaps of the very weakness here of seigniorial power). By contrast with the cities of northern Europe, 'the quintessential burgher ... is not identifiable' in Italy (Waley, p. 118).

12. G. Holmes, *Europe: Hierarchy and Revolt, 1320–1450*, Glasgow 1975, p. 81.

13. The procedure for the election of the Venetian Doge comprised no less than *five* ballots in succession, each one (except the last) immediately stymied by a further selection by lot. See Hay, p. 120, and for further examples, Waley, p. 37.

14. See Waley, pp. 42–3.

15. Ibid., p. 43.

16. Anderson, *Passages from Antiquity to Feudalism*, p. 192.

17. A. Sereni, *The Italian Conception of International Law*, New York 1943, p. 42.

18. '[M]edieval treaty law was usually contained in the glosses and commentaries on contract law ... individuals rather than sovereign states were the principal subjects of international law.' (J.L. Holzgrefe, 'The Origins of Modern International Relations Theory', *Review of International Studies*, 15 (1), 1989, pp. 13–14.)

19. Mattingly, p. 53.

20. Waley, p. 68.

21. For a brief but pregnant discussion of the operation of religious legitimation in hierarchical modes of domination, see Wolf, p. 83.

22. Cited in Sereni, p. 14.

23. Waley, p. 88.

24. Ibid., p. 49

25. Sereni, p. 11.

26. Giddens observes the simultaneous and interlinked emergence of domestic and international political structures with respect to the rise of the nation-state. See especially *The Nation-State and Violence*, chapter 4.

27. Waley, p. 42.

28. Holmes, pp. 81–2.

29. Matteo Visconti secured the Imperial Vicariate in 1294 (Hay, p. 167).

30. Among the exceptions were Venice and Florence, which had expanded sufficiently to secure their own defences.

31. Cited in Waley, p. 158. For a discussion of the formal survival of republican institutions, see L. Martines, *Power and Imagination: City-States in Renaissance Italy*, New York 1979, pp. 102ff.

32. Martines (p. 103) observes that 'For all their original violence, *signori* knew that they could endure only by regularizing procedures and affecting to side with the rule of law ... The major legislative bodies survived in nearly all the cities that fell subject to signorial rule.'

33. Cosimo held supreme public office for only three two-month terms during the entire period of his ascendancy (H. Hearder and D.P. Waley, *A Short History of Italy*, Cambridge 1963, p. 85).

34. Marx, 'Critique of Hegel's *Rechtsphilosophie*', reprinted in *Readings from Karl Marx*, p. 116.

35. See Holzgrefe, p. 12.

36. Mattingly, p. 53.

37. 'On the Jewish Question', reprinted in *Readings From Karl Marx*, p. 125.

38. See, for example, 'The Critique of Politics and Political Economy: Capitalism, Communism and the State in Marx's Writings of the mid-1840s', *Sociological Review*, 33 (2), 1985.

39. *Readings from Karl Marx*, p. 124.

40. Ibid.

41. For a discussion of the last three of these, drawn from the same texts, see Sayer, 'The Critique of Politics and Political Economy', pp. 230–3.

42. Hill's phrase, Vol. I, London 1905, p. 359. Butterfield similarly allows that for many commentators 'the states of the Renaissance ... formed a neat closed area ... an arena of limited size ... a field of interacting forces such as can be envisaged for the most part in isolation.' ('The Balance of Power', in *Diplomatic Investigations*, London 1966, p. 133.) Mattingly's gripping history, by concentrating on the emergence of ambassadors, has this disadvantage. And viewed from the other side of the Alps, this geopolitical isolation has a similarly deceptive effect: Renaissance Italy is one of the stranger silences of Mann's *Sources of Social Power*.

43. The lack of a common culture does not appear to have inhibited the growth of a flourishing 'international society' in the eastern Mediterranean at this time: 'It must be especially stressed that Italian states attributed more or less the same legal value to agreements concluded with Mohammedan sovereigns as to those concluded with Christian states.' (Sereni, p. 28.) On the contrary, all the cultural and political authority of the Church itself seems to have been unable to *suppress* Christian intercourse with the Muslim world: 'This constant repetition of ecclesiastical prohibitions was an indication of the laxity with which they were observed.' (Ibid.)

44. Waley, p. 8.

45. Braudel, p. 109.

46. H. Adelson, *Medieval Commerce*, Princeton 1962, p. 74.

47. Waley, p. 23.

48. For the following, see Adelson, pp. 76–7.

49. Sereni, p. 22.

50. Ibid., pp. 19–20.

51. Braudel, p. 143. The Portuguese, however, never established effective control over supply in the Far East. And, in addition, Levantine demand for European products such as copper helped divert the flow of eastern spices back into their old caravan routes. (K. Glamann, 'European Trade 1500–1750', in C. Cipolla, ed., *The Fontana Economic History of Europe: Vol. II: The Sixteenth and Seventeenth Centuries*, Glasgow 1974, pp. 478–9.) Hence, by the middle of the century, the Levant trade, measured by volume, had returned to its old levels. See J.H. Parry, *The Age of Reconnaissance*, London 1973, p. 69.

52. Hobsbawm, 'The Crisis of the Seventeenth Century', p. 16.

53. Holmes, p. 71.

54. Braudel (p. 136) avers of Venice, 'probably the leading industrial centre in Europe', that '[t]he primacy of commercial capitalism over industrial capitalism until at least the eighteenth century is not seriously challenged.'

55. R. Davis, *The Rise of the Atlantic Economies*, London 1973, pp. 26–7.

56. Waley, p. 23.

57. Holmes, p. 72. Braudel describes how 'all the international aspects of the Champagne fairs were controlled on the spot or at a distance by Italian merchants' (p. 112), while Davis (p. 27) gives an instance of their more long-lived financial dominance: as late as the sixteenth century, 'At Lyon, the most important financial centre in the West, 143 out of 169 leading houses ... were Italian.'

58. Holmes, pp. 68–9, Hay, p. 376.

59. Holmes, p. 95.

60. Anderson, *Passages from Antiquity to Feudalism*, p. 193.

61. Holmes, p. 96.

62. Which itself, as Anderson notes, was made possible by the 'parcellization

NOTES TO PAGES 73-76

of sovereignty' characterizing the feudal mode of production. (*Passages from Antiquity to Feudalism*, p. 193.)

63. He ploughs not, he sows not, he reaps not. (Braudel, p. 108.)

64. Francesco Gucciardini, 1536, reprinted in J. Ross and M. McLaughlin, eds, *The Portable Renaissance Reader*, Harmondsworth 1968, pp. 280–81.

65. One of the most dramatic (though slightly later) demonstrations of this came when the merchants of Genoa, which 'was constantly surrendering to other powers, either forcibly, voluntarily or out of prudence' (Braudel, p. 158), imposed terms on the King of Spain: 'When in 1575, the king of Spain quarrelled with them and decided to do without their services, they succeeded in blocking the circulation of gold. The unpaid Spanish troops mutinied and sacked Antwerp in November 1576. And the king was eventually obliged to give in.' (Ibid., p. 168.)

66. These included not only textiles and eastern luxuries, but, in the case of Milan especially, a considerable quantity of weapons.

67. See Waley, p. 92, Adelson, pp. 74 and 79–80, respectively.

68. Marx, *Capital*, Vol. III, chapter XX, p. 325. The full sentence is worth reproducing: 'Since merchant's capital is penned in the sphere of circulation, and since its function consists exclusively of promoting the exchange of commodities, it requires no other conditions for its existence – aside from the undeveloped forms arising from direct barter – outside those necessary for the simple circulation of commodities and money.' This contrasts drastically with modes of *production*, feudal, capitalist, etc., which require very extensive economic and political conditions for their existence.

69. See Waley (p. 23), who says that 'the population was certainly not rooted to its home city. In the case of the larger cities much involved in long-distance trade … a quite sizeable proportion of the adult male citizens must have been away on business.'

70. Anderson, *Lineages of the Absolutist State*, p. 153.

71. Mattingly, p. 65.

72. Ibid., pp. 186–7.

73. Waley, p. xvi.

74. Sabine's charge (*A History of Political Theory*, London 1941, p. 352) that Machiavelli misread the spirit of the age insofar as he advocated *raison d'état* on the eve of the Wars of *Religion* is thus not wholly satisfactory: if these conflicts brought religion to the fore, it was precisely because they mediated the final collapse of Christendom and the rise of the secular state-system. Every confessional dispute, by receiving a secular settlement, itself became part of the emergence of the 'political state'. Thus Mattingly (p. 266) notes of the new doctrines of extraterritoriality which emerged in the sixteenth century: 'Probably the largest single factor in preparing men's minds to accept this extraordinary fiction was the embassy chapel question'. Something similar applies to the precept of *cujus regio, ejus religio*, another secular principle founded explicitly upon a reorganization of religious authority.

75. R. Gilpin, 'The Richness of the Tradition of Political Realism', in R. Keohane, ed., *Neorealism and Its Critics*, New York 1986, p. 306.

76. Dougherty and Pfaltzgraff, p. 469.

77. Thucydides, *History of the Peloponnesian War*, ed. M. Finley, Harmondsworth 1972, p. 49.

78. Ibid., pp. 400ff.

79. *Systems of States*, p. 66.
80. M. Wight, 'Western Values in International Relations', in H. Butterfield and M. Wight, eds, *Diplomatic Investigations*, London 1966, p. 127.
81. For example, R. Purnell, 'Theoretical Approaches to International Relations: The Contribution of the Graeco-Roman World', in T. Taylor, ed., *Approaches and Theory in International Relations*, Harlow 1978, pp. 19–20. The lack of Greek discussions of a balance of power has of course not prevented writers, from David Hume onwards, from trying to read this institution back into the Classical world. Hume's reasoning visibly strains as he attempts to understand the Greek silence: 'the maxim of preserving the balance of power is founded so much on common sense and obvious reasoning that it is impossible it could altogether have escaped antiquity.' 'Of the Balance of Power', reproduced in M. Wright, ed., *Theory and Practice of the Balance of Power, 1486–1914*, London 1975, p. 189.
82. Purnell,'Theoretical Approaches to International Relations', pp. 27–8. Sabine (p. 109) observes similarly: 'The modern distinction between the state and society is one which no Greek thinker made clearly and adequately.'
83. *Passages from Antiquity to Feudalism*, p. 43.
84. For example, by Weber in chapter XVI of *Economy and Society*, ed. G. Roth and C. Wittich, Berkeley 1978, and more concisely by Anderson in *Lineages of the Absolutist State*, pp. 150–56.
85. For the latter, see R.J. Hopper, *Trade and Industry in Classical Greece*, London 1979, p. 74.
86. Ibid., p. 11.
87. M.I. Finley, *The Ancient Greeks*, London 1963, p. 28. It seems also to be the case that the waves of colonization in the eighth and seventh centuries which created the multipolar Greek system were undertaken not in pursuit of trade but under the pressure of demographic and agrarian crisis in the early communities. See ibid., pp. 26–7.
88. See Hopper, p. 57. Philip Curtin suggests that by the fifth century BC there were perhaps ten thousand *metics* in Athens compared to roughly twenty-one thousand citizens (*Cross-Cultural Trade in World History*, Cambridge 1984, p. 77).
89. Ibid., p. 65.
90. Finley, p. 78.
91. Anderson, *Passages from Antiquity to Feudalism*, p. 19.
92. Ibid., p. 22.
93. Finley, pp. 65–6.
94. A.R. Burn, *The Pelican History of Greece*, Harmondsworth 1982, p. 245.
95. Finley, p. 66.
96. Ibid., p. 36; Anderson, *Passages from Antiquity to Feudalism*, p. 36.
97. Weber, *The City*, p. 214.
98. The Doge's speech is reprinted in Adelson, pp. 188–90.
99. This comparison is perhaps less arbitrary than at first it appears, inasmuch as there is no evidence that Greek equivalents of the Doge's balance-sheet were systematically maintained: 'It is to be regretted that the Athenians, and indeed the Greeks in general, were so uninterested in economic statistics.' (Hopper, p. 53.) Tribute lists were a different matter.
100. See Anderson, *Lineages of the Absolutist State*, pp. 150ff, where these points and others are fleshed out.
101. Thucydides, p. 145. The Athenians went to the remarkable length of using

Scythian slave police 'so that no citizen might have to lay violent hands upon another' (Burn, p. 239).

102. See Burn, p. 213.

103. Finley, p. 33.

104. Ibid. p. 56.

105. Thucydides, pp. 212–23. Diodotus says of the inhabitants of Mytilene whose fate is to be decided following the crushing of their revolt against Athens: 'I might prove that they are the most guilty people in the world, but it does not follow that I shall propose the death penalty, unless that is in your interests; I might argue that they deserve to be forgiven, but should not recommend forgiveness unless that seemed to me the best thing for the state. ... [T]his is not a law-court, where we have to consider what is fit and just; it is a political assembly, and the question is how Mytilene can be most useful to Athens.' (Ibid., pp. 219–20.) Compare this with Anderson's observation that in feudalism 'justice ... was the ordinary name of power' (*Passages from Antiquity to Feudalism*, p. 153) – i.e. political rule was legitimated and exercised via legal right ('privilege' in the sense used by Marx in the earlier discussion above) not common interest and the votes of political equals.

106. 'There was no bureaucracy or civil service and despite the large number of officials, no hierarchy of offices – everyone being responsible solely to the *demos* itself.' (Finley, pp. 68-9.)

107. Marx, 'Critique of Hegel's Doctrine of the State', in *Early Writings*, ed. L. Colletti, Harmondsworth 1975, p. 138.

108. Same text, different translation: *Pre-capitalist Socio-economic Formations*, Moscow 1979, p. 29. For the alternative translation, see *Early Writings*, p. 91.

109. See Hopper, p. 74.

110. Ibid., pp. 54 and 58 respectively.

111. Finley, p. 80.

112. Notably the Corinthians. See Thucydides, pp. 73–7.

113. M.W. Doyle clearly distinguishes the mechanisms of Athenian and Spartan external power, calling the one imperial and the other hegemonic (*Empires*, Ithaca, New York 1986, chapter 2).

114. Thucydides, p. 46.

115. Doyle, *Empires*, p. 68.

116. Thucydides, p. 77.

117. Ibid. p. 95. See also Burn's treatment of this incident, pp. 210–11.

118. 'Potidaea', the Corinthians protested, 'is the best possible base for any campaign in Thrace, and Corcyra might have contributed a very large fleet to the Peloponnesian League.' (Thucydides, p. 74.)

119. Burn, p. 261. Of the 150-odd *poleis* in the Athenian Empire, all but three were, or were obliged to become, democracies. See Doyle, *Empires*, p. 56.

120. Thucydides, pp. 36 and 38.

121. As Doyle puts it: 'Athenian power was not only large relative to any one of its subordinate allies in the Delian League, it was also different from that of Sparta and different from, and not just larger than, that of the subordinate allies.' (*Empires*, p. 65.)

122. M.W. Doyle, 'Thucydidean Realism', *Review of International Studies*, 16 (3), 1990, p. 237.

123. Finley, p. 88.

124. *Capital*, Vol. III, p. 791.

125. See E. Wood, 'The Separation of the Economic and the Political in Capitalism', *New Left Review*, 127, May/June 1981, for an illuminating exploration of these pitfalls. Incidentally, it might be argued in this context that Gramsci chased the will-o'-the-wisp of 'power' back and forth across the modern institutional frontier between state and civil society so many times that it finally became unclear whether his intellectual legacy was one of social revolution or social democracy. See Anderson's 'The Antinomies of Antonio Gramsci', *New Left Review*, 100, November/January 1976/77, especially the section entitled 'Illusions of Left Social-Democracy', pp. 27-9.

126. As Wolf calls it (chapter 2).

127. See Anderson's discussion of this in the 'Conclusions' to *Lineages of the Absolutist State*.

128. Reproduced in *Readings from Karl Marx*, p. 122. Both senses of the word freedom are implied: the general sense of politically emancipated, and the technical sense of having been prized free from the land and hence compelled to sell itself. See also *Capital*, Vol. I, p. 874.

129. *Readings from Karl Marx*, p. 116.

130. See Finley, p. 49.

131. See the *Critique of Hegel's Philosophy of Right*: 'just as the Christians are equal in heaven, but unequal on earth, so the individual members of the nation are *equal* in the heaven of their political world, but unequal in the earthly existence of *society*.' (*Readings from Karl Marx*, p. 120.) In Italy and Classical Greece, 'heaven' and 'earth' also exist but do not share the same membership. Their co-extension in capitalist societies makes modern citizenship problematic in ways quite foreign to these two historical civilizations.

132. E. Wood, 'The Separation of the Economic and the Political in Capitalism', p. 82.

133. Public in the double sense, referring both to the visibility of the contract and to its legal status sanctioned by the 'public political' state.

134. *Capital*, Vol. III p. 331. In this connection, Marx also observed: 'So long as merchant's capital promotes the exchange of products between undeveloped societies, commercial profit not only appears as outbargaining and cheating, but also largely originates from them.' (Ibid., p. 330.) The Greeks, for their part, mapped out the complex relations involved in a different, but hardly less penetrating, idiom: Hermes, the god of trade, was also the patron of (among other things) messengers, boundary stones – and thieves.

135. Wood, 'The Separation of the Economic and the Political in Capitalism', p. 82.

136. To these structural limits we can also add some more circumstantial, though no less real, impediments to any generalization of the Clasical Greek or Renaissance Italian systems. Among these are the restrictions on geographical and demographic scale due to the need for face-to-face contact in a pre-industrial participatory polity, and relatedly the unique facilitating role of the Mediterranean Sea as a medium of communication in both civilizations. These observations should not, however, license a fetishizing of technology: after all, the emergence of agrarian capitalism in England *preceded* the Industrial Revolution.

137. *Pre-capitalist Economic Formations*, London 1964, pp. 77-8.

138. 'Goodbye to All That?', *Marxism Today*, October 1990, p. 21.

139. One suspects that advocates of 'the critical turn in international theory', insofar as they seek to ground their anticipations in contemporary political realities, would indicate such a possibility as crucial. This, however, is speculative, since these writers persistently shy away from identifying concrete historical agencies of change at the international level. See, for example, Linklater's discussion of Habermas, especially Linklater, pp. 26–7.

140. Conversely, this suggests why sovereignty could not be admitted as a doctrine of external relations in the feudal world, where territorial expansion premissed upon labour tied to land was the key mechanism of intra-seigniorial accumulation, and why it remained moot and unrealized within the Soviet system.

141. For a sympathetic critique of one attempt to square this circle (that is, to promote capitalist representative government as the lever of a wider realization of democracy), see P. Anderson, 'The Affinities of Noberto Bobbio', *New Left Review*, 170, July/August 1988.

142. *The German Ideology*, reprinted in *Readings from Karl Marx*, p. 130.

4. Trade and Expansion in Early Modern Europe

1. 'The emergence of the European world-economy in the "long" sixteenth century (1450–1640) was made possible by a historical conjuncture ... which created a dilemma that could only be resolved by a geographic expansion of the division of labour.' (I. Wallerstein, *The Capitalist World Economy*, Cambridge 1979, p. 25.)

2. See P. O'Brien's 'Europe in the World Economy' for a powerful, empirically based attack on the very idea of an international economy before the nineteenth century (in H. Bull and A. Watson, eds, *The Expansion of International Society*, Oxford 1984).

3. This theme will be developed in chapter 6 below.

4. *Capital*, Vol. I, p. 915.

5. From the opening lines of *The Lusiads* by Luiz Vas de Camoens, extract reproduced in D. O'Sullivan, *The Age of Discovery*, Harlow 1984, p. 95.

6. Ibid., p. 11. Prince Henry, a son of the Portuguese King John I, is celebrated for his role in promoting the early exploration of the West African coastline. However, he did not himself participate in the voyages of discovery.

7. J.H. Elliott, *Imperial Spain, 1469–1716*, London 1970, p. 57.

8. Wolf, pp. 38–9.

9. See O'Sullivan, pp. 13–14.

10. Ibid., p. 22.

11. *The Age of Reconnaissance*, p. 55.

12. See Wolf, p. 111, and Davis, pp. 3–4.

13. Curtin, p. 139. Vasco da Gama himself 'was not a professional seaman, but a nobleman, a soldier and a diplomat' (Parry, *The Age of Reconnaissance*, p. 179).

14. Compare, for example, Davis, pp. 3–4, with O'Sullivan, p. 10, and Wolf, p. 112. Braudel (p. 140) makes the remarkable claim that the Aviz dynasty was brought to power in 1385 by 'a "bourgeois" revolution', and adds that 'all things considered, [Portugal] was already halfway' to becoming 'a modern state'. C.R. Boxer describes thirteenth-century Portugal as 'the first of the modern European nation-states' (*The Portuguese Seaborne Empire 1415–1825*, Harmondsworth 1973, p. 4); but he appears to indicate by this only the early attainment of the present

national borders, following the destruction of the last of the Moorish kingdoms in the Algarve in 1249.

15. Curtin, p. 139.

16. Cited in Boxer, p. 321.

17. Ibid., p. 215.

18. Ibid., p. 219.

19. O'Sullivan, p. 20.

20. Cited in Boxer, p. 53.

21. Ibid., pp. 49–51.

22. Curtin, p. 137.

23. Parry, *The Age of Reconnaissance*, p. 62.

24. Figure calculated from the table on p. 381 of Boxer.

25. Curtin, p. 143.

26. Ibid., p. 142.

27. Ibid., p. 144.

28. Boxer, p. 59.

29. *The Modern World-System*, Vol. I, London 1974, p. 326.

30. Boxer, p. 324. Boxer goes on to note that 'King John V's spectacular extravagances were achieved at the cost of letting his army, navy and many other essential services decline in penurious neglect.' Royal profligacy by itself, however, does not account for the distinctive *form* of Portuguese failure outlined below.

31. *The Age of Reconnaissance*, p. 64.

32. Cited in Wallerstein, *The Modern World-System*, Vol. I, p. 331. Something similar applied to slave-dominated sugar production in Brazil, in which 'the Portuguese transferred to the New World an agricultural complex of long standing in the European Mediterranean'. (Wolf, 149.)

33. Wallerstein, *The Modern World-System*, Vol. I, p. 328.

34. Wolf, p. 79.

35. *Studies in the Development of Capitalism*, New York 1963, p. 8.

36. *Capital*, Vol. III, p. 329.

37. Cited in ibid., p. 331n.

38. Ibn Khaldun, cited in Wolf, p. 120.

39. Glamann, p. 475.

40. Davis, p. 181.

41. Wallerstein, *The Modern World-System*, Vol. II, London 1980, pp. 52 and 53. The Dutch were also able to exploit their *geographical* position to facilitate and engross the exchange of Portuguese spices for Baltic grain. See Glamann, p. 446.

42. Koenigsberger, pp. 171–3.

43. Davis, pp. 190–91. The Dutch had themselves, over the previous half-century, prised the Portuguese out of the spice trade by a combination of financial and military manoeuvres and assaults. See Braudel, *The Perspective of the World*, pp. 211–13.

44. *Capital*, Vol. III, p. 330.

45. Ibid., p. 328.

46. An exception which proves this rule is that impressive work of Karl Polanyi, *The Great Transformation* (first published in 1944). There, Polanyi associates capitalism with the predominant role played in the organization of modern societies by 'the self-regulating market'. However, not only is he emphatic that 'previously to our time no economy has ever existed that, even in principle, was controlled by

markets' (ibid., p. 43); he is also crystal clear that the 'self-regulation' which distinguishes this market from its politically- or custom-regulated forbears is itself an effect of the commodification of labour-power (and secondarily of land). Thus although Polanyi does not discuss Marx's social theory, his own attention to the historical and structural specificity of the capitalist market allows him to identify the structural break between precapitalist and capitalist commercial activity in remarkably similar terms: 'Up to the end of the eighteenth century, industrial production in Western Europe was a mere accessory to commerce' (ibid., p. 74). It might be added that the anthropological idiom of Polanyi's thought lends it two special strengths in this area: a powerful instinct for theorizing societies as social totalities; and a wide range of comparative empirical knowledge of (tribal) non-capitalist societies – wide enough to make him wary of extrapolating conditions peculiar to 'the market economy' into transhistorical and cross-cultural assumptions shaping the analysis of other societies. On the other hand, despite identifying the historical novelty of the capitalist market, Polanyi never provided a *social theory* of it. He simply detailed its practical effects as a mechanism of social organization. The next step – the apprehension of the value relations between persons which lie 'behind' yet are accomplished only through exchange relations between things – was taken by Marx alone. For Polanyi, the commodification of labour might be an outrage, but it was never a mystery. For a searching yet sympathetic probing of the limitations of Polanyi's theoretical framework, see M. Godelier, 'Karl Polanyi and the "Shifting Place" of the Economy in Societies', in *The Mental and the Material*, London 1986.

47. See, for example, the discussion of imperialism reproduced in *From Max Weber: Essays in Sociology*, eds H.H. Gerth and C.W. Mills, London 1948, pp. 166–9.

48. Curtin, p. 136.

49. See O'Sullivan, pp. 15–16.

50. Parry, *The Age of Reconnaissance*, p. 173.

51. And in more ways than one: under the terms of the Treaty Castile had been allowed to retain the Canary Islands, which, as would soon be found, lay on the northern fringe of the North East Trade Wind zone.

52. The broad division of East and West between Spain and Portugal was later consolidated in the famous Treaty of Tordesillas (1494) which moved the longitude of demarcation proclaimed by the papal bull 'Inter Caetera' to a line 370 leagues west of the Cape Verde islands. The Spanish Crown, however, persisted in the attempt to find a competing *western* route to the Spice Islands, renouncing this goal only in 1529 (Treaty of Saragossa) after Magellan had failed to discover westerly winds in the Pacific which could drive the homeward journey to Mexico of a Pacific trade in spices. (See O'Sullivan, p. 44.) When the winds were finally discovered in 1565, their net effect, ironically enough, was not to yield Spain a cut in Portugal's spice trade but rather to produce an uncontrollable haemorrhage of American silver in the direction of China (via Manila).

53. Braudel (p. 142) cites contemporary estimates of returns on the Guinea gold trade at 500 per cent. As to the spice trade, a comparison of its weight/value ratio with that of the Baltic trade in staples makes the point: for the years around 1600, an average annual total of some 126,109.4 tons of grain was imported into Europe, at a value equivalent to 87.5 tons of silver; at the same time the annual imports of 2,712 tons of spices were worth 136.8 tons of silver. (P. Kriedte, *Peasants, Landlords*

and Merchant Capitalists, Leamington Spa 1983, p. 41.) The difference in the weight/
value ratio is a factor of 72.

54. Parry, *The Age of Reconnaissance,* p. 73.

55. Braudel, p. 143.

56. Glamann, p. 486.

57. Boxer, p. 61. This latter innovation was apparently unsuccessful, but its very
appearance is startling.

58. Braudel, p. 149.

59. Ibid., p. 149.

60. Pierre Chaunu calculated that the overall terms of trade between East and
West in this period were very favourable to Europe: '120 to 150,000 tons of spices
were bought, almost without merchandise in return, for 150 tons of gold, which
the weight of domination had seized from the feeble African societies, and a
quantity of specie difficult to calculate, but not at all comparable to the 6,000 tons
of equivalent silver which remained to be made up.' (Cited in Wallerstein, *The
Modern World-System,* Vol. I, p. 329.)

61. Boxer, p. 69. Nor did the Portuguese exercise any control over the land
routes. According to Boxer (p. 60), by the end of the century, larger quantities of
pepper 'were reaching Europe by the overland route to the Levant' than the
Portuguese were carrying by sea. Finally, Boxer also notes (p. 59) that for strategic
reasons (principally the desire to cultivate Persia as a counterweight to the
Ottomans) the Gulf sea-route was never completely closed to Muslim traders.

62. Parry, *The Age of Reconnaissance,* p. 240.

63. As was noted in chapter 2 above, India's spice consumption was double that
of Europe (Braudel, p. 219).

64. Boxer, p. 60. Spanish exploitation of the Mexican silver mines provided the
other important source of specie facilitating Western entry into Asian circulation.
See Wallerstein, *The Modern World-System,* Vol. I, p. 329, especially footnotes 132
and 133.

65. Parry, *The Age of Reconnaissance,* pp. 241–2.

66. Boxer, p. 324.

67. For examples, see Boxer pp. 61–3 and chapter 14.

68. Sansom, cited in Wallerstein, *The Modern World-System,* Vol. I, p. 331n. In
fact it was not only the penetration of Asian social orders which was superficial.
The Portuguese success in cornering the country trade was itself modest relative
to the whole. Curtin suggests (p. 145) that 'the value of Gujarat customs revenues
was still three times the total revenue of the Portuguese empire in Asia [in the
1570s], though many Gujarat merchants worked within the Portuguese *cartaz*
system'.

69. H. Kamen, *Spain, 1469–1714: A Society of Conflict,* Harlow 1983, p. 91.

70. 'The Continuing Tradition of Reconquest' in H.B. Johnson, ed., *From
Reconquest to Empire: The Iberian Background to Latin American History,* New York 1970,
p. 43.

71. J. Lang, *Conquest and Commerce: Spain and England in the Americas,* New York and
London 1975, p. 10.

72. *Passages from Antiquity to Feudalism,* p. 168.

73. See J.H. Parry, *The Spanish Seaborne Empire,* London 1966, pp. 30–31.

74. Anderson, *Passages from Antiquity to Feudalism,* pp. 168–9.

75. E. Lourie, 'A Society Organized for War: Medieval Spain', *Past and Present,*
December 1966, p. 69.

76. Lang, pp. 27–8.

77. See J.W. Thompson, *Economic and Social History of the Middle Ages*, Vol. II, New York 1959, pp. 556–7.

78. In Castile itself, the parallel result of this orientation of the town towards booty and privileged military consumption was the retarded growth of an urban bourgeoisie. And one of the strongest indicators of this skewed development is that whereas elsewhere in Europe the later consolidation of royal absolutism was typically pursued in the face of noble resistance and with urban support, in Spain the pattern was reversed: 'the Spanish monarchy's most fundamental victory over corporate resistance to royal absolutism – indeed its only actual armed contest with any opposition in that realm – was the military defeat of the towns, rather than the nobles.' (Anderson, *Lineages of the Absolutist State*, p. 68.)

79. Lourie, p. 60.

80. See J.W. Thompson, pp. 554–5.

81. See 'Introduction' to H.B. Johnson, ed., *From Reconquest to Empire: The Iberian Background to Latin American History*, New York 1970, pp. 9–10.

82. Elliott, p. 59.

83. For an exhaustive contrast of the *encomienda* of the Indies with its multiple Castilian forebears, see R.S. Chamberlain, 'The Roots of Lordship: The *Encomienda* in Medieval Castile', in H.B. Johnson, ed., *From Reconquest to Empire: The Iberian Background to Latin American History*, New York 1970.

84. Elliott affirms (p. 60) that 'the municipal organization of medieval Castile was faithfully transplanted to the overseas colonies'.

85. Lang, pp. 27–8.

86. See Parry, *Age of Reconnaissance*, p. 211, and O'Sullivan, p. 46.

87. 'Every leader of a conquering army made it his first care to establish towns, to get them legally incorporated and to install his own immediate followers as the officers of municipal government.' (J.H. Parry, 'The New World, 1521–1580', in G.R. Elton, ed., *The New Cambridge Modern History: Vol. II: The Reformation, 1520–1559*, Cambridge 1965, p. 563.)

88. 'Every township established by the Spaniards in Mexico, with the exception of Mexico City and perhaps Vera Cruz, lost most of its Spanish population within a few years of its foundation.' (Davis, p. 42.)

89. '[D]own to the Avis revolution of 1383, the annual income of the monarchy was approximately equal to that of the church, and the two combined were between four and eight times larger than the total revenues of the nobility'. (Anderson, *Passages from Antiquity to Feudalism*, p. 172.)

90. See Elliott, p. 26.

91. For the content of some of these struggles, see Holmes, pp. 61–3.

92. Johnson, p. 10.

93. Perhaps by the Moors (as Kamen suggests, p. 50), perhaps by the Castilians at the instigation of Italian merchants (Johnson, p. 10).

94. Elliott, p. 33. It had always been true of Castile that 'Ranching was almost the sole occupation of the inhabitants.' (J.W. Thompson, p. 555.)

95. Johnson, p. 11.

96. See Wolf, p. 135, and Davis, p. 46.

97. O'Sullivan, p. 55.

98. Cortés, cited in Kamen, p. 92.

99. See O'Sullivan , p. 32.

100. Ibid., p. 34.
101. Elliott, p. 32.
102. Johnson, p. 17.
103. Ibid.
104. Anderson, *Passages from Antiquity to Feudalism*, pp. 199–200.
105. Davis, p. 98.
106. Ibid., p. 69; C. Kindleberger, *Historical Economics: Art or Science?*, Hemel Hempstead 1990, p. 37; Glamann, p. 430. Davis later adds (p. 145): 'During much of the sixteenth century, pressure on real resources had been largely responsible for pushing Spanish prices upward, and the influence of rapidly growing money supply had added little to it.'
107. Davis, p. 98.
108. Kindleberger, p. 40.
109. *The Conquest of New Spain*, ed. J.M. Cohen, Harmondsworth 1963, p. 274.
110. Isabella's 'dying request [in 1504 was] that her husband should devote himself "unremittingly to the conquest of Africa and to the war for the Faith against the Moors"' (Elliott, p. 53).
111. O'Sullivan, p. 27.
112. Kindleberger, p. 40.
113. This was true of the discoveries of the Reconnaissance as a whole. Parry, discussing the simultaneous rise of Portuguese and Spanish long-distance trade in the sixteenth century, remarks that 'Much of the exploring activity of other nations during the century was inspired by the hope of breaking or circumventing one or other of these monopolies.' (*The Age of Reconnaissance*, p. 224.) Similarly, most land exploration in the Americas in the sixteenth century was undertaken by individuals hoping to emulate Cortés and Pizarro by discovering further empires to conquer. For examples, see ibid., pp. 221–2.
114. Ibid., p. 40.
115. See Parry, *The Age of Reconnaissance*, pp. 253–6. Parry describes this search as 'another story of heroism, of failure in its main purpose, and, later, of successful results in unexpected directions'. (Ibid., p. 255.)
116. See Johnson, p. 23.
117. O'Sullivan, p. 33.
118. Ibid, p. 24.
119. Johnson, p. 34. Elliott also briefly discusses Columbus's personal failure in the context of the tension between Mediterranean (trading post) and Iberian (territorial) approaches (pp. 61–2). Parry, however, implies that the contrast was not, at this stage, explicit: 'The immediate object of the voyage was not to open a new trade or to conquer Oriental kingdoms, but to settle the island of Hispaniola, to found a mining and farming colony which could produce its own food, pay the cost of the voyage by remitting gold to Spain, and serve at the same time as a base for further exploration in the direction of Cipangu [Japan], Cathay and India.' (*The Age of Reconnaissance*, p. 194.)
120. Johnson p. 23.
121. *The Age of Reconnaissance*, pp. 207 and 222.
122. Ibid., p. 211.
123. See Diaz, pp. 245–77. Of the contents of the royal treasury, immediately melted down for distribution among the *conquistadores*, Diaz says: 'There was so much of it that after it was broken up it made three heaps of gold weighing over

six hundred thousand pesos in all, not counting the silver and many other valuables, or the ingots and slabs of gold, or the gold from the mines.'(Ibid., pp. 271–2.)

124.   Parry, *The Age of Reconnaissance*, p. 213.

125.   'There were 15,000 kilometers of paved roads!' exclaims Mann. (*The Sources of Social Power*, p. 122.) The Andean 'Royal Road' traversing the Inca territories from north to south was, at 3,250 miles, 'until the nineteenth century, the longest arterial road of history'. (V.W. von Hagen, *The Ancient Sun Kingdoms of the Americas*, London 1962, p. 308.) It was supplemented by a parallel 2,520 mile coastal road, the two being linked at numerous points by cross-cutting lesser roads. These roads were, wherever possible, built to a standard 24-foot gauge and lined on either side by a low wall. Pre-positioning of food and other resources at regular intervals enabled not only rapid massing and movement of forces, but also a runner-based messenger relay-system which composed 'the fastest communication system the world had seen, not excepting the Roman' (ibid., p. 317). Mann is, perhaps wisely, sceptical of some of the early records on which such judgements as the last must have been based. See *The Sources of Social Power*, p. 122.

126.   Hagen (p. 328) suggests that once again the Spaniards were mistaken for returning gods. On the other hand, any commander of an 80,000-strong army confronted with 180 travel-weary intruders might normally be forgiven a certain amount of complacency.

127.   Pizarro's secretary reported that 'During the whole time no Indian raised his arms against a Spaniard.' (See O'Sullivan, p. 53.) This paralysis is reminiscent of Montezuma's stupefaction at being kidnapped by Cortés: so incredulous was he of this development that, it seems, he could more easily believe that he was being imprisoned of his own free will – a delusion which Cortés fostered assiduously, to great manipulative effect. (See Diaz, pp. 246–7.)

128.   See O'Sullivan, p. 53.

129.   Hagen, p. 300. By comparison, in 1550, the total value of the ordinary taxes of Castile (principally the domestic sales tax) was equivalent to just over 1m pesos. See Kamen, p. 87, for the figure in ducats, and ibid., pp. x–xi, for the conversion ratios.

130.   See Parry, *The Age of Reconnaissance*, pp. 218–20.

131.   For the following, see idem, 'The New World, 1521–1580', pp. 562–72.

132.   See Lang, pp. 33–4.

133.   Ibid., p. 35.

134.   Wolf, p. 134. The Peruvian silver mine at Potosi, 'king of mountains, envy of kings', as the town's coat of arms proclaimed, consumed the surrounding population with a ghastly voracity. By 1660 the provinces of the *altiplano* had been depopulated by some 80 per cent. By the time it was closed in 1823, this operation may have cost 8 million lives. (See L. Potts, *The World Labour Market: A History of Migration*, London 1990, pp. 22–3.)

135.   See Lang, pp. 18–24, for an excellent discussion of these processes.

136.   For a cautious discussion along these lines, see M. Donelan's 'Spain and the Indies' in H. Bull and A. Watson, eds., *The Expansion of International Society*, Oxford 1984. Kamen (p. 93) suggests that Francisco de Vitoria's 'study of the Indian problem enabled him to develop principles on the relationship between peoples that created a framework for international law and the rights of man'.

137.   J.H. Parry, *The Spanish Theory of Empire in the Sixteenth Century*, New York, p. 21.

216 NOTES TO PAGES 119–125

138. Idem., *The Age of Reconnaissance*, p. 347.
139. See ibid., p. 386, and *The Spanish Theory of Empire*, p. 27, respectively.
140. Idem, *The Age of Reconnaissance*, p. 291.
141. Ibid., p. 222.
142. Idem, *The Spanish Theory of Empire*, pp. 49–56.
143. Ibid.
144. Wight, *Power Politics*, pp. 144 and 149.
145. For a treatment of the modern international system in terms of separately constituted markets, states and societies, see R. Gilpin, *The Political Economy of International Relations*, Princeton 1987, chapter 1. This conception, however, also marked the boundary of Polanyi's social thought. By contrast, C. Wright Mills vigorously rejected the resultant reduction of sociology to 'a sort of odd job man among the social sciences, consisting of miscellaneous studies of academic left-overs'. See his *The Sociological Imagination*, Oxford 1959, p. 23.
146. 'The economists have a singular way of proceeding. For them, there are only two kinds of institutions, artificial and natural. The institutions of feudalism are artificial institutions, those of the bourgeoisie are natural institutions. ... Thus there has been history, but there no longer is any.' (Marx, quoting *The Poverty of Philosophy*, in *Capital*, Vol. I, p. 175n.)

5. The Empire of Civil Society

1. *Capital*, Vol. III, p. 790.
2. Often, upholding a rule of law in connection with the capitalist labour contract is a bloody affair – drawing out the coercive arm of the state in routine acts of violent repression. South Korea still provides not infrequent examples of this. However – and here is the point – the pitched battles between police and workers in South Korea take place not in the courtyards of state-owned factories, but on the premises of Hyundai and Samsung corporations, non-governmental organizations. And if it sometimes takes bayonets and tear gas to drive workers into factories, the rule to which they submit once inside is not that of the state, but rather that of so-called 'management'.
3. 'The social world of capitalism appears as something we inhabit ... rather than some ways we are.' (Sayer, *Capitalism and Modernity*, p. 88.)
4. For an exposition of the labour theory of value as a social theory, see Isaac Rubin's classic of the 1920s, *Essays on Marx's Theory of Value*, introduced by F. Perlman, Montreal 1973. See also Perlman's fine introduction to that volume.
5. Eduard Heimann, referring to the Greek distinction between *oikonomia* and *chrematistike*, notes that 'the modern name "economics" which has been taken over from the ancients now denotes the exact opposite of what they meant by it' (*History of Economic Doctrines: An Introduction to Economic Theory*, New York 1964, p. 23). This distinction is also discussed briefly by Marx in *Capital*, Vol. I, pp. 253–4n. See also Therborn, chapter 2, for an admirably clear discussion of these points. As he puts it: 'Economic discourse emerged as a concomitant of the rise of what this discourse was about: the capitalist economy. This should be understood in a strong sense.' Ibid., p. 77.)
6. In the *Grundrisse*, Marx alludes to this by joking with the etymology of the word 'capital': 'If the concern is the word, capital, which does not occur in

antiquity, then the still migrating hordes with their herds on the Asiatic plateau are the biggest capitalists, since capital originally means cattle.' (Ibid., p. 513.)

7. This contrasts with the 'parcellized sovereignty' of feudal Europe, where local jurisdiction was a direct source of revenue and social power for the noble estate. As Anderson put it, justice, far from entailing an impersonal rule of law among legal equals, 'was the ordinary name of power' (*Passages from Antiquity to Feudalism*, p. 153).

8. Wood, 'The Separation of the Economic and the Political in Capitalism', p. 82.

9. As noted earlier, Polanyi was insistent on the novelty of this: 'Nineteenth-century society, in which economic activity was isolated and imputed to a distinctive economic motive, was, indeed, a singular departure.' (Polanyi, p. 71.)

10. See, for example, J. Stoessinger, 'The Anatomy of the Nation-State and the Nature of Power', reprinted in M. Smith et al., eds, *Perspectives on World Politics*, Beckenham 1981; H. and M. Sprout, 'Tribal Sovereignty vs Interdependence', in ibid.; and G. Goodwin, 'The Erosion of External Sovereignty?', *Government and Opposition*, 9 (1), Winter 1974. For a brief, though highly selective, survey of definitions of sovereignty in IR, see A. James, *Sovereign Statehood: The Basis of International Society*, London 1986, chapter 2. James himself opts for a definition of external sovereignty as 'constitutional separateness' (ibid., p. 24), a somewhat unhistorical formulation which leads him at one point to the curious observation that 'an empire [is] a form of sovereign state' (ibid., p. 31). However, James's purpose is to explicate sovereignty not as a particular form of rule but rather as a term 'used by states when referring to what it is about themselves that fits them for international life' (ibid., p. 51). This is in step with the work of the English School as a whole. Wight (who rarely uses the term at all), Bull and Watson have all remained content with a very general definition in terms of internal primacy and external independence. (See Wight, *Systems of States*, pp. 129–30; Bull, *The Anarchical Society*, p. 8; and Watson, p. 316.) Even Carr could not rise to a clear definition of modern sovereignty: 'One prediction may be made with some confidence. The concept of sovereignty is likely to become in the future even more blurred and indistinct than it is in the present.' (*The Twenty Years' Crisis*, 2nd edn, p. 230.)

11. Waltz, in Keohane, ed., p. 90.

12. Or even where it redresses imbalances of power within production through constraining the freedom to 'hire and fire' or assuaging the rigours of unemployment.

13. And, one could say, 'legitimation crisis' enforces a limit to change which social democracy cannot overleap. For a lucid and not uncritical discussion of Habermas's theory of legitimation crisis, a theory whose appearance towards the end of the 1970s reflected unmistakably the strains building up within West European social democracy after the end of the long boom, see D. Held, 'Crisis Tendencies, Legitimation and the State' in J. Thompson and D. Held, eds, *Habermas: Critical Debates*, London 1982.

14. See, for example, the account given in G. Goodman, *The Miners' Strike*, London 1985, chapter 2.

15. This assumes that they are not interrupted by direct state intervention.

16. It would not be possible to make such a jigsaw out of feudal Europe, in which each piece corresponded to a single, exclusive jurisdiction. Jeremy Black notes

(even of the absolutist period) that 'It was usually beyond the ingenuity of even the most skilful cartographer to indicate on one map alone areas of mixed jurisdictions, owing allegiance to different rulers for different aspects of their existence.' (*The Rise of the European Powers, 1679–1793*, London 1990, p. 194.) Black gives an example of one treaty (Turin, 1760) which required no less than eight different maps of the same area in order to render fully its complex political identity (ibid., p. 194). Ironically, in the light of our discussion in chapter 2, the dispute resolved here concerned the delineation of boundaries by the Treaty of Utrecht.

17. One of the effects of this realization is to show up the inadequacy of ahistorical discussions of 'international ethics' which unwittingly universalize social forms peculiar to capitalist modernity into 'natural' starting assumptions. A clear example arising from the present discussion concerns the question of borders. The fact of borders between 'national' political communities is held by communitarian thinkers to mark a fundamental obstacle to the extension of ethical reasoning to IR – a claim contested by writers of a cosmopolitan stamp. Which side is right? If the argument put forward above is correct, then the debate itself is simply not worth having until we have understood the historical and structural specificity of territoriality in a capitalist states-system.

18. 'Universal interdependence of nations' as a result of these specific social relations (rather than as a novelty of the 1970s) was described by Marx and Engels in the *Communist Manifesto* – reprinted in *The Revolutions of 1848*, ed. D. Fernbach, Harmondsworth 1973, p. 71.

19. In fact, we shall see in the last section of this chapter that what we have here is not only a differentiation of the spheres of social power, but also a radical, epochal transformation in the character of that power in both spheres. In Marx's formulation, 'relations of personal dependence' are replaced by 'personal independence based on dependence mediated by things'. But this belongs to the redefinition of anarchy.

20. 'Civil society' here is used to denote the social totality, including the state, a connotation which its French (*bourgeois*) and German (*bürgerliche Gesellschaft*) equivalents have not lost. In Anglo-Saxon usage, however, the term has come to be defined not in contrast to other kinds of society, but rather over against the state within capitalist society – a device which assigns the exercise of political power exclusively to the public sphere of the state and allows the private political sphere of capital to represent itself as the realm of individual freedom. For a powerful and systematic critique of this usage, see E. Wood, 'The Uses and Abuses of "Civil Society"', *Socialist Register* 1990 (special issue: R. Miliband and L. Panitch, eds, *The Retreat of the Intellectuals*).

21. For a brief account of the NIEO campaign, see J. Spero, *The Politics of International Economic Relations*, London 1985, pp. 207ff.

22. Susan George, LSE seminar, January 1989.

23. *This*, it may be argued, is the deep sense in which realism is ideological. It is not just that it provides politicians with a convenient language with which to justify their policies; rather, by reifying and naturalizing the alienated social forms of modernity, it reproduces at the cognitive level the separation of economics and politics which is constitutive of the specifically capitalist form of international power.

24. Marx and Engels, *The German Ideology*, p. 57. In other words, the political and material incorporation of humanity into the global system studied by IR was

accomplished through the expansion of Europe in the era of capitalist industrialization. In the overall schema of *Capital* as set out in the 'General Introduction' of 1857, this theme was marked out for development: 'World history has not always existed; history as world history as a result.' (*Grundrisse*, p. 109.)

25. Bull, *The Anarchical Society*, p. 8.

26. The Pope's response to Westphalia, *Zelo Domus Dei*, ends with the following pronouncement: 'we assert and declare by these presents that all the said articles in one or both of the said treaties which in any way impair or prejudice in the slightest degree, or that can be said, alleged, understood, or imagined to be able in any way to injure or to have injured the Catholic religion, divine worship, the salvation of souls, the said Roman apostolic see, the inferior churches, the ecclesiastical order or estate, their persons, affairs, possessions, jurisdictions, authorities, immunities, liberties, privileges, prerogatives, and rights whatsoever, – all such provisions have been and are of right, and shall perpetually be, null and void, invalid, iniquitous, unjust, condemned, rejected, frivolous, without force or effect, and no one is to observe them, even when they be ratified by oath.' (Reprinted P. Limm, *The Thirty Years' War*, Harlow 1984, p. 107.)

27. As with most historical references cited in IR, it is remarkably difficult to find any systematic research – even of chapter length – into the actual context, provisions and significance of Westphalia. A valuable recent exception is K.J. Holsti's discussion in chapter 2 of *Peace and War*.

28. F.H. Hinsley, *Sovereignty*, London 1966, p. 121. 'Although the word 'sovereignty' had gained currency by the beginning of that century, Bodin in his *Six Livres de la république* of 1577 was perhaps the first man to state the theory behind the word.' (Ibid., p. 71.)

29. See E. Wood, *The Pristine Culture of Capitalism*, London 1991.

30. Ibid., p. 25.

31. Ibid., pp. 54–5.

32. The same is true later, as Wood notes, of that other liberal great power, the US. The reason is the same in each case: 'It is not at all as paradoxical as it may seem that the concept of the state has been least well defined precisely where the formal separation of state and civil society characteristic of capitalism occurred first and most "naturally".' (Ibid., p. 34.) Exactly the same could be said with respect to the geopolitical definition of the state. It is remarkable that Britain and the US – the only two truly world powers there have been – both had to import the idiom of *raison d'état* from abroad. This is especially clear in the role of Niebuhr and Morgenthau in the development of US realism. But Carr too derives utopianism above all from Anglo-American liberalism, and cites two Europeans (Mannheim and Niebuhr) as the most important intellectual influences on *The Twenty Years' Crisis*. See the Preface to the first edition.

33. '[T]he truth is that legal sovereignty, exercised by the "Crown in Parliament", was becoming a reality in England long before it existed even as a gleam in the eyes of French legal scholars.' (Wood, *The Pristine Culture of Capitalism*, p. 48.)

34. Ibid., p. 28.

35. Ibid., p. 55.

36. D. Sayer, 'A Notable Administration: English State Formation and the Rise of Capitalism', *American Journal of Sociology*, 97 (5), March 1992, p. 1393. Sayer, like Wood, goes so far as to suggest a direct reversal of the (sociological) assumptions of historical research in this matter: 'From the point of view of its contribution to

the rise of capitalism, there would appear to be every reason for regarding such a polity as paradigmatic rather than peculiar.' (Ibid., p. 141.) For a more detailed comparative history of European state-building written in the spirit of these observations, see C. Mooers, *The Making of Bourgeois Europe*, London 1991.

37. In other words, the absolutist doctrine of sovereignty as the centralization of political power would be unable to explain its *disaggregation* into public and private spheres. One writer who has recognized very clearly the disjuncture between the absolutist and the liberal versions of sovereignty is Roy Jones: 'An achievement of the liberal tradition is to have constructed a notion, and a structure, of statehood which is the antithesis of sovereignty. The liberal state was inspired by a passion to regulate, even do away with, sovereigns.' (R. Jones, 'The English School of International Relations: A Case for Closure', *Review of International Studies*, 7(1), 1981, p. 6.) The implied suggestion that the term itself should also be done away with is logical enough. However, since this is unlikely to happen in IR, the alternative path of theoretical and historical redefinition has been preferred in this work.

38. See Holmes, pp. 28–47.

39. Morgenthau, p. 5.

40. 'If there is any distinctively political theory of international politics, balance-of-power theory is it.' (Waltz, in Keohane, ed., p. 116.)

41. Bull's work *The Anarchical Society* probably provides the most explicit and consistent version of this account. Bull observes: 'The classical argument against world government has been that ... it is destructive of liberty or freedom: it infringes the liberties of states and nations.' (Ibid., pp. 252–3.) However, the nostrums are general. In a section entitled 'The Virtues of Anarchy', Waltz comments that 'States, like people, are insecure in proportion to the extent of their freedom. If freedom is wanted, insecurity must be accepted.' (Keohane, ed., p. 110.)

42. Marx, *Capital*, Vol. I, p. 477. Italics added.

43. 11 July 1868, reproduced in *The Correspondence of Marx and Engels*, ed. D. Torr, London 1934, p. 245. It would be wrong to suggest that it is more central than the better-known analysis of the despotism of the workplace; as suggested in the earlier quotation, they are two sides of the same coin.

44. Well-known instances of these include Gilpin, *War and Change in World Politics*, and the work of Kenneth Waltz. Indeed, Waltz uses the analogy to justify the traditional realist segregation of domestic and international politics: 'With both systems-level and unit-level forces in play, how can one construct a theory of international politics without simultaneously constructing a theory of foreign policy? The question is exactly like asking how an economic theory of markets can be written in the absence of a theory of the firm. The answer is "very easily."' (Keohane, ed., p. 60.)

45. For a critique of this traditional view, see Wood, 'Marxism and the Course of History'.

46. The so-called 'Formen', *Grundrisse*, pp. 471–514.

47. On the contrary, Marx is quite clear that '[e]quality and freedom presuppose relations of production as yet unrealized in the ancient world and in the Middle Ages' (ibid., p. 245). And his condemnation of the 'undignified, stagnatory and vegetative life' of the Indian village is well known. (See Marx and Engels, *On Colonialism*, Moscow and London 1980, p. 36.)

48. *Grundrisse*, cited by Sayer, *Capitalism and Modernity*, pp. 13–14. This translation is here preferred over the Nicolaus version which substitutes 'objective dependence' for 'dependence mediated by things'. (*Grundrisse*, p. 158.)
49. *Grundrisse*, p. 161.
50. *Capital*, Vol. I, p. 173.
51. *Grundrisse*, p. 649.
52. Ibid., pp. 164 and 84, respectively.
53. 'Why Is There No International Theory?', p. 26.
54. See his discussion of these points in Sayer, *Capitalism and Modernity*, pp. 13–22.
55. Marx to Kugelmann, referring to the *Grundrisse*, cited by Nicolaus in his introduction to the Penguin edition (p. 59).
56. Marx's method here is very clearly elaborated by Sayer in *The Violence of Abstraction*, chapter 6.
57. *Grundrisse*, p. 88.
58. Ibid., p. 105.
59. The other key site of analysis is 'the chapter on money', and the discussions of competition in the *Grundrisse*. See especially pp. 649–52.
60. Either that, or products are consumed directly by their producer.
61. Letter to Kugelmann, *The Correspondence of Marx and Engels*, p. 246.
62. For the English School of IR, the defining questions of international theory are generally posed in such terms as 'How can there be an international society without an international government? If all states are sovereign, how can they be bound by a common law?' etc.
63. Marx to Kugelmann, *The Correspondence of Marx and Engels*, p. 246.
64. *Grundrisse*, p. 135.
65. Ibid., p. 161.
66. Marx describes precapitalist social relations as 'much more transparent and simple' than those organizing generalized commodity production (ibid., p. 172).
67. *Capital*, Vol. I, pp. 167–8.
68. *Grundrisse*, p. 241.
69. Ibid., p. 242.
70. Or as Marx puts it 'they recognize one another reciprocally as proprietors, as persons whose will penetrates their commodities.' (Ibid., p. 243.)
71. Ibid., p. 245. Marx goes on to note that this sharply distinguishes the character of modern freedom from its predecessors in history: 'Equality and freedom as developed to this extent are exactly the opposite of the freedom and equality in the world of antiquity, where developed exchange value was not their basis.'
72. *Grundrisse*, p. 485. Marx describes the predecessors of this new social form of the individual as 'rooted to the spot, ingrown' (ibid., p. 494).
73. Ibid., p. 85.
74. For Marx the caveat to this proviso is a third social form, lying beyond 'dependence mediated by things': 'Free individuality, based on the universal development of individuals and on their subordination of their communal, social productivity as their social wealth.' (*Grundrisse*, p. 158.)
75. Ibid., pp. 157–8.
76. 'I believe that the desire and the motive for large and mighty empires; for gigantic armies and great navies ... will die away; I believe that such things will

cease to be necessary, or to be used when man beomes one family, and freely exchanges the fruits of his labour with his brother man. I believe that, if we could be allowed to reappear on this sublunary scene, we should see, at a far distant period, the governing system of this world revert to something like the municipal system.' (Quotation from a speech of 1846; in Bourne, ed., pp. 269–70.)

77.   For example, in the House of Commons Debate on 'Russia and the Porte', 16 August 1853: 'We went to war, not for the purpose of increasing the export of our commodities, but in defence of the liberty and independence of nations, and for the maintenance of that balance of power, which, however the hon. Gentleman may treat it with contempt and sneer at it, because he does not understand it – everybody else considers to be a point deserving of assertion, and essential to the liberty and well-being of mankind.' (Cited in ibid., p. 329.)

78.   Cited in ibid., p. 85.

79.   See also Palmerston's response to the overthrow of the French Restoration monarchy in 1830: 'We shall drink the cause of Liberalism all over the world ... This event is decisive of the ascendancy of Liberal principles throughout Europe; the evil spirit has been put down and will be trodden under foot.' [Cited in ibid., p. 29.)

80.   House of Commons Speech on the Corn Laws, 1842, extracted in ibid., p. 255.

81.   Palmerston, 1 March 1848, extracted in ibid., pp. 292–3.

82.   In the end, Carr maintained, utopianism ran far deeper than the childish fantasies of deluded international lawyers. He traced it *inter alia* to the father of the 'invisible hand' himself: Adam Smith. (*The Twenty Years' Crisis*, 2nd edn, p. 43.) In other words, modern utopianism, like modern realism, is rooted in the experience of anarchical social forms.

83.   If our argument were following the rhetorical structure of *Capital*, we would have reached no further than the fifth of thirty-three chapters in the first of three volumes.

84.   *Capital*, Vol. I, p. 733. The quotation cited earlier from the *Grundrisse* which eulogized the 'spontaneous interconnection' of the market goes on to insist: 'But it is an insipid notion to conceive of this merely *objective bond* as a spontaneous, natural attribute inherent in individuals and inseparable from their nature. ... This bond is their product. It is a historic product.' (*Grundrisse*, p. 162.)

85.   *Capital*, Vol. I, p. 729.

86.   Ibid., p. 730.

87.   *Grundrisse*, p. 247.

88.   For this reason, Marx also chides 'the foolishness of those socialists ... who demonstrate that exchange and exchange-value etc. are *originally* ... or *essentially* ... a system of universal freedom and equality, but that they have been perverted by money, capital etc.' (Ibid., p. 248.)

89.   Rubin, p. 6.

90.   Cited by S. Lukes, 'Saint-Simon (1760–1825)', in A. Donini and J. Novak, eds, *Origins and Growth of Sociological Theory*, Chicago 1982, p. 59.

91.   'The better theory will be able to specify in more detail the causal processes at work and the situations in which causal mechanisms come into operation.' (Craib, p. 26.) In this case, if value theory can illuminate underlying social relations which are opaque to realism and yet which can be shown to be constitutive of the balance of power as a historically specific social form, then the claim holds that

it is a superior social theory. For it can explain everything that realism can, and much more besides.

92. *Capital*, Vol. I, p. 280.

93. It is striking that most IR critiques of realism operate by stressing the *mitigation* of the state of nature, not by uncovering its historicity as a social form. This holds even of the finest critiques, such as Charles Beitz's *Political Theory and International Relations*, Princeton 1979.

94. Frisby and Sayer, p. 120.

95. Polanyi, p. 114.

96. *The Division of Labour*, cited in Frisby and Sayer, p. 44.

97. Frisby and Sayer, p. 28.

98. For a brief discussion of Simmel's treatment of this question, see ibid., chapter 3.

99. Grotius, Prolegomena to *On the Law of War and Peace*, in M. Forsyth et al., eds, *The Theory of International Relations: Selected Texts from Gentili to Treitschke*, London 1970, p. 48.

100. Ibid., pp. 42 and 50.

101. *Power Politics: An Introduction to the Study of International Relations and Post-War Planning*, London 1941, p. 35.

102. *Community and Association (Gemeinschaft und Gesellschaft)*, London 1955, p. 39.

103. Manning's brief discussion of these terms abstracts them from both their historical and their theoretical context: 'international society at the present time being so palpably *not* a *Gemeinschaft*, a *Gesellschaft* it therefore is taken to be.' (*The Nature of International Society*, London 1975, p. 176.)

104. Schwarzenberger, pp. 35 and 42.

105. Tönnies, p. 87.

106. *Grundrisse*, p. 652.

6. *Tantae Molis Erat*

1. *Capital*, Vol. 1, p. 925n: 'The full quotation is *Tantae molis erat Romanam condere gentem*' ('So great was the effort required to found the Roman race'), from Virgil, *Aeneid*, Bk I, line 33.'

2. Ibid., p. 874.

3. One of the most effective interrogations of this form of reasoning can be found in Robert Brenner's critique of Sweezy, Frank and Wallerstein. See 'The Origins of Capitalist Development'. The analytical core of the argument is set out more briefly in Brenner's 'The Social Basis of Economic Development', in J. Roemer, ed., *Analytical Marxism*, Cambridge 1986. More recently, Brenner has argued that Marx himself fully escaped the Smithian model of capitalist origins only in the mature writings, from the *Grundrisse* onwards. See 'Bourgeois Revolution and the Transition to Capitalism' in A. Beier et al., eds, *The First Modern Society: Essays in English History in Honour of Lawrence Stone*, Cambridge 1989.

4. *The Anarchical Society*, pp. 13–14.

5. Letter to the editor of the *Otyecestvenniye Zapisky*, reproduced in *The Correspondence of Marx and Engels*, p. 354.

6. *Capital*, Vol. I, pp. 874–5.

7. Marx hints at this political dimension but does not develop it here: 'The industrial capitalists, these new potentates, had on their part not only to displace

the guild masters ... but also the feudal lords.' (Ibid., p. 875.) Sayer develops the argument much more clearly in 'The Critique of Politics and Political Economy', concluding: 'state formation is an essential facet of *bourgeois* society' (p. 234).

8. Ibid., p. 875.

9. Ibid., p. 876.

10. Ibid., p. 915.

11. Ibid., pp. 915–16.

12. *The Correspondence of Marx and Engels*, pp. 105 and 119.

13. *Grundrisse*, p. 109.

14. *The Eastern Question*, eds. E. Marx and E. Aveling, London 1897.

15. V. Kubulkova and A. Cruickshank, *Marxism and International Relations*, Oxford 1985, p. 27.

16. *Capital*, Vol. I, p. 876.

17. Wight sets out the trio of Hobbes, Grotius and Kant as comprehending, albeit schematically, the range of approaches available within political theory for thinking about international relations. See 'An Anatomy of International Thought', *Review of International Studies*, 13 (3), 1987.

18. For the claim that 'more than any other figure Weber established the discourse of the realist approach to international relations', see M.J. Smith, chapter 2 (quotation from p. 53).

19. Wight's is in fact a remarkable selection. For Hobbes, as we saw above, articulated philosophically the social forms of agrarian capitalism; Kant's universalism is the very signature of liberal thought. Meanwhile the inclusion of Grotius, most of whose work is now inaccessible except to the specialist, sometimes took on the air of an enigma to Wight himself. (At one point he remarks with disarming candour: 'Trying to pick a path once again through the baroque thickets of Grotius's work, where profound and potent principles lurk in the shade of forgotten arguments and obsolete examples like violets beneath overgrown gigantic rhododendrons, I find that he does not say what I thought he said.' [*Systems of States*, p. 127.]) A possible explanation is suggested by the fact that what is generally drawn from Grotius (or rather from the *Prolegomena* to his *De jure belli ac pacis* published in 1625) is the feasibility of an (international) society of sovereign individuals (states) based upon the observance of contract: could Grotius be a front for Locke here? Certainly, most of Wight's exposition of 'the Grotian conception' in this article is explicitly a discussion of Locke. Whatever the answer, all three figures antedate the Industrial Revolution. For this reason, their 'modernity', which in fact derives from the specificities of their historical locations, is made to seem evidence rather of a timeless spectrum of political possibilities, not associated with any particular kinds of society.

20. *The World Crisis, 1911–1914*, (1923), extracted in Wright, ed., p. 137.

21. 'Politics as a Vocation', in *Weber: Selections in Translation*, ed. W.G. Runciman, Cambridge 1978, p. 224.

22. See, for example, Hinsley's *Power and the Pursuit of Peace*; and Ian Clarke's *The Hierarchy of States: Reform and Resistance in the International Order*, Cambridge 1989.

23. Only one major non-European polity, Japan, fully succeeded in organizing its entry in such a manner – and this was only by virtue of a self-imposed crash programme of Westernization. For a brief account of the Meiji Restoration, see E. Hobsbawm, *The Age of Capital*, London 1977, chapter 8, section II.

24. Ibid., p. 231.

25. Ibid., p. 228.

26. In most countries of the modern world much of this labour of 'modernity' is yet to come, even though the formal 'external marks' of sovereign statehood are in place. Declarations of sovereignty and legal recognition cannot magic away the gruesome reality of what state-building involves, or overleap the trauma of expropriation which the commodification of social reproduction entails. Eric Hobsbawm has observed that: 'the period from 1950 to 1975 … saw the most spectacular, rapid, far-reaching, profound and worldwide social change in global history … [This] is the first period in which the peasantry became a minority, (not merely in industrial developed countries, in several of which it had remained very strong, but even in Third World countries)'. (Cited by Giovanni Arrighi in 'World Income Inequalities and the Future of Socialism', *New Left Review*, 189, September/October 1991, p. 39.)

27. Wolf, p. 360.

28. W. Woodruff, *Impact of Western Man: A Study of Europe's Role in the World Economy, 1750–1960*, London 1966, p. 666.

29. Wolf, p. 276.

30. Cited in the Introduction to S. Marks and P. Richardson, eds, *International Labour Migration: Historical Perspectives*, Hounslow 1984, p. 17.

31. Hobsbawm, *The Age of Revolution*, p. 91. See also Fohlen, 'The Industrial Revolution in France, 1700–1914', in C.M. Cipolla, ed., *The Fontana Economic History of Europe, Vol. IV: The Emergence of Industrial Societies*, Glasgow 1973, pp. 28–31. For a general survey of European land reform between 1789 and 1848, see Hobsbawm, *The Age of Revolutions*, chapter 8.

32. For a brief discussion of the 'Great Reform', see Gregory Grossman's account in C.M. Cipolla, ed., *The Fontana Economic History of Europe, Vol. IV: The Emergence of Industrial Societies*, Glasgow 1973, pp. 493–6.

33. Just how different has been the subject of an important debate on the uneven social and political development of nineteenth- and twentieth-century Europe. See in particular, Arno Mayer's *The Persistence of the Ancien Régime*, London 1981 – an argument carried forward into the interwar period by *Why Did the Heavens Not Darken?*, London 1990. Mayer has also elaborated his account of uneven political development into a stimulating treatment of the character of European warfare in the same period. See 'Internal Crisis and War since 1870', in C. Bertrand, ed., *Revolutionary Situations in Europe, 1917–1922*, Montreal 1977.

34. *Capital* Vol. I, p. 940.

35. Wolf, p. 364.

36. Potts, p. 131.

37. See the table in A. Kenwood and A. Lougheed, *The Growth of the International Economy, 1820–1980*, London 1983.

38. See Wolf, p. 364.

39. Kenwood and Lougheed, p. 62.

40. Ibid., p. 67.

41. Woodruff, *Impact of Western Man*, p. 64.

42. Idem, 'The Emergence of an International Economy, 1700–1914', in C.M. Cipolla, ed., *The Fontana Economic History of Europe, Vol. IV: The Emergence of Industrial Societies*, Glasgow 1973.

43. Ibid., p. 664.

44. Wolf, pp. 280–84.

45. Woodruff, 'The Emergence of an International Economy, 1700–1914', p. 659.

46. Wolf, p. 279.

47. Ibid., pp. 313 and 319.

48. As Bull regards it in *The Anarchical Society*, chapter 9.

49. 'The economic development of the United States is itself a product of the large-scale industry of Europe, or, to be more precise, of England.' (Marx, *Capital*, Vol. I, p. 580n.)

50. *Grundrisse*, p. 245. Two qualifying points should be made here. First, the preindustrial emergence of the English colonies was already a by-blow of the emergence of English agrarian capitalism. The US was thus, as it were, born twice. Second, the discussion above is not meant to diminish the importance of either Southern slavery or Northern homestead farming in the making of the United States. However, since the latter was based on private property and exchange relations, it did not constitute the structural block on capitalist development which European peasant production did. And the alternative ideological identity promoted by the Southern slave-based mode of production was submerged by the outcome of the Civil War.

51. Max Weber, *The Protestant Ethic and the Spirit of Capitalism*, introduced by Anthony Giddens, London 1985, pp. 48–50.

52. *The German Ideology*, p. 60. In the *Grundrisse*, Marx describes the US as 'the most modern form of existence of bourgeois society' (p. 104).

53. *Grundrisse*, p. 884.

54. Cited in T. von Laue, *The World Revolution of Westernization*, Oxford 1987, p. 15. Or as Marx put it of the British in India, twenty-five years earlier: 'They are the defenders of property, but did any revolutionary party ever originate agrarian revolutions like those in Bengal, in Madras, and in Bombay?' 'The Future Results of the British Rule in India', in Marx and Engels, *On Colonialism*, p. 81.

55. Cobden had predicted that 'the speculative philosopher of a thousand years hence will date the greatest revolution that ever happened in the world's history from the triumph of the principle [of free trade]'. (Bourne, ed., p. 270.)

56. cf. Potts, pp. 71–3.

57. 'Marx and India', in R. Miliband and J. Saville, eds, *Socialist Register*, 1967, p. 164. Kiernan continues: 'Even before the unsuccessful revolutions of 1848 he was writing as if the bourgeoisie were already firmly in the saddle in Europe at large. He remembered the blight that had fallen on the hand-weavers of England, he watched English manufactures creating a "latent proletariat" in backward Germany, and in his mind's eye, rather than in any statistical mirror, he saw the same process not merely at work, but completed, in India.'

58. 'The Future Results of the British in India', in *On Colonialism*, p. 77.

59. The terms and effectiveness of Habsburg jurisdiction varied widely between provinces. The key point, however, is that Habsburg power – unlike its British and American successors – could not be exercised without formal political submission.

60. See P. O'Brien, 'The Costs and Benefits of British Imperialism 1846–1914', *Past and Present*, August 1988. However, Gallagher and Robinson suggest that studies of the Empire which are concentrated on the areas under formal rule may be compared to 'judging the size and character of icebergs solely from the parts above the water-line'. ('The Imperialism of Free Trade', *Economic History Review*, second series, VI (1), 1953, p. 1.) Something similar may apply to O'Brien's calculations in this article, empirically sound though they may be.

61. As Stedman Jones observed, US imperialism has been distinctive on two counts: 'its non-territorial character ... and its possession of a formally anti-imperialist ideology'. See 'The History of US Imperialism', in R. Blackburn, ed, *Ideology in Social Science: Readings in Critical Social Theory*, Glasgow 1973, p. 212.

62. Barraclough, writing perceptively but too close to the events, mistook decolonization for a decisive reversal of power in the world: 'Never before in the whole of human history had so revolutionary a reversal occurred with such rapidity.' (*An Introduction to Contemporary History*, London 1964, p. 148.)

63. Such speculation did not of course begin in 1942. For the imperial prehistory of this 'special relationship', see C. Hitchens, *Blood, Class and Nostalgia*, London 1990.

64. Quotations taken from CFR deliberations excerpted in Shoup and Mintner, pp. 146 and 149.

65. Gallagher and Robinson, p. 6.

66. Cited in ibid., p. 8.

67. Ibid, pp. 9–10.

68. Ibid., p. 9.

69. R. Robinson, 'Non-European Foundations of European Imperialism: Sketch for a Theory of Collaboration', in R. Owen and R. Sutcliffe, eds, *Studies in the Theory of Imperialism*, London 1972, p. 129.

70. See Potts, chapter 7.

71. *Capital*, Vol. I, p. 875.

72. Ibid., p. 165.

Bibliography

Adelson, H. *Medieval Commerce*, Princeton 1962.

Anderson, P., 'The Affinities of Noberto Bobbio', *New Left Review*, 170, July/August 1988.

Anderson, P., 'The Antinomies of Antonio Gramsci', *New Left Review*, 100, 1976/7

Anderson, P., *Lineages of the Absolutist State*, London 1974.

Anderson, P., *Passages from Antiquity to Feudalism*, London 1974.

Anderson, P., *A Zone of Engagement*, London 1992.

Arrighi, G. 'World Income Inequalities and the Future of Socialism', *New Left Review*, 189, September/October 1991.

Aston, T., *Crisis in Europe, 1560–1660*, London 1965.

Barraclough, G., *An Introduction to Contemporary History*, London 1964.

Beetham, D., *Max Weber and the Theory of Modern Politics*, 2nd edn, Cambridge 1985.

Beitz, C., *Political Theory and International Relations*, Princeton 1979.

Berghahn, V., *Militarism: History of an International Debate*, Cambridge 1984.

Black, J. *The Rise of the European Powers, 1679–1793*, London 1990.

Bourne, K., ed., *The Foreign Policy of Victorian England*, Oxford 1970.

Boxer, C.R., *The Portuguese Seaborne Empire*, Harmondsworth 1973.

Braudel, F. *The Perspective of the World (Capitalism & Civilization, 15th –18th Centuries*, Vol. III), London 1979.

Brenner, R., 'Bourgeois Revolution and the Transition to Capitalism', in A. Beier et al., eds, *The First Modern Society: Essays in English History in Honour of Lawrence Stone*, Cambridge 1989.

Brenner, R., 'The Origins of Capitalist Development: A Critique of Neo-Smithian Marxism', *New Left Review*, 104, July/August 1977.

Brenner, R., 'The Social Basis of Economic Development', in J. Roemer, ed., *Analytical Marxism*, Cambridge 1986.

Bull, H., *The Anarchical Society*, London 1977.

Bull, H., 'International Theory: The Case for a Classical Approach', *World Politics*, 18 (3), 1966.

Burn, A.R., *The Pelican History of Greece*, Harmondsworth 1982.

Butterfield, H., 'The Balance of Power', in H. Butterfield and M. Wright, eds, *Diplomatic Investigations*, London 1966.

Cammack, P., 'Bringing the State Back In?', *British Journal of Political Science*, April 1989.

Carr, E.H., *Nationalism and After*, London 1945.

Carr, E.H., *The Twenty Years' Crisis*, 1st edn London 1939; 2nd edn London 1946, reprinted Basingstoke 1981.

Chamberlain, R.S., 'The Roots of Lordship; The *Encomienda* in MedievalCastile', in H.B. Johnson, ed., *From Reconquest to Empire: The Iberian Background to Latin American History*, New York 1970.

Chomsky, N., *Towards a New Cold War*, New York 1982.

Clarke, I., *The Hierarchy of States: Reform and Resistance in the International Order*, Cambridge 1989.

Corbridge, S., *Capitalist World Development*, Basingstoke 1986.

Craib, I., *Modern Social Theory*, Brighton 1984.

Curtin, P.D., *Cross-Cultural Trade in World History*, Cambridge 1984.

Davis, R., *The Rise of the Atlantic Economies*, London 1973.

Dehio, L., *The Precarious Balance*, London 1963.

Diaz, B., *The Conquest of New Spain*, ed J.M. Cohen, Harmondsworth 1963.

Dobb, M., *Studies in the Development of Capitalism*, New York 1963.

Donelan, M., 'Spain and the Indies', in H. Bull and A, Watson, eds, *The Expansion of International Society*, Oxford 1984.

Dougherty, J.E. and Pfaltzgraff, R.L., *Contending Theories of International Relations*, New York 1981.

Doyle, M.W., *Empires*, Ithaca, New York 1986.

Doyle, M.W., 'Thucydidean Realism', *Review of International Studies*, 16(3), 1990.

Elliott, J.H., *Imperial Spain 1469–1716*, London 1970.

Evans, P., Rueschmeyer, D., and Skocpol, T., eds, *Bringing the State Back In*, Cambridge 1985.

Finley, M.I., *The Ancient Greeks*, London 1963.

Fohlen, C., 'The Industrial Revolution in France, 1700–1914', in C.M. Cipolla, ed., *The Fontana Economic History of Europe, Vol. IV: The Emergence of Industrial Societies*, Glasgow 1973.

Forsyth, M., et al.,eds, *The Theory of International Relations: Selected Texts from Gentili to Treitschke*, London 1970.

Frisby, D. and Sayer, D., *Society*, London 1986.

Gallagher, J., and Robinson, R., 'The Imperialism of Free Trade', *Economic History Review*, Second Series, VI(1), 1953.

Giddens, A., *A Contemporary Critique of Historical Materialism*, Basingstoke 1981.

Giddens, A., *The Constitution of Society*, Cambridge 1984.

Giddens, A., *The Nation-State and Violence*, Cambridge 1985.

Gilpin, R., *The Political Economy of International Relations*, Princeton 1987.

Gilpin, R., 'The Richness of the Tradition of Political Realism', in R. Keohane, ed., *Neorealism and Its Critics*, New York 1986.

Gilpin, R., *War and Change in World Politics*, Cambridge 1981.

Glamann, K., 'European Trade, 1500–1750' in C.M. Cipolla, ed., *The Fontana History of Europe, Vol. II: The Sixteenth and Seventeenth Centuries*, Glasgow 1974.

Godelier, M., *The Mental and the Material*, London 1986.

Goodman, G., *The Miners' Strike*, London 1985.

Goodwin, G. 'The Erosion of External Sovereignty?', *Government and Opposition*, 9(1), Winter 1974.

Gramsci, A., *Selections from Prison Notebooks*, ed. Q. Hoare and G.N. Smith, London 1971.

Grossman, G., 'Russia and the Soviet Union', in, C.M. Cipolla, ed., *The Fontana History of Europe, Vol. IV: The Emergence of Industrial Societies*, Glasgow 1973.

Hagen, V. W. von, *The Ancient Sun Kingdoms of the Americas*, London 1962.

Hall, J., 'They Do Things Differently There, or, The Contribution of British Historical Sociology', *The British Journal of Sociology*, 40(4), December 1989.

Halliday, F., *The Making of the Second Cold War*, London 1983.

Halliday, F., '"The Sixth Great Power": On the Study of Revolution and International relations', *Review of International Studies*, 16(3), July 1990.

Halliday, F., 'State and Society in International Relations: A Second Agenda', *Millennium*, Summer 1987.

Halliday, F., 'Theorizing the International', *Economy and Society*, 18(3), August 1989.

Hay, D., *Europe in the Fourteenth and Fifteenth Centuries*, London 1966.

Header, H., and Waley, D.P., *A Short History of Italy*, Cambridge 1963.

Heimann, E., *History of Economic Doctrines: An Introduction to Economic Theory*, New York 1964.

Held, D., 'Crisis Tendencies, Legitimation and the State', in J. Thompson and D. Held, eds., *Habermas: Critical Debates*, London 1982.

Heller, E., *The Artist's Journey into the Interior*, London 1966.

Hill, D.J., *A History of Diplomacy in the International Development of Europe*, 3 vols, London 1905–14.

Hilton, R., ed., *The Transition from Feudalism to Capitalism*, London 1976.

Hinsley, F.H., *Power and the Pursuit of Peace*, Cambridge 1963.

Hinsley, F.H., *Sovereignty*, London 1966.

Hitchens, C., *Blood, Class and Nostalgia*, London 1990.

Hobsbawm, E., *The Age of Capital*, London 1975.

Hobsbawm, E., *The Age of Empire*, London 1987.

Hobsbawm, E., *The Age of Revolutions*, London 1962.

Hobsbawm, E., 'The Crisis of the Seventeenth Century', in T. Ashton, ed., *Crisis in Europe 1560–1660*, London 1965.

Hobsbawm, E., 'Goodbye to All That?', *Marxism Today*, October 1990.

Hoffman, S., 'An American Social Science: International Relations', *Daedalus*, Summer 1977.

Holmes, G., *Europe: Hierarchy and Revolt, 1320–1450*, Glasgow 1975.

Holsti, K. J., *Peace and War: Armed Conflicts and International Order, 1648–1989*, Cambridge 1991.

Holzgrefe, J.L., 'The Origins of Modern International Relations Theory', *Review of International Studies*, 15(1), 1989.

Hopper, R.J., *Trade and Industry in Classical Greece*, London 1979.

Howard, M., 'The Concept of Peace', *Encounter*, 61(4), December 1983.

James, A., *Sovereign Statehood: The Basis of International Society*, London 1986.

Jarvis, A., 'Societies, States and Geopolitics: Challenges from Historical Sociology', *Review of International Studies*, 15(3), 1989.

Jenkins, B. and Minnerup, G., *Citizens and Comrades*, London 1984.

Johnson, H.B., 'Introduction' to H.B. Johnson, ed., *From Reconquest to Empire: The Iberian Background to Latin American History*, New York 1970.

Jones, R., 'The English School of International Relations: A Case for Closure', *Review of International Studies*, 7(1), 1981.

Kamen, H., *Spain, 1469–1714: A Society of Conflict*, Harlow 1983.

Kant, I., *Perpetual Peace and Other Essays*, ed. T. Humphrey, Indianapolis 1983.

Kaplan, M., 'The New Great Debate: Traditionalism vs. Science in International Relations', *World Politics*, 19(1), 1966.

Kennedy, P., *The Realities behind Diplomacy*, London 1981.

Kenwood, A. and Lougheed, A., *The Growth of the International Economy, 1820–1980*, London 1983.

Keohane, R., ed., *Neorealism and its Critics*, New York 1986.

Keohane, R. and Nye, J., *Power and Interdependence*, Boston 1977.

Kiernan, V. 'Marx and India', in R. Miliband and J. Saville, eds, *Socialist Register*, 1967.

Kindleberger, C.P., *Historical Economics: Art or Science?*, Hemel Hempstead 1990.

Knutsen, T., *A History of International Relations Theory*, Manchester 1992.

Koenigsberger, H., *Early Modern Europe, 1500–1789*, Harlow 1987.

Kriedte, P., *Peasants, Landlords and Merchant Capitalists*, Leamington Spa 1983.

Kubalkova, V. and Cruickshank, A., *Marxism and International Relations*, Oxford 1985.

Lang, J., *Conquest and Commerce: Spain and England in the Americas*, New York and London 1975.

Laue, T. von, *The World Revolution of Westernization*, Oxford 1987.

Limm, P., *The Thirty Years' War*, Harlow 1984.

Linklater, A., *Beyond Realism and Marxism: Critical Theory and International Relations*, London 1990.

Lourie, E., 'A Society Organized for War: Medieval Spain', *Past and Present*, December 1986.

Mann, M., 'The Autonomous Power of the State: Its Origins, Mechanisms and Results', in J. Hall, ed., *States in History*, Oxford 1986.

Mann, M., 'Capitalism and Militarism', *War, State and Society*, London 1984.

Mann, M., *The Sources of Social Power*, Vol. I, Cambridge 1986.

Mann, M., 'War and Social Theory: Into Battle with Classes, Nations and States', in M. Shaw and C. Creighton, eds, *The Sociology of War and Peace*, London 1987.

Manning, C., *The Nature of International Society*, London 1975.

Marks, S., and Richardson, P., 'Introduction', to S. Marks and P. Richardson, eds, *International Labour Migration: Historical Perspectives*, Hounslow 1984.

Martines, L., *Power and Imagination: City-States in Renaissance Italy*, New York 1979.

Marx, K., *Capital*, Vol. I, introduced by E. Mandel, Harmondsworth 1976.

Marx, K., *Capital*, Vol. III, Moscow 1959.

Marx, K., *Early Writings*, ed. L. Colletti, Harmondsworth 1975.

Marx, K., *The Eastern Question*, eds E. Marx and E. Aveling, London 1897.

Marx, K., *Grundrisse*, foreword by M. Nicolaus, Harmondsworth 1973.

Marx, K., *Pre-Capitalist Economic Formations*, ed. E. Hobsbawm, Moscow 1964.

Marx, K., *Readings from Karl Marx*, ed. D. Sayer, London 1989.

Marx, K., *The Revolutions of 1848*, ed. D. Fernbach, Harmondsworth 1973.

Marx, K., *Surveys From Exile: Political Writings*, Vol. II, ed. D Fernbach, Harmondsworth 1973.

Marx, K. and Engels, F., *The Correspondence of Marx and Engels*, ed. D. Torr, London 1934.

Marx, K. and Engels, F., *The German Ideology*, (Parts I and II), ed. R. Pascal, New York 1947.

Marx, K. and Engels, F., *On Colonialism*, Moscow and London 1980.

Marx, K. and Engels, F., *Pre-capitalist Socio-economic Formations*, Moscow 1979.

Mattingly, G., *Renaissance Diplomacy*, Harmondsworth 1965.

Mayer, A., 'Internal Crisis and War since 1870', in C. Bertrand, ed., *Revolutionary Situations in Europe, 1917–1922*, Montreal 1977.

Mayer, A., *The Persistence of the Ancien Régime*, London 1981.

Mayer, A., *Why did the Heavens Not Darken?*, London 1990.

Merrington, J., 'Town and Country in the Transition to Capitalism', in R. Hilton, ed., *The Transition from Feudalism to Capitalism*, London 1965.

Mills, C.W., *The Sociological Imagination*, Oxford 1959.

Minchinton, W.E., *The Growth of English Overseas Trade in the 17th and 18th Centuries*, London 1969.

Mommsen, W., *The Age of Bureaucracy*, Oxford 1974.

Mooers, C., *The Making of Bourgeois Europe*, London 1991.

Morgenthau, H., 'Another "Great Debate": The National Interest of the US', in M. Smith et al., eds, *Perspectives on World Politics*, Beckenham 1981.

Morgenthau, H., *Politics among Nations*, 6th edn, New York 1985.

O'Brien, P., 'Europe in the World Economy', in H. Bull and A. Watson, eds, *The Expansion of International Society*, Oxford 1984.

O'Brien, P., 'The Costs and Benefits of British Imperialism, 1846–1914', *Past and Present*, August 1988.

Olsen, W., 'The Development of a Discipline', in B. Porter, ed., *The Aberystwyth Papers: International Politics, 1919–1969*, London 1972.

O'Sullivan, D., *The Age of Discovery*, Harlow 1984.

Parry, J.H., *The Age of Reconnaissance*, London 1973.

Parry, J.H., 'The New World, 1521–1580' in G.R. Elton, ed., *The New Cambridge Modern History, Vol. II: The Reformation, 1520–1559*, Cambridge 1965.

Parry, J.H., *The Spanish Seaborne Empire*, London 1966.

Parry, J.H., *The Spanish Theory of Empire in the Sixteenth Century*, New York 1974.

Polanyi, K., *The Great Transformation*, Boston 1957.

Potts, L., *The World Labour Market: A History of Migration*. London 1990.

Purnell, R., 'Theoretical Approaches to International Relations: The Contribution of the Graeco-Roman World', in T. Taylor, ed., *Approaches and Theories in International Relations*, Harlow 1978.

Robinson, R., 'Non-European Foundations of European Imperialism: Sketch for a Theory of Collaboration', in R. Owen and R. Sutcliffe, eds, *Studies in the Theory of Imperialism*, London 1972.

Rosenberg, J., 'Giddens' *Nation-State and Violence*: A Non-Realist Theory of Sovereignty?', *Millennium*, Summer 1990.

Ross, J., and McLaughlin, M., eds, *The Portable Renaissance Reader*, Harmondsworth 1968.

Rubin, I., *Essays on Marx's Theory of Value*, introduced by F. Perlman, Montreal 1973.

Sabine, G., *A History of Political Theory*, London 1941.

Sanchez-Albornoz, C., 'The Continuing Tradition of Reconquest', in H.B. Johnson, ed., *From Reconquest to Empire: The Iberian Background to Latin American History*, New York 1970.

Sayer, D., *Capitalism and Modernity*, London 1991.

Sayer, D., 'The Critique of Politics and Political Economy: Capitalism, Communism and the State in Marx's Writings of the Mid-1840s', *Sociological Review*, 33 (2), 1985.

Sayer, D., 'A Notable Administration: English State Formation and the Rise of Capitalism', *American Journal of Sociology*, 97(5), March 1992.

Sayer, D., 'Reinventing the Wheel: Anthony Giddens, Karl Marx and Social Change' in J. Clark et al., eds, *Anthony Giddens: Consensus and Controversy*, London 1990.

Sayer, D., *The Violence of Abstraction*, Oxford 1987.

Schwarzenberger, G., *Power Politics: An Introduction to the Study of International Relations and Post-war Planning*, London 1941.

Sereni, A., *The Italian Conception of International Law*, New York 1943.

Shoup, L., and Minter, W., 'Shaping a New World Order: The Council on Foreign Relations' Blueprint for World Hegemony', in H. Sklar, ed., *Trilateralism*, Boston 1980.

Smith, M. J., *Realist Thought from Weber to Kissinger*, Baton Rouge and London 1986.

Spero, J., *The Politics of International Economic Relations*, London 1985.

Sprout, H., and Sprout, M., 'Tribal Sovereignty vs Independence', in M. Smith at al., eds, *Perspectives on World Politics*, Beckenham 1981.

Stedman Jones, G., 'The History of US Imperialism', in R. Blackburn, ed., *Ideology in Social Science: Readings in Critical Social Theory*, Glasgow 1972.

Stoessinger, J., 'The Anatomy of the Nation-State and the Nature of Power', in M. Smith et al., eds, *Perspectives on World Politics*, Beckenham 1981.

Taylor, T., 'Power Politics', in T. Taylor, ed., *Approaches and Theory in International Relations*, Harlow 1978.

Therborn, G., *Science, Class and Society*, London 1976.

Thompson, J.W., *Economic and Social History of the Middle Ages*, Vol. II, New York 1959.

Thompson, K., 'Toward a Theory of International Politics', in S. Hoffman ed., *Contemporary Theory in International Relations*, Englewood Cliffs, New Jersey 1960.

Thucydides, *History of the Peloponnesian War*, ed. M. Finley, Harmondsworth 1972.

Tönnies, F., *Community and Association (Gemeinschaft und Gesellschaft)*, London 1955.

Vasquez, J., *The Power of Power Politics: A Critique*, London 1983.

Viner, J., 'Power versus Plenty as Objectives of Foreign Policy in the Seventeenth and Eighteenth Centuries', *World Politics*, 1(1), 1948.

Waley, D., *The Italian City-Republics*, 3rd edn, Harlow 1988.

Wallerstein, I., *The Capitalist World Economy*, Cambridge 1979.

Wallerstein, I., *The Modern World-System, Vol. I: Capitalist Agriculture and the Origins of the European World-Economy in the Sixteenth Century*, London 1974.

Wallerstein, I., *The Modern World-System, Vol. II: Mercantilism and the Consolidation of the European World-Economy, 1600–1750*, London 1980.

Waltz, K., *Man, the State and War*, New York 1959.

Waltz, K., *Theory of International Politics*, Reading, Mass. 1979.

Watson, A., *The Evolution of International Society*, London 1992.

Weber, M., *Economy and Society*, ed. G. Roth and C. Wittich, Berkeley 1978.

Weber, M., *From Max Weber: Essays in Sociology*, eds H.H. Gerth and C.W. Mills, London 1948.

Weber, M., *The Protestant Ethic and the Spirit of Capitalism*, introduced by A. Giddens, London 1985.

Weber, M., *Weber: Selections in Translation*, ed. W.G. Runciman, Cambridge 1978.

Wight, M., 'An Anatomy of International Thought', *Review of International Studies*, 13(3), 1987.

Wight, M., *Power Politics*, 2nd edn, Harmondsworth 1986.

Wight, M., 'Western Values in International Relations', in H. Butterfield and M. Wight, eds, *Diplomatic Investigations*, London 1966.

Wight, M., *Systems of States*, Leicester 1977.

Wight, M., 'Why Is There No International Theory?', in H. Butterfield and M. Wight, eds, *Diplomatic Investigations*, London 1966.

Wolf, E., *Europe and the People without History*, Berkeley 1982.

Wood, E., 'Marxism and the Course of History', *New Left Review*, 147, September/October 1984.

Wood, E., *The Pristine Culture of Capitalism*, London 1991.

Wood, E., 'The Separation of the Economic and the Political in Capitalism', *New Left Review*, 127, May/June 1981.

Wood, E., 'The Uses and Abuses of "Civil Society"', *Socialist Register*, 1990 (Special issue: R. Miliband and L. Panitch, eds, *The Retreat of the Intellectuals*).

Woodruff, W., 'The Emergence of an International Economy, 1700–1914', in C.M. Cipolla, ed., *The Fontana Economic History of Europe: Vol. IV: The Emergence of Industrial Societies*, Glasgow 1973.

Woodruff, W., *Impact of Western Man: A Study of Europe's Role in the World Economy, 1750–1960*, London 1966.

Wright, M., ed., *Theory and Practice of the Balance of Power, 1486–1914*, London 1975.

Index

utopianism, critique of, 15
Utrecht, Treaty of 1713, 38, 39–43, 91, 179 n20

Valencia, 110
Venice, 70–72, 73, 75, 78, 104, 107
Vera Cruz, 110
Vespucci, Amerigo, 113
Vietnam War, 173
Visconti, 67
Vitoria, Francisco de, 91, 118–19

wage-labour, 151–2
Waley, D., 83
Wallerstein, Immanuel, 91, 97–8, 99, 102
Waltz, Kenneth, 5, 9, 23–9, 30, 32, 36, 53, 55, 127, 175 n2, 177 n24, 202 n44
war, 74; explanation, 24, 27; predatory, 56
War of Spanish Succession, 42, 91

Weber, Max, 9, 23, 52, 102, 162, 166
West Africa, 96; gold, 94, 98
West Indies, 114
Westphalia, Treaty of 1648, 39, 44, 75, 136, 137, 138
wheat, 166
Wight, Martin, 9, 35, 39, 43–6, 55, 59, 61, 76, 144, 162, 175 n10, 180 n28, 206 n19
Wilhelm II, Kaiser, 19
William of Orange, 74
'Winter of Discontent', 128, 134
Wolf, Eric, 50–51, 99, 166
Wood, Ellen, 85, 128, 137, 179 n20
Woodruff, W., 166
wool, 111
world economy, capitalist see capitalist world economy
World Systems Theory, 91–2
World War II, 162, 169

Yucatan, 115